Uneven Economic Development

RENEWALS 458-4574
DATE DUE

NOTES ON THE EDITORS

JOSÉ ANTONIO OCAMPO is Professor in the Professional Practice of International and Public Affairs at Columbia University, New York. At the time of writing he was Under-Secretary General for Economic and Social Affairs at the United Nations.

ROB VOS is Director of the Development Policy and Analysis Division at the Department of Economic and Social Affairs of the United Nations, New York, and Affiliated Professor of Finance and Development at the Institute of Social Studies, The Hague.

Uneven Economic Development

Edited by
José Antonio Ocampo and Rob Vos

Zed Books
London and New York

TWN
Third World Network

Published in association with the UNITED NATIONS

Uneven Economic Development was first published in 2008.

Published in association with the United Nations

Published in the Indian Subcontinent, South East Asia (except Malaysia and Singapore) and Africa by
ORIENT LONGMAN PRIVATE LIMITED
Registered Office: 3-6-752 Himayatnagar, Hyderabad 500 029 (A.P.), India
Email: orientswan@gmail.com
Other Offices: Bangalore, Bhopal, Bhubaneshwar, Chennai, Ernakulam, Guwahati, Hyderabad, Jaipur, Kolkata, Lucknow, Mumbai, New Delhi and Patna

Published in the UK, Europe, USA, Canada and Australia by
ZED BOOKS LIMITED
7 Cynthia Street, London N1 9JF, UK and
Room 400, 175 Fifth Avenue, New York, NY 10010, USA
www.zedbooks.co.uk
Distributed in the USA on behalf of Zed Books by
Palgrave Macmillan, a division of St Martin's Press, LLC
175 Fifth Avenue, New York, NY 10010, USA

Published in Malaysia and Singapore by
THIRD WORLD NETWORK
131 Jalan Macalister, 10400 Penang, Malaysia
www.twnside.org.sg

Published worldwide by the United Nations and distributed worldwide via the UN specialized network of agents
United Nations Publications
2 United Nations Plaza Room DC2-853, New York, NY 10017, USA
https://unp.un.org Email: publications@un.org

Copyright © United Nations 2008

All rights reserved

No part of this publication may be reproduced, stored in a retrieval system or transmitted, in any form or by any means, electronic or otherwise, without the prior permission of the copyright holder.

United Nations' sales number: E.08.II.A.8
ISBN: 978 81 250 3525 1 Pb (Orient Longman)
ISBN: 978 1 84813 194 1 Hb (Zed Books)
ISBN: 978 1 84813 195 8 Pb (Zed Books)

A catalogue record for this book is available from the British Library
US CIP data is available from the Library of Congress

Cover design by Rogue Four Design
Printed in India by Graphica Printers, Hyderabad 500 013

Contents

Explanatory Notes	vi
Acknowledgements	x

CHAPTER I
GROWTH AND DEVELOPMENT TRENDS, 1960-2006 1

CHAPTER II
STRUCTURAL CHANGE AND ECONOMIC GROWTH 33

CHAPTER III
HAS TRADE INTEGRATION CAUSED GREATER DIVERGENCE? 59

CHAPTER IV
MACROECONOMIC POLICIES AND GROWTH DIVERGENCE 103

CHAPTER V
GOVERNANCE, INSTITUTIONS AND GROWTH DIVERGENCE 147

APPENDICES

A. Technical note on the decomposition of labour productivity
   growth and of the employment-to-population ratio 177

B. On data and methodology for the analysis
   of trade patterns and growth in Chapter III 179

C. Annex tables 182

REFERENCES 201

INDEX 219

Explanatory Notes

The following symbols have been used in the tables throughout the book:

..	**Two dots** indicate that data are not available or are not separately reported.
–	**A dash** indicates that the amount is nil or negligible.
-	**A hyphen** (-) indicates that the item is not applicable.
-	**A minus sign** (-) indicates deficit or decrease, except as indicated.
.	**A full stop** (.) is used to indicate decimals.
/	**A slash** (/) between years indicates a crop year or financial year, for example, 1990/91.
-	**Use of a hyphen** (-) between years, for example, 1990-1991, signifies the full period involved, including the beginning and end years.

Reference to "dollars" ($) indicates United States dollars, unless otherwise stated.

Reference to "tons" indicates metric tons, unless otherwise stated.

Annual rates of growth or change, unless otherwise stated, refer to annual compound rates.

Details and percentages in tables do not necessarily add to totals, because of rounding.

The following abbreviations have been used:

BIS	Bank for International Settlements
CIS	Commonwealth of Independent States
DAC	Development Assistance Committee (OECD)
EBRD	European Bank for Reconstruction and Development
ECE	Economic Commission for Europe
ECLAC	Economic Commission for Latin America and the Caribbean
EMU	European Monetary Union
EPZ	export processing zone
EU	European Union
FDI	foreign direct investment
GATT	General Agreement on Tariffs and Trade
GDP	gross domestic product
GFCF	gross fixed capital formation
GNI	gross national income

HT	high-tech
ICT	information and communication technologies
ILO	International Labour Organization
IMF	International Monetary Fund
IPN	integrated production network
LIBOR	London Interbank Offered Rate
LT	low-tech
M&A	mergers and acquisitions
MT	medium-tech
NAFTA	North American Free Trade Agreement
NBER	National Bureau of Economic Research (Cambridge, Massachusetts)
NIE	newly industrialized economies
NRB	natural resource-based
ODA	official development assistance
OECD	Organization for Economic Cooperation and Development
OPEC	Organization of the Petroleum Exporting Countries
PP	primary products
PPP	purchasing power parity
R&D	research and development
SITC	Standard International Trade Classification
UNCTAD	United Nations Conference on Trade and Development
UN/DESA	Department of Economic and Social Affairs of the United Nations Secretariat
UNIDO	United Nations Industrial Development Organization
WGP	world gross product
WIDER	World Institute for Development Economics Research (United Nations University)

Country groupings

For analytical purposes, the following country groupings and subgroupings have been used:

Developed economies (developed market economies):

European Union, Iceland, Norway, Switzerland, Canada, United States of America, Australia, Japan, New Zealand.

Major developed economies (the Group of Seven):

Canada, France, Germany, Italy, Japan, United Kingdom of Great Britain and Northern Ireland, United States of America.

European Union (EU):

Austria, Belgium, Cyprus, Czech Republic, Denmark, Estonia, Finland, France, Germany, Greece, Hungary, Ireland, Italy, Latvia, Lithuania, Luxembourg, Malta, Netherlands, Poland, Portugal, Slovakia, Slovenia, Spain, Sweden, United Kingdom of Great Britain and Northern Ireland.

EU-10:

Cyprus, Czech Republic, Estonia, Hungary, Latvia, Lithuania, Malta, Poland, Slovakia, Slovenia.

EU-8:

All countries in EU-10, excluding Cyprus and Malta.

Economies in transition:

South-eastern Europe:

Albania, Bosnia and Herzegovina, Bulgaria, Croatia, Romania, Serbia and Montenegro, the former Yugoslav Republic of Macedonia.

Commonwealth of Independent States (CIS):

Armenia, Azerbaijan, Belarus, Georgia, Kazakhstan, Kyrgyzstan, Republic of Moldova, Russian Federation, Tajikistan, Turkmenistan, Ukraine, Uzbekistan.

Net fuel exporters:

Azerbaijan, Kazakhstan, Russian Federation, Turkmenistan, Uzbekistan.

Net fuel importers:

All other CIS countries.

Developing economies:

Latin America and the Caribbean, Africa, Asia and the Pacific (excluding Japan, Australia, New Zealand and the member States of CIS in Asia).

Subgroupings of Latin America and the Caribbean:

South America:

Argentina, Brazil, Chile, Colombia, Ecuador, Paraguay, Peru, Uruguay, Venezuela (Bolivarian Republic of).

Mexico and Central America:

Costa Rica, El Salvador, Guatemala, Honduras, Nicaragua, Panama, Mexico.

Caribbean:

Barbados, Cuba, Dominican Republic, Guyana, Haiti, Jamaica, Trinidad and Tobago.

Subgroupings of Africa:

Northern Africa:

Algeria, Egypt, Libyan Arab Jamahiriya, Morocco, Tunisia.

Sub-Saharan Africa, excluding Nigeria and South Africa (commonly contracted to "sub-Saharan Africa"):

All other African countries except Nigeria and South Africa.

Subgroupings of Asia and the Pacific:

Western Asia:

Bahrain, Iraq, Israel, Jordan, Kuwait, Lebanon, Oman, Qatar, Saudi Arabia, Syrian Arab Republic, Turkey, United Arab Emirates, Yemen.

East and South Asia:

All other developing economies in Asia and the Pacific (including China, unless stated otherwise). This group is further subdivided into:

South Asia:

Bangladesh, India, Iran (Islamic Republic of), Nepal, Pakistan, Sri Lanka.

East Asia:

All other developing economies in Asia and the Pacific.

For particular analyses in Chapters II, III and IV (section entitled "Macroeconomic imbalances and growth"), a sample of developing countries has been subdivided into the following groups:

Asia:

First-tier newly industrialized economies:

Hong Kong Special Administrative Region of China,[a] Republic of Korea, Singapore, Taiwan Province of China.

South-East Asia:

Indonesia, Malaysia, Philippines, Thailand, Viet Nam.

South Asia:

Bangladesh,[b] India, Mongolia,[a] Pakistan, Sri Lanka.

Latin America and the Caribbean:

Argentina, Brazil, Chile, Colombia, Mexico, Uruguay, Venezuela (Bolivarian Republic of).

Low- and middle-income Latin America (Smaller Andean countries):

Bolivia, Ecuador, Peru, Paraguay.[a]

Central America and the Caribbean:

Costa Rica, Cuba,[a] Dominican Republic, El Salvador, Guatemala, Honduras,[a] Jamaica, Nicaragua,[a] Panama,[a] Trinidad and Tobago.[a]

Commonwealth of Independent States (CIS):

Russian Federation, Ukraine.

Central and Eastern Europe:

Albania,[a] Bulgaria, Czech Republic, Hungary, Poland, Romania, Slovakia.

Sub-Saharan Africa:

Cameroon, Congo,[a] Côte d'Ivoire, Ethiopia, Gabon,[a] Ghana, Kenya, Mauritius,[a] Mozambique, Nigeria, Seychelles,[a] Uganda, United Republic of Tanzania, Zimbabwe.

Middle East and Northern Africa:

Algeria, Bahrain,[a] Egypt, Iran (Islamic Republic of), Iraq, Israel,[a] Jordan, Kuwait,[a] Lebanon,[a] Libyan Arab Jamahiriya,[a] Morocco, Oman,[a] Saudi Arabia, Syrian Arab Republic, Tunisia, United Arab Emirates,[a] Yemen.

Semi-industrialized countries:

Argentina, Brazil, Chile, Colombia, Mexico, South Africa, Turkey, Venezuela (Bolivarian Republic of).

Least developed countries not included in regional groupings:

Afghanistan, Angola, Benin, Burkina Faso, Burundi, Cambodia, Central African Republic, Chad, Democratic Republic of the Congo,[b] Djibouti, Equatorial Guinea, Gambia, Guinea, Guinea-Bissau, Haiti, Lao People's Democratic Republic, Liberia, Madagascar, Malawi, Mali, Mauritania, Myanmar, Nepal, Niger, Rwanda, Senegal, Sierra Leone, Somalia, Sudan, Togo, Zambia.

The designation of country groups in the text and the tables is intended solely for statistical or analytical convenience and does not necessarily express a judgment about the stage reached by a particular country or area in the development process.

a Added in the analysis in Chapter III.
b Not considered in Chapter III owing to lack of data.

Acknowledgements

This book presents a revised version of the *World Economic and Social Survey 2006: Diverging Growth and Development*, issued by the United Nations Department of Economic and Social Affairs in June 2006. It has been revised and updated by José Antonio Ocampo and Rob Vos, who were also responsible for the original edition of the *Survey*. The following contributed to the original versions of the chapters of the *Survey*: Jomo K.S., Richard Kozul-Wright and Codrina Rada to Chapter I; Codrina Rada to Chapter II; Ana Cortez, Richard Kozul-Wright, Maria Angela Parra, Roland Mollerus and David O'Connor to Chapter III; Pingfan Hong, Stefania Piffanelli, Oumar Diallo, Keiji Inoue, Grigor Agabekian, Sergio Vieira and Anke Green to Chapter IV; and Simon Cunningham and Hiroshi Kawamura to Chapter V. Valuable support to the original Survey was also provided by June Chesney, Michael Brodsky, and Valerian Monteiro.

Chapter I
Growth and Development Trends, 1960-2006

By many measures, world inequality is high and rising. The average citizen in Ethiopia today is 35 times poorer than that citizen who happens to have been born in Europe or the United States of America.[1] In 1950, the income level of an Ethiopian (measured at purchasing power parity) was one sixteenth that of an average citizen of the industrialized world. Similarly, the average citizen of the United States now has an income that is 27 times that of the average Nepalese, up from 19 times the income of the average Nepalese around 1950. Most of the world's poorest nations have fallen behind in more or less similar degrees. The main reason is that in the industrialized world, the income level for the last five decades has grown steadily, while it has failed to do so in many developing countries. Periods of growth for developing countries have alternated with prolonged periods of stagnation and volatility, especially since the mid-1970s. Only a few developing countries have been growing at sustained rates in recent decades, but these include, most notably, the world's two most populous countries, China and India. Considering that these two countries alone account for almost half of world population, inequality across the globe is beginning to decline (Milanovic, 2005). However, when these countries are left out, global inequality is seen as having continued to rise strongly from already high levels.

These developments are at odds with the conventional economic wisdom about how income differentials between countries change over time in a more integrated world economy. During the 1980s and 1990s, there had developed the promise that giving more space to the global market would lead to a closing of the income gap between the poor and the rich. In reality, income convergence took place only for a small number of countries; it did not occur in the case of many others, despite the fact that countries across the globe had opened up their trade and financial systems to the global market. In fact, the more successful countries tended to be rather cautious in pursuing trade and financial reforms. Attempts over decades by multilateral and bilateral donors alike to bridge the gap between rich and poor countries through development assistance also had outcomes that have remained modest, at best.

How concerned should one be about greater global inequality? Inequality matters especially within developing countries, not only because it signals injustice, but also, and particularly, because unequal opportunities make it so much more difficult, as economic potential stays unutilized, to achieve human development objectives, including the major development goals recognized today by the international community, the Millennium Development Goals. The rich tend to be healthier and better educated. Better education and greater wealth are "assets" that help people gain influence in society and take fuller advantage of economic opportunities. At the other end of the spectrum, inequality makes it more difficult for those who lack such assets to grow out of poverty. In short, inequality breeds more inequality. Further, it is now also more broadly maintained that wide income disparities within countries tend to impair the pursuit of sustainable long-term prosperity. Several important recent studies, such as the 2005 UN report "The Inequality Predicament" (United Nations, 2005a) and the World Development Report 2006 (World Bank, 2005a), have examined extensively the detrimental impact on development of widening income disparities within countries.

The present study, in contrast, focuses on the causes and possible implications of the growing inequality among countries.[2] There are several reasons why one should be equally concerned with the growing disparities in welfare between the world's nations. First, when considering income inequality among all the people in the world, available studies have shown that about 70 per cent is explained by differences in incomes between countries (Bourguignon and Morrisson, 2002; Milanovic, 2005). The same studies indicate that before the Second World War, it was inequality within countries that appeared to be more important. While this does not make the disparities within countries any less important, it is striking that global inequality increasingly has become a problem conditioned to where one happens to live.

Second, what we see at the national level also applies to the global level, where the better "endowments" enjoyed by richer countries give them preferential access to capital markets and makes them less vulnerable to shifts in global commodity markets. This is so because world markets are far from equitable. Global investors generally prefer to invest in countries with better endowments in terms of wealth and institutions, which ensure lower investment risk. Poorer countries have less diversified economies and export structures, making them much more vulnerable to shifts in commodity prices and shocks in international financial markets. Patent protection may increase the costs incurred by poor countries in securing access to innovation, as in the case of medicines; moreover, most resources are being invested in new research oriented towards combating diseases with a higher prevalence in richer societies.

Third, economic power and political power tend to be reinforcing. Also, in this sense, the rules governing global markets are likely to be less advantageous for developing countries, as these countries tend to have less of a voice in the negotiation processes leading to the establishment of those rules. This tendency has been recognized in the Monterrey Consensus of the International Conference on Financing for Development (United Nations, 2002a), which gave a clear mandate to the international community to improve participation of developing countries in international economic decision-making. However, progress in this area has been slow. This also affects the way in which and the extent to which global market imperfections are "corrected", leading world markets to work less favourably for developing countries.

Fourth, widening global asymmetries can in turn harm growth and prevent poorer countries from reaping the full gains of global development and thus from utilizing their full economic potential. This should be considered a welfare loss for the world economy at large. Lower growth in turn obstructs the efforts to eradicate poverty and, in some contexts, this has been shown to be a major source of regional conflicts, domestic strife and social instability (Murshed, 2008).

Ignoring growing international income inequality means ignoring all of the above phenomena. This book explores the patterns of growth divergence and the income inequality among countries, examining its origins and its implications. The present chapter indicates which countries are falling behind and which countries are catching up. The subsequent chapters will address in more detail the international and domestic causes of inequality and the policy options that may be available to countries to enable them to avoid falling further behind.

This chapter begins by examining the trends in income growth across countries that explain particular patterns of convergence and divergence. Determining the causes of such patterns typically requires going a long way back in history; however, because of data limitations, the main focus will be on trends since 1960. This is a symbolic starting point, given that on 19 December 1961, the General Assembly proclaimed the First United Nations Development Decade. Income inequality between what we now call developing and developed countries has been on the rise for many decades. Divergence in income levels had not widened much in the aftermath of the Second World War during the period labelled the "golden age" (1950-1973) when world economic growth was broad-based, including also most developing countries. In contrast, during the 1980s and 1990s, international inequality increased sharply between developed countries and all developing-country regions, except for East and South Asia. These patterns of divergence and convergence are explained by growth failures and successes that appear to have clustered in time and space. Thus, income levels and economic growth also have become more polarized across groups of neighbouring countries.

The section of this chapter entitled "Growth divergence and human development" broadens the economics focus by introducing the linkages that exist between human development and growth, with a special emphasis on the implications of the high level of international inequality for achieving the Millennium Development Goals. The final section focuses on the causes and implications of the increasing global asymmetries. It is argued that world markets are inequitable and that the rising global inequality is in part explained by market imperfections that characterize global markets and which are inadequately countered by global policies and rules. That section also shows not only that developing countries remain highly vulnerable to external shocks, but also that their growth path closely follows the trends and fluctuations in the economic performance of developed economies. To a considerable degree, developing-country growth depends on what happens in the world's largest economy, namely, the United States. However, with continued fast growth in East Asia, and in China in particular, that part of the world could become the engine of global economic growth. One cannot be sure, of course, whether China can sustain its rapid expansion. However, if it does, an important question is whether the current pattern of widening global asymmetries will continue or whether, in contrast, sustained high growth in China could improve growth opportunities for other developing countries as well and thereby soften the inequality predicament.

PATTERNS OF ECONOMIC GROWTH DIVERGENCE

The renewed interest in the determinants of economic growth heightened after it was observed that many developing countries had gone through a prolonged period of poor growth performance and that there was increasing evidence that only a few countries appeared able to "catch up" with the developed world. The standard economic model of growth focused primarily on the role of savings and investment and predicted that, in the long run, rich and poor economies would eventually converge in terms of income levels. To explain the lack of observed convergence, the model was extended to include other factors of growth such as human capital and endogenous technological change.

Based on these building blocks, the new economic growth theory has also addressed the issue of income convergence among countries (see, for example, Barro and Sala-i-Martin, 1992). Nobel Prize winner Robert Lucas (2000) has estimated that the diffusion of technology and ideas will allow income distribution across nations to narrow and make everyone "equally rich and growing" by the year 2100. This may or may not happen, and there are still more than nine decades years to go before Lucas's previsions are proved accurate or not. Meanwhile, however, the trend is mainly in the opposite direction with the unprecedented widening of income distribution across countries driven largely by the poor economic performance of the economies at the bottom end. The pattern is one of divergence not only between developed countries and developing countries, but also between the developing countries that have experienced growth successes and other developing countries that have undergone growth collapses.

The big divide: developing versus developed countries

Taking a long view, convergence between the rest of the world and the advanced regions of 1820—Western Europe and its Western offshoots (the United States, Australia and New Zealand)—never took place. The countries that had been most advanced in 1820 grew faster in terms of gross domestic product (GDP) per capita throughout the nineteenth and twentieth centuries. The one notable exception was Japan which, having seen growth accelerate from the 1890s onward and enjoyed a period of spectacular growth after the Second World War, went on to reach, by 1970, the same income level as that of other industrialized countries.

In terms of purchasing power parity (PPP), commonly used when making such comparisons, the developed world had managed to increase its GDP per capita 19-fold between 1820 and 2001 (see table I.1).[3] The performance of the rest of the world was much more modest. The mean incomes of countries in Eastern Europe increased nine times, while those of the countries in Latin America and Asia showed, respectively, an eight- and a sevenfold increase during the same period. African countries witnessed much more modest welfare increases: their GDP per capita in 2001 was only three and a half times that observed for 1820. In consequence, when looking at the broader picture for the entire period, it is clear that over the past two centuries, there has been a very large divergence of the average income levels of developed and developing countries.

Table I.1.
The Big Divergence: developing versus developed countries, 1820-2002

	GDP per capita - 1990 International Geary-Khamis dollars					
	1913	1950	1973	1980	2002	1820
Developed World	3,989	6,298	13,376	15,257	23,384	1,204
Eastern Europe	1,695	2,111	4,988	5,786	6,238	683
Former USSR	1,488	2,841	6,059	6,426	5,006	688
Latin America	1,481	2,506	4,504	5,412	5,754	692
Asia	883	918	2,049	2,486	4,127	584
China	552	439	839	1,067	4,197	600
India	673	619	853	938	2,012	533
Japan	1,387	1,921	11,434	13,428	20,969	669
Africa	637	894	1,410	1,536	1,513	420
	Ratio of GDP per capita of all regions relative to developed world					
	1913	1950	1973	1980	2002	1820
Eastern Europe	0.42	0.34	0.37	0.38	0.27	0.57
Former USSR	0.37	0.45	0.45	0.42	0.21	0.57
Latin America	0.37	0.40	0.34	0.35	0.25	0.58
Asia	0.22	0.15	0.15	0.16	0.18	0.48
China	0.14	0.07	0.06	0.07	0.18	0.50
India	0.17	0.10	0.06	0.06	0.09	0.44
Japan	0.35	0.30	0.85	0.88	0.90	0.56
Africa	0.16	0.14	0.11	0.10	0.06	0.35
	Per capita GDP growth (annual average compound growth rates, percentage)					Fold increase
	1820-1913	1913-50	1950-73	1973-80	1980-2002	1820-2002
Developed World	1.3	1.2	3.3	1.9	2.0	19.4
Eastern Europe	1.0	0.6	3.8	2.1	0.3	9.1
Former USSR	0.8	1.8	3.3	0.8	-1.1	7.3
Latin America	0.8	1.4	2.6	2.7	0.3	8.3
Asia	0.4	0.1	3.6	2.8	2.3	7.1
China	-0.1	-0.6	2.9	3.5	6.4	7.0
India	0.3	-0.2	1.4	1.4	3.5	3.8
Japan	0.8	0.9	8.1	2.3	2.0	31.3
Africa	0.4	0.9	2.0	1.2	-0.1	3.6

Sources: Maddison (2001) and UN/DESA.

Note: 1990 International Geary-Khamis dollars are purchasing power parities (PPPs) used to evaluate output which are calculated based ona specific method devised to define internationally comparable prices. Incormation on the computation of the PPPs in Geary-Khamis dollars is available from hhtp://unstats.un.org/unsd/methods/icp/ipc7_htm.htm.

Country groupings are as specified in Maddison (2001).

The pace at which the gap widened had slowed down during the quarter-century that followed the Second World War (1950-1973) and during this period several regions (Eastern and Central Europe and Asia) and the Union of Soviet Socialist Republics managed to catch up in modest terms with the developed countries. As noted above, this period is sometimes also referred to as the "golden age", since rapid growth took place in a large number of countries and regions across the world. At the time, optimism was running high, as many considered the widely observed good economic performance as the first signs of the beginning of a process of sustained growth in developing countries and of a convergence across countries.

During this period, all regions recorded an average GDP per capita growth rate of at least 2 per cent (see lowest subdivision of table I.1). India was the only large developing country showing slower growth, with a rate of 1.4 per cent per annum. The fastest-growing economy was Japan, with an impressive 8.1 per cent GDP per capita growth rate, followed by Eastern Europe, Asia and the Soviet Union, all attaining growth rates of 3.4 per cent or higher. Latin America experienced lower growth. It may be noted that Latin America and the former Soviet Union were the only two regions that had achieved some degree of catching up with the developed world in the period between and during the two World Wars (1913-1950). Africa, for its part, continued to diverge relative to developed countries even during the golden age. In this sense, one may speak of a process of "upward growth divergence" during 1950-1973, as the income gap for some developing countries widened despite the fact that those countries had achieved fairly satisfactory growth rates themselves, albeit more slowly than did the industrialized countries.

This relatively good economic performance had come to an end with the second oil price shock, the sudden increase in world interest rates at the end of the 1970s and the collapse of non-oil commodity prices in the 1980s. These factors triggered the debt crisis of the 1980s, which hit African and Latin American countries particularly hard. Although the period between the two oil shocks had been marked by a rising frequency of growth collapses, particularly in sub-Saharan Africa, it was the combination of these external shocks that sparked a large number of growth collapses among developing economies in the 1980s. Hence, in the 1980s, a renewed trend of divergence set in, with Latin America, Africa, Eastern Europe and the Soviet Union falling farther behind the developed world, only this time owing to a lack of growth of their own economies.

As symptoms of this "downward divergence", annual average growth rates of GDP per capita dropped to values below 1 per cent for Latin America and Africa and turned negative for the former Soviet Union. In the latter case, the growth collapse actually took place during the transition from socialist to market economies in the 1990s. Output growth also slowed down for Asia but the region still recorded a decent per capita income growth rate of 2.4 per cent. China leaped forward at a speed of 5.3 per cent per year, while India, shedding its low but steady "Hindu" rate of per capita growth, moved up to a new and much higher steady pace of 3 per cent. The increased divergence in growth performance across countries left the inequality in the distribution of world income across countries (excluding China) at an all-time high.

If we exclude China, between 1960 and 1980, the share of world population living in countries with a GDP per capita less than half the mean for the world had stayed constant at 47 per cent. By 2001, however, this share had increased to 52 per cent (see the upper part of figure I.1). In this sense, as one study has pointed out, the world income distribution, in being polarized between rich and poor, is taking the form of "twin peaks" (Quah, 1996) or, as others have indicated, the distribution is becoming one in which there is no longer a "middle class" of countries (Milanovic, 2005; Milanovic and Yitzhaki, 2001). Figure I.1 confirms this to some extent. The concept of a disappearing middle class applies specifically to the group of upper middle income countries.

After the golden age, a major new element in the dynamics of global income distribution was thus the growing divergence within the group of developing countries. Many countries in the middle-income group either moved up the ladder, catching up with the rich countries, or moved down to become part of the lower-income group. In explaining these dynamics, a great deal is attributed to the tendency of growth successes and collapses to cluster within specific time periods as well as regionally.

Growth successes and collapses have been concentrated in time

Since the golden age, patterns of growth among developing countries have become more diverse. A dual pattern of divergence emerged in which, on the one hand, developing countries as a group lagged behind the developed countries in terms of economic growth and, on the other hand, there were strikingly different growth experiences within the group of developing countries (figure I.2). Diverging growth experiences among developing countries or areas have been in part the result of the fact that several success stories, like the Republic of Korea, Taiwan Province of China, Singapore and Hong Kong Special Administrative Region (SAR) of China, outpaced the rest. The dual divergence observed in the last quarter-century, however, has been much more strongly associated with a significant increase in the frequency of growth collapses and a decline in the number of growth successes.

Figure I.1.
World income inequality, 1960, 1980 and 2001

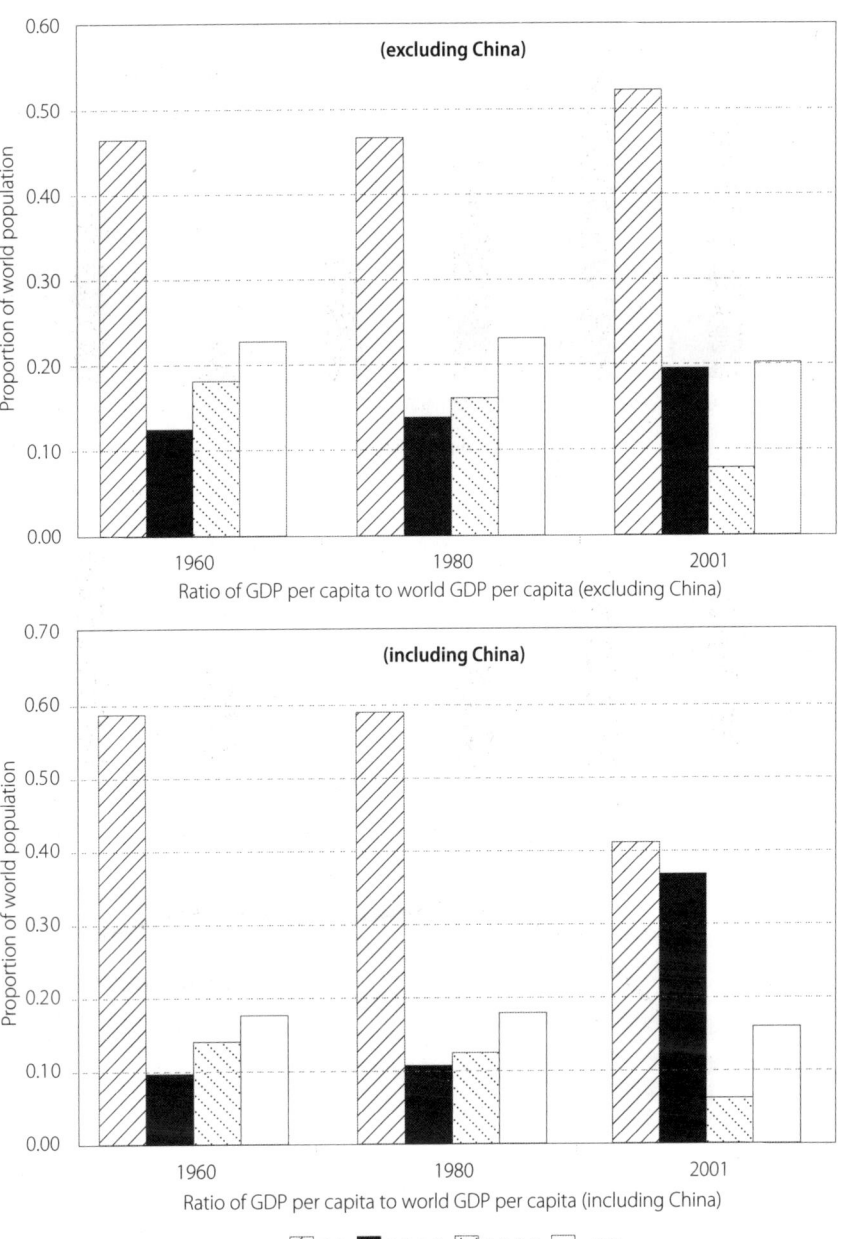

Sources: World Bank, World Development Indicators 2005 database; and UN/DESA.

Figure I.2.
Per capita GPD growth, developing countries and OECD member countries, 1950-2006

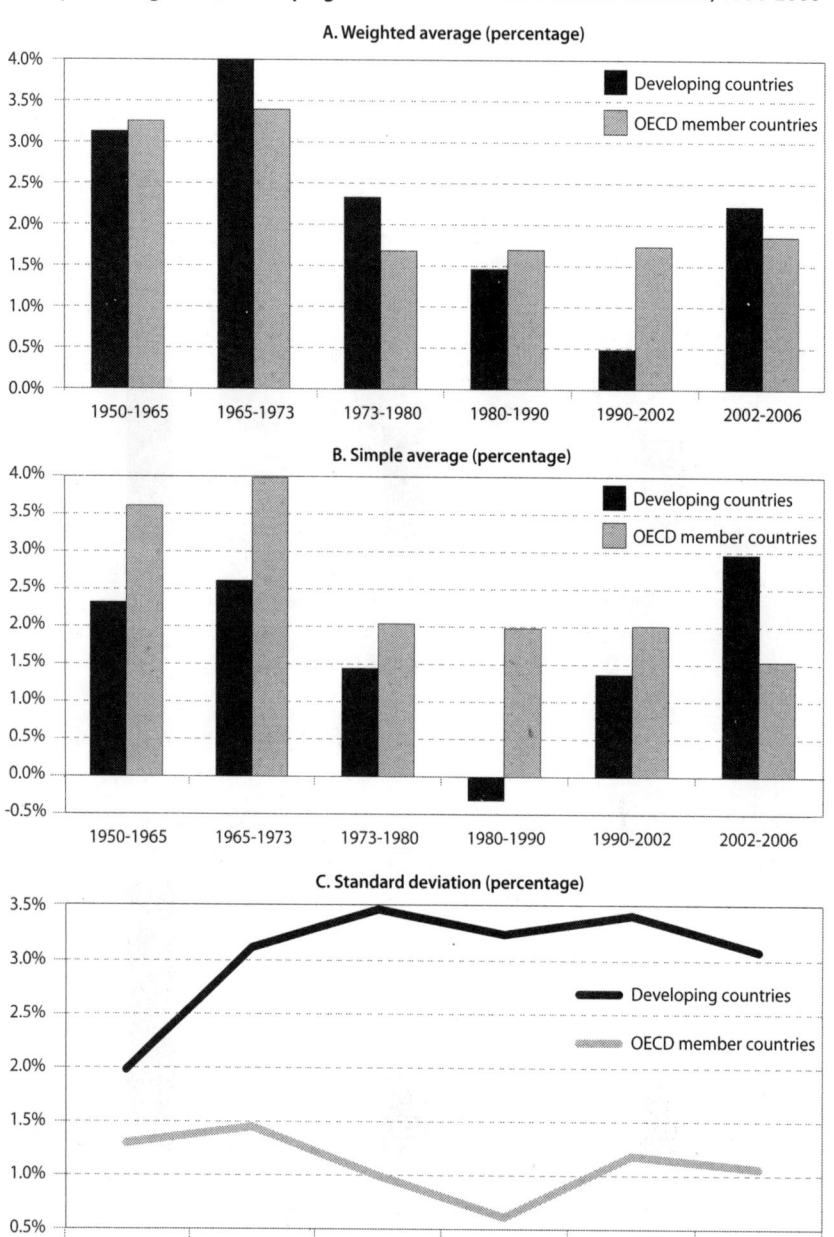

Sources: Maddison (2001) and UN/DESA.

In the 1960s and 1970s, nearly 50 of the 106 developing countries included in the analysis had experienced sustained expansion (defined as four consecutive five-year moving average periods with growth of over 2 per cent per capita). In contrast, during the past quarter–century, only 20 developing countries enjoyed sustained growth (figure I.3 A). While those experiences had been widespread in the developing world during the golden age, they by and large disappeared in the 1980s, except in Asia. Sustained growth occurred more often again in the 1990s, but at levels far below those of the golden age, in part because depression set it in most of the developing world after the Asian and Russian crises of 1997-1998.[4]

The decrease in the number of countries experiencing periods of accelerated growth in the last decades of the twentieth century was mirrored by increasing episodes of growth failure or "sustained contractions" (defined as four consecutive five-year periods with negative GDP growth per capita). Such growth failures had been rare before the first oil shock. They became more frequent in the 1970s, between the two oil price shocks, and mainly affected least developed countries, especially those in Africa. Sustained contractions then became widespread among developing countries during the "lost decade" of the 1980s and continued well into the 1990s (figure I.3 B).[5]

In sum, over the past 45 years, growth successes and collapses have tended to cluster in specific time periods. It is unlikely that domestic factors alone, abundantly explored in the growth literature, can explain a pattern common to many countries at the same time. Indeed, global economic developments played an important role in this outcome. In recent decades, these developments arose from major external shocks that affected the developing world around 1980: the strong increase in real interest rates, which affected many developing countries disproportionately, and a steep and prolonged decline in the terms of trade for non-oil primary commodity exporters.

The oil shock of 1973 had disturbed the normal functioning of the economies of developed countries, generating inflation and recession, and had important effects on developing countries as well (adversely, through the demands for exports from industrialized countries, but with indirect benefits through the temporary easing of external financing conditions). Nonetheless, the dynamics of oil prices had different effects on different groups of developing countries and thus generated a slowdown but not the steep downturn in growth in most developing countries which took place around 1980 (see table I.1 and figure I.4).

Two major and largely unexpected shocks explain this generalized downturn in the developing world in the 1980s. The first was the permanent effect of the interest rate shock of 1979. Real interest rates in the United States

12 • Uneven Economic Development

Figure I.3.
Episodes of sustained expansion or contraction in GDP per capita, by number of countries per region or country group, 1951-2006

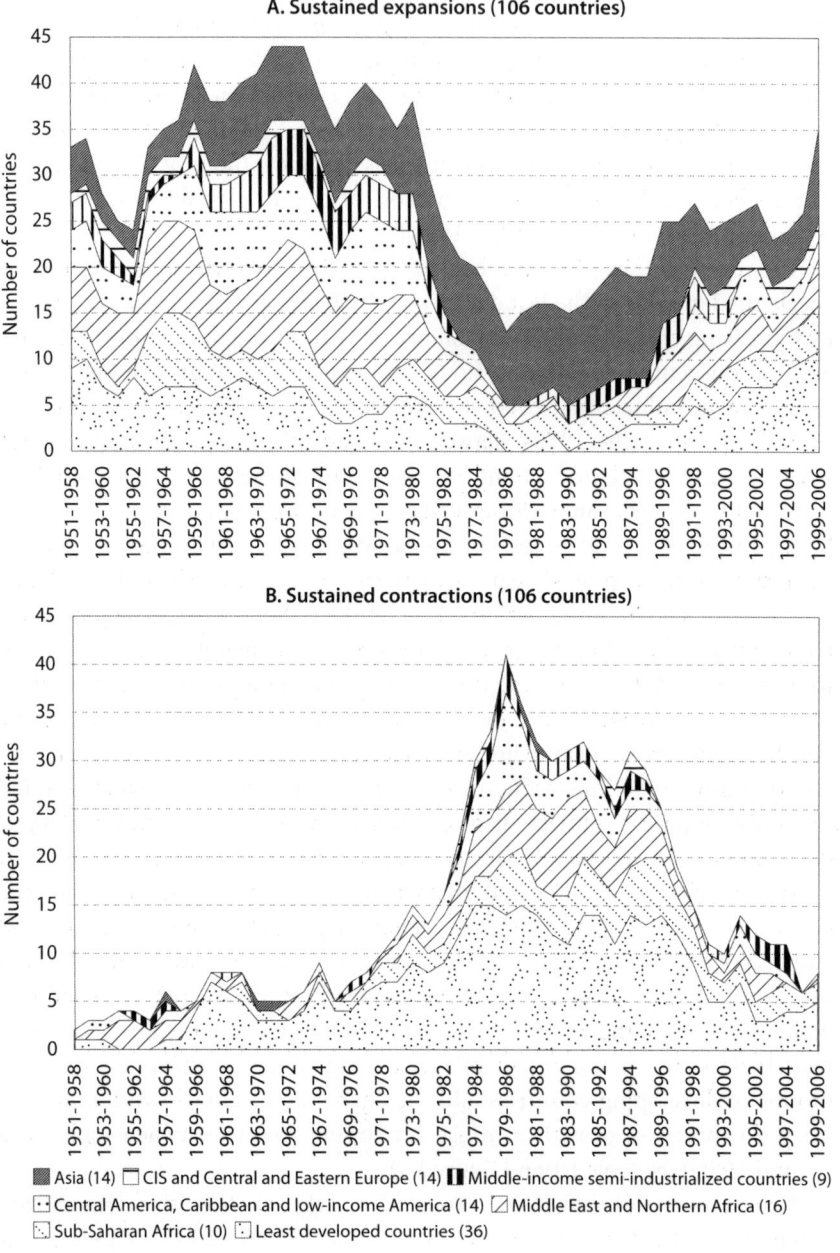

Asia (14) □ CIS and Central and Eastern Europe (14) ▮▮ Middle-income semi-industrialized countries (9)
Central America, Caribbean and low-income America (14) ⊘ Middle East and Northern Africa (16)
Sub-Saharan Africa (10) Least developed countries (36)

Sources: Maddison (2001) and UN/DESA.

Figure I.4.
Growth in GDP per capita of 106 developing countries, 1951-2006 (*percentage*)

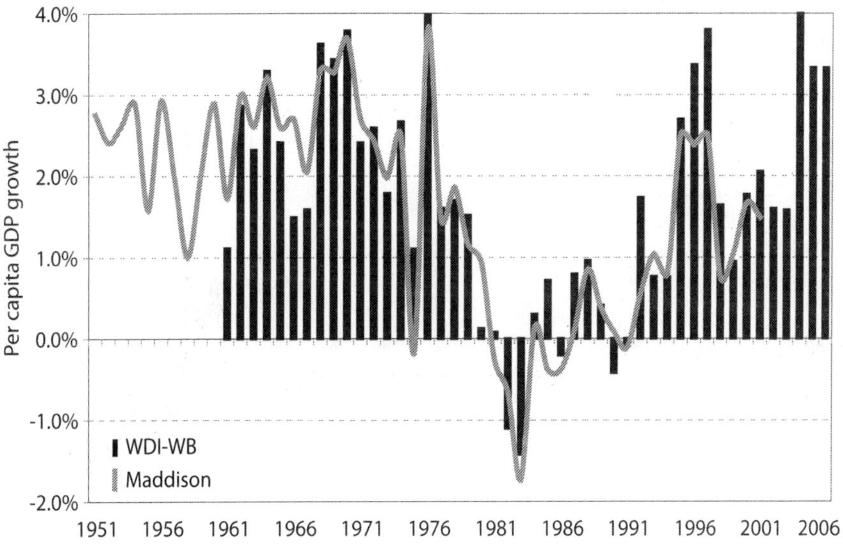

[Chart showing per capita GDP growth from 1951 to 2006, with WDI-WB and Maddison data series]

Sources: Maddison (2001) and UN/DESA.

(using the rate on 10-year Treasury Bills as the benchmark) had increased from -1.8 per cent in 1979 to 3.6 per cent in 1981, reaching a peak of 8.2 per cent in 1984. The cost of borrowing for developing countries was even higher as the average risk premium (over the London Interbank Offered Rate (LIBOR)) paid by developing countries had risen in real terms from 2.5 to 22.0 percentage points between 1979 and 1981. Having profited from the previous eased external financing conditions, developing countries suffered a sudden and substantial shock leading, for many of them, to debt crises which affected them for one or two decades and even until today. The second shock was the steep and prolonged decline in the terms of trade for non-oil primary commodity exporters. Real non-oil commodity prices experienced a permanent drop by more than 30 per cent, after having fluctuated without a clear trend for a long period of time between 1920 and 1980 (see figure I.5).

Both the terms-of-trade and interest-rate shocks were outcomes of the macroeconomic adjustments taking place in developed countries. However, they were also associated with boom-bust cycles in international financing directed to developing countries. Combined, these phenomena in the global economy had a decisive impact on the divergence trajectory for many developing countries.

Interestingly, since 2003 we have seen, in turn, an unprecedented period of rapid growth in most developing countries (see figure I.4), fuelled by

Figure I.5.
Terms of trade for non-fuel commodities and for developing-country manufactures, 1900-2005

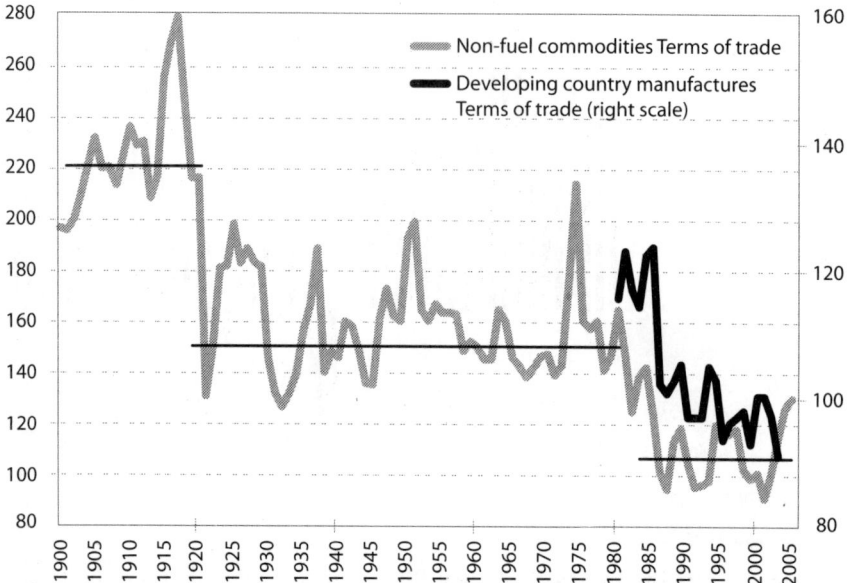

Source: Grilli and Yang (1988); Ocampo and Parra (2003); and United Nations, 2003.
Note: The terms of trade for non-fuel commodities correspond to the aggregate commodity price index versus manufactures, excluding oil, with year 2000 as the base year. The terms of trade for developing-country manufactures were calculated as the ratio of the price index of manufactures exported by developing countries to the price index of manufactures exported by developed countries, with year 2000 as the base year.

favourable conditions in international financial and commodity markets which are the polar opposites of the two adverse shocks that the developing world faced in the 1980s. This recent period is the only one in history in which we can talk of worldwide convergence in incomes between developed and developing countries (see table I.1). However, based on the measures of sustained success used in this book, it is still too soon to judge whether this is the beginning of a long-term convergence.

The strong impact of the shocks in global commodity and financial markets does not mean that region- and country-specific factors are not important. There is a close relationship, however, between the relevant country- and region-specific factors and elements that are particular to a specific conjuncture. Whether a country experiences rapid growth or not during periods of economic expansion in the developing world as a whole, or whether it can mitigate or avoid a growth collapse during the downward cycle, depends on the interaction between domestic conditions, and the way in which the country is affected by the global or regional market dynamics.

In this regard, for example, macroeconomic policy can play an essential role in diminishing the adverse effects of external shocks. This is not always easy, however, since the "policy space" for redressing the impact of such shocks is not the same for each country. This has been clearly shown in comparisons of macroeconomic policy between Latin America and East Asia, whose macroeconomic adjustments since the 1980s debt crisis have been shaped by very different policy choices and constraints.

There have also been differences within regions. For instance, both Cambodia and the Lao Peoples Democratic Republic, the poorest countries in East Asia, suffered severe economic setbacks related to the Asian financial crisis. In contrast, Thailand and the Republic of Korea, the countries first hit by the crisis, managed to recover fairly quickly. Not only were these countries helped by an external financial rescue operation, but they could also build on a tradition of counter-cyclical macroeconomic policies and the institutional framework within which to make adjustments in financial regulations. The strong devaluation of their respective currencies boosted growth in established export industries (see chapter III). In Cambodia and the Lao People's Democratic Republic, the policy response needed to be more halting and painful, as these countries had their currencies pegged to the Thai baht. The devaluation of Thailand's currency by 70 per cent had strong inflationary effects leading to dramatic declines in real incomes, which could not be counteracted because of insufficient external finance, poorly developed financial systems, and a lack of instruments with which to conduct counter-cyclical fiscal and monetary policy. This inequality in terms of policy space is discussed at greater length in chapter IV.

Geographical concentration of growth successes and collapses

Growth successes and collapses not only appear to be concentrated in particular time periods, but also tend to coincide in particular regions of the world. Most of the successful growth stories have occurred in East Asia, while most growth collapses have been seen in Africa. Also, growth performance in Latin America has been rather uniform among the countries of the region, but different when the region is compared with other regions in the world. Thus, we see widening international inequality (divergence), which coexists with greater similarity in growth patterns within regions (convergence). The existence of "regional convergence clubs" is of particular interest, as it sheds light on the growing importance of initial conditions in explaining uneven global development. Capabilities, attitudes, social institutions and economic

16 • Uneven Economic Development

potential differ across regions and explain persistent differences in economic performance which, if unchecked, perpetuate the global asymmetries.

Table I.2 confirms that China's fast growth led to a decline in overall international inequality after 1980, but the trend is observed to have continued to move starkly upward when the world's most populous country is not taken into account. That upward trend is due, for the most part, to the fact that differences between geographical regions have been widening. As table I.2 shows, 84 per cent of international income inequality (excluding China) is explained by differences between regions and only 16 per cent by differences within regional groups (see table I.3).[6] Income disparities within regions have

Table I.2.
Theil decomposition of international income inequality, 1960-2001

	Theil coefficient of inequality			*Contribution to inequality*		
	1960	1980	1999	1960	1980	1999
All countries						
Between regions	0.447	0.509	0.449	87%	91%	85%
Within regions	0.066	0.052	0.079	13%	9%	15%
Total	0.512	0.561	0.528			
All countries without China						
Between regions	0.354	0.424	0.476	84%	89%	84%
Within regions	0.068	0.053	0.088	16%	11%	16%
Total	0.422	0.477	0.565			

Source: UN/DESA, based on Maddison (2001), See annex table A.1 for further details.

Note: The inequality index considers only inequality between countries and not inequality within countries. The inequality measure is weighted for the population of each country.

Table I.3.
Theil decomposition of developing-world income inequality, 1960-2001

	Theil coefficient of inequality			*Contribution to inequality*		
	1960	1980	2000	1960	1980	2000
All countries						
Between regions	0.25	0.26	0.08	81%	74%	35%
Within regions	0.06	0.09	0.15	19%	26%	65%
Total	0.32	0.36	0.23			
All countries without China						
Between regions	0.17	0.17	0.12	70%	64%	38%
Within regions	0.07	0.10	0.19	30%	36%	62%
Total	0.24	0.27	0.31			

Source: UN/DESA, based on Maddison (2001), See annex table A.1 for further details.

Note: The inequality index considers only inequality between countries and not inequality within countries. The inequality measure is weighted for the population of each country.

become more important in recent decades, however, and are relatively more important in explaining income inequality among developing countries.

Convergence clubs appear to assemble at the extremes of the income spectrum. There is one for wealthier nations, largely located in Western Europe and Northern America, and one for poorer countries, predominantly in Africa, with both clubs attracting new members. As one study (Ben-David, 1995, p. 12) observes: "The wealthier clubs exhibit upward convergence where the poorer members essentially catch up with the richest members. Among the poorest countries, the situation is one of downward convergence, where the decline in income disparity is brought about by very low growth among the clubs' better-off members." European countries such as Greece, Portugal, Spain and Ireland are examples of upward convergence to the industrialized countries club. Their geographical location and geopolitics in terms of membership in the European Union (EU) created positive spillover effects; and the transfer of technology, intensification of trade and integration policies in general played a decisive role in their catching-up story. Sub-Saharan Africa and subregions within Latin America (notably those comprising several of the Andean and Central American countries) are examples of downward divergence, with initially richer countries regressing to the lower income levels of surrounding neighbours.

A visual snapshot of geographical club formation is presented in figure I.6 A, B and C where 164 countries are grouped by the ratio of their income (GDP) per capita to the world average. Countries are grouped in one of four clubs according to their score on this indicator. Countries with an income that is less than half of per capita world gross product (WGP) are classified as belonging to the poorest club designated by the figure. The lower middle income club includes countries with a GDP per capita ranging from one half the mean world income to the mean itself. The upper middle income countries have a GDP per capita that is higher than the average but less than double WGP per capita. The rich countries are those with a GDP per capita that is more than twice the average.

Graphically, the results confirm the statement above that convergence occurs at the extremes, that is to say, among members of the rich country club on the one hand and among members of the poor country club on the other, suggesting greater growth polarization. In 1960, the poorest group consisted of 63 countries, of which 43 were in Africa, 18 were in Asia and 2 were in Latin America. The number of countries in this category had decreased to 58 by 1980 with the largest number still in Africa. The Republic of Korea, Thailand, Tunisia, the Dominican Republic and Oman were among the countries that had exited the poorest group. Swaziland, the Democratic Republic of Korea

18 • Uneven Economic Development

Figure I.6.
Geographical distribution of GDP per capita, 164 countries, 1960, 1980 and 2000

A. 1960 Geographical distribution of GDP per capita (ratio of country to world GDP per capita)

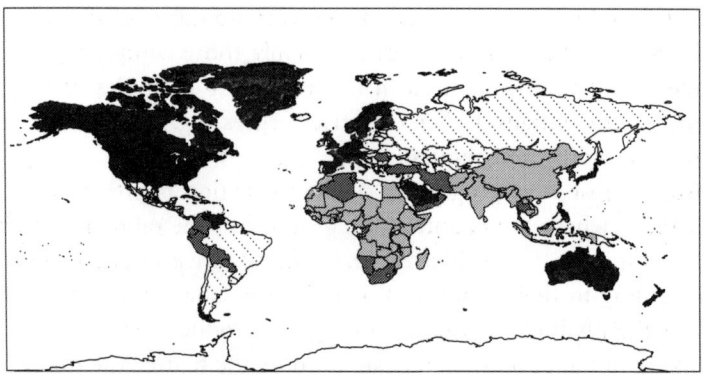

B. 1980 Geographical distribution of GDP per capita (ratio of country to world GDP per capita)

C. 2000 Geographical distribution of GDP per capita (ratio of country to world GDP per capita)

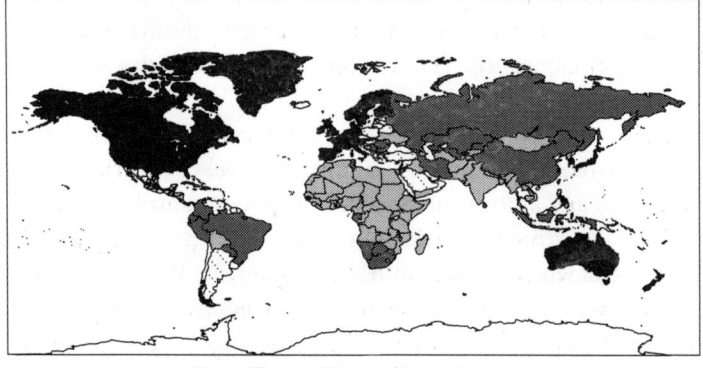

■ <0.5 ■ 0.5-1.0 ▨ 1.0-2.0 ■ >2.0 ☐ No data

Sources: Maddison (2001) and UN/DESA.

and Yemen had also left the poorest group in the first half of the period, although they returned to the poorest group in the subsequent period.

Because of the generally poor growth performance of developing countries during the 1980s and part of the 1990s, membership in the lowest-income group had increased to 75 countries by 2001, with several countries members of the Commonwealth of Independent States (CIS) as well as some Latin American countries having joined the group. The latter group included Bolivia, which had faced a period of hyperinflation in the 1980s, as well as El Salvador and Nicaragua, which had suffered from prolonged periods of civil strife in the 1970s and 1980s. Polarization of growth took place also at the other end of the spectrum, with the group of rich countries and areas having increased in number from 22 in 1960 to 29 in 2001, after welcoming Hong Kong SAR, Japan, Israel, the Republic of Korea, Portugal, Puerto Rico, Singapore, Slovenia, Spain and Ireland. In contrast, Argentina, the Bolivarian Republic of Venezuela, Qatar and Kuwait dropped to a lower income category.

Most East and South Asian countries and areas had belonged to the poorest group in 1960, with the exception of Taiwan Province of China, Singapore, the Philippines, Malaysia and Japan which already had by then a GDP per capita that was higher than half of the world average. By 2001, nearly all of them had exited the poorest group. Subregional convergence clubs appeared to have formed. By 1980, following active export-oriented industrial policies and sustained growth, the Republic of Korea had managed to catch up with the slower-growing economies of Malaysia and the Philippines. GDP per capita has also grown rapidly in Thailand and the Democratic Republic of Korea, albeit at more modest rates than that of the Republic of Korea.

During this long period, Singapore, Taiwan Province of China and Japan crossed the income threshold of the rich country club. Japan had already joined the industrialized country club by 1970, with a level of GDP per capita three times higher than the mean income for the world. A "flying geese formation" emerged in the region (Okita, 1985): Japan led the group, followed by: the first-tier newly industrialized economies, namely, the Republic of Korea, Taiwan Province of China and Singapore; and the second-tier newly industrialized economies, namely, Malaysia, Thailand, Indonesia and then China and Viet Nam. Once in motion, the geese were able to continue flying after their leader (Japan) slowed its pace and—if one wishes to develop the metaphor—a new formation emerged in recent years with China as its leader. However, it is through the rise of China and India, as the most dynamic centres during those years, that the pattern of growth in Asia has been entirely reshaped.

Bangladesh, Pakistan and Sri Lanka in South Asia sustained an almost uninterrupted per capita growth rate of 2 per cent or higher during the period 1980-2001. The only significant disappointment in that region was the Philippines, which did not manage to divest itself of its status as a lower middle income country.

The story for the other continents is only slightly more diverse. The trend towards regional convergence predominated, though in the opposite direction: the initially richer countries converged downward following unsatisfactory growth. In CIS and Eastern and Central European countries, upward convergence had occurred during 1960-1980 and up to 1990 (not shown in figure I.6) when the dismantling of the communist bloc took place. During their transition to becoming market economies, two trends emerged. On the one hand, the Central European countries and the Baltic States, which by now had acceded to EU membership, retained their position in the upper middle income group. The rest, on the other hand, experienced an absolute decrease in GDP per capita which caused them to converge downward to a lower income group.

In Latin America and the Caribbean, Brazil's economy had strongly expanded during the golden age at a rate of 3.8 per cent per year in per capita terms and by 1980 its income level surpassed the average for the world. This also held for Mexico. Argentina, Honduras and Peru, on the other hand, dropped into lower income groups. Figure I.6 B shows that Argentina's income level did become similar to that of Brazil, Chile, Colombia, Uruguay and Mexico, all of which had a GDP per capita between one and two times WGP per capita. Argentina's average living standard had used to be more than double that of the average for the world in 1960. For the region as a whole, the lost decade of the 1980s and the several financial crises in the 1990s served to cancel much of the effect of earlier growth gains and the slowdown in the widening of the income gap relative to the industrialized world achieved in the previous buoyant period (see figure I.6 C). In this period, GDP growth slowed down considerably in all countries, with the exception of Chile.

On the African continent, in contrast, the trend has been one of downward convergence of income levels following slow growth in nearly all of the countries over the last four decades. Only the southern tip of the continent, comprising Botswana, Mauritius, South Africa and Namibia, as well as Gabon on the west coast and Tunisia in the north, had avoided membership in the lowest income club as of 2001. Among these, only Botswana, Mauritius and Tunisia grew steadily for prolonged periods. Botswana's success was due to its richness in natural resources and its good institutions (see chapter V). Mauritius, whose GDP per capita grew at an average annual rate of 4.2 per cent over the period 1970-2003, redirected its development strategy away from the primary sector to focus on strengthening the industrial sector, largely through protectionist measures (see chapter III). Positive but very low growth rates over that period were recorded in a few other countries, including Kenya, Ghana, Uganda, Mozambique, Zimbabwe and Mauritania.

Finally, Western Europe and the Western offshoots became more homogeneous as well only in their case this was the result of upward convergence, with the countries that had been poorer in 1960 having joined the club by 2001. Growth rates in the industrialized country club for the recent period have slowed down to an annual average of 2 per cent per capita.

Growth Divergence and Human Development

The large inequalities in income are paralleled by huge disparities in other indicators of well-being. In 2002, the life expectancy of a child born in Japan (82 years), Switzerland (80 years) or the United States (77 years) was more than double that for a child born in Zambia (37 years), Malawi (38 years) or Botswana (38 years). Similarly, opportunities in education show huge disparities across countries. Educational attainment measured in years of schooling amounted to less than 4 years in sub-Saharan Africa but to more than 12 years in developed countries. As in the case of incomes, such major differences in education and health between citizens of different countries are mostly larger than those between various groups within countries.

While these disparities are still very large, over the last four decades most parts of the world have seen progress in terms of higher life expectancy and more schooling. In fact, there has been more convergence across countries in outcomes for health and education than in outcomes for incomes. In 1960, for instance, there were 73 countries whose citizens had a life expectancy of less than 50 years and 45 countries whose citizens had a life expectancy of 65 years or more. These "twin peaks" had disappeared by 2002; population data from the United Nations indicates that the number of countries in which a newborn was expected to live less than 50 years had dropped to 32 (all in sub-Saharan Africa), and the number of countries where he or she was expected to survive for at least 65 years had increased to 128. At the same time, inequalities in life expectancy at the extremes increased during the 1980s and 1990s, mainly because of the toll taken on lives in Africa by the HIV/AIDS epidemic. Progress has also been evident in education: the average number of years of schooling for all citizens almost doubled between 1960 and 2002, from 3.4 to 6.3 and disparities across countries fell (Schady, 2005). For many countries, however, the pace of this convergence in indicators of well-being has slowed considerably since 1980 and it has stagnated from the beginning of the 1990s (United Nations Development Programme, 2005).

Thus, though global income inequality is reflected in other indicators of well-being, divergence in education and health outcomes has become less pronounced. What does this tell us about the relationship between human development and economic growth? When associating life expectancy and infant mortality with per capita income levels across countries, one finds that at low levels of development, health improves strongly with increase in income but improves more slowly above a certain threshold per capita income level (about $3,000 in constant 2000 dollars, according to figure I.7). Such a non-linear relationship can also be found for education.

Figure I.7.
The relation between level of income and life expectancy, 2002

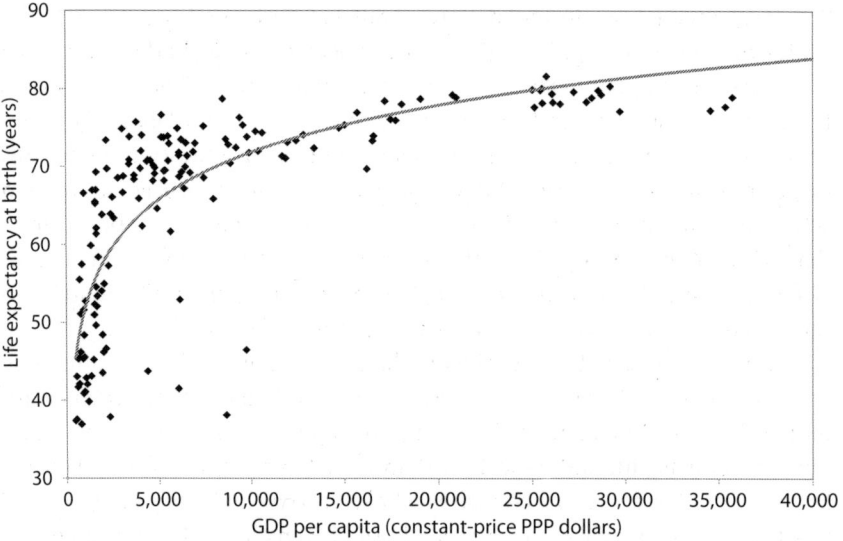

Sources: World Bank, World Development Indicators 2005 database; and UN/DESA.

The links between growth and human development are complex and they probably stand in a two-way relationship, implying that both must be promoted to sustain progress in either.[7] Economies may find themselves in a virtuous cycle with growth and human development reinforcing each other or they may be trapped in a vicious cycle. Based on empirical evidence for 84 countries, Ranis and Stewart (2005) identified two additional scenarios of country performance: one characterized by strong human development (HD) and weak economic growth (EG), which the authors call HD-lopsided, and the other characterized by weak human development and strong economic growth, styled EG-lopsided.[8] Most of the countries selected for the study were experiencing either a virtuous or a vicious cycle, with only one in the EG-lopsided group, and a few others displaying an HD-lopsided pattern. In the context of growth divergence patterns, it is of interest to see which countries had moved towards a virtuous cycle over the four decades, which had not and had actually moved into other groups, and which had been able to escape from the vicious cycle.

The results showed that the only countries that had remained consistently within the virtuous cycle were the Republic of Korea and Singapore. A few other countries, mostly in Asia, managed to move over time into the virtuous cycle group, namely, China, in the 1970s, and Viet Nam and Malaysia, in the 1990s, as well as Chile in the 1990s. All of these countries were also identified above as convergence success stories. Many other countries, following the debt crises in Latin America or the financial crises of the 1990s, moved from the virtuous cycle to the HD-lopsided category. The study also revealed that most of the countries that had been in a vicious cycle in the 1960s tended to remain there, reinforcing the idea of the low-equilibrium growth trap discussed earlier. Only those countries that had been initially affected by civil wars advanced, once these conflicts were resolved, to better performance categories. These findings indicate that a number of the countries that had been HD-lopsided managed to enter the stage of sustained economic growth and converge upward but that those that were EG-lopsided typically did not. The fact, however, that not all countries with relatively higher levels of human development managed to reach higher levels of long-term economic growth suggests that human development is a necessary but not a sufficient condition for economic growth.

Figure I.8 attempts to capture the relationship between convergence and human development for the period 1960-2003. In a slight modification of Ranis and Stewart (2005), the figure plots a convergence parameter instead of GDP growth. The convergence parameter reflects the difference between the annual change in the ratio of GDP per capita of the country in question to average WGP per capita. The indicator for human development measures the annual change in the infant mortality rate (number of infant deaths per 1,000 live births). The negative slope suggests that faster income convergence will also accelerate the decrease in the infant mortality rate.

Increasing income inequality among countries has an indirect impact on human development. A country that sees its relative income decline will be more affected by global asymmetries as represented, for example, by less access to external finance and weaker international bargaining power (see below) and this will affect the country's growth potential. Lower growth, in turn, may negatively affect income inequality within the country if it leads, for instance, to a shrinkage in government revenues and therefore in the

Figure I.8.
The relation between income convergence and the decrease in infant mortality rate, 1960-2003

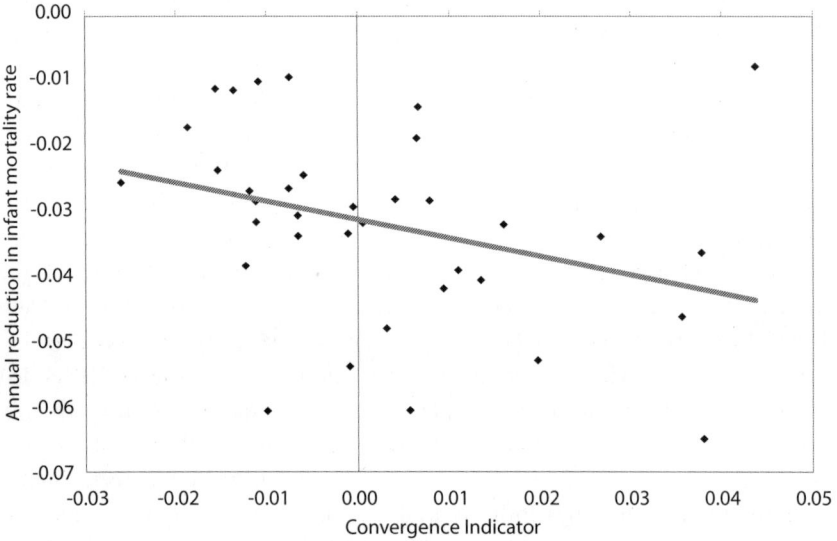

Sources: World Bank, World Development Indicators 2005 database; and UN/DESA.

availability of resources necessary for investment in human development. Insufficient human capital investment will feed back into lower growth and further divergence.

PERPETUATION OF INEQUALITY AND ITS IMPLICATIONS FOR WORLD DEVELOPMENT

Some observers, such as Robert Lucas (quoted earlier), argue that we have endured the worst of global inequality. As technology spreads more easily with globalization and institutions across the world become more similar, income levels will also eventually converge. In this sense, one could interpret China's spectacular growth over the past 20 years as the first major break in the trend towards rising global inequality. But is it really a break in that trend? There is no guarantee that soon other poor countries in the region, like Bangladesh or Pakistan, will also shift towards a high and sustained growth path, in a new flying geese formation led by China. Yet, even if this does not happen, one could still ask what impact the continued growth of China's economy would have on different developing countries.

Again, the implications are hard to predict. Since economic growth in developing countries closely follows that of the world's largest economy, poor countries could benefit from a more dynamic engine of world economic growth. Figure I.9 shows that developing countries have followed the trends in economic growth of the United States America, though with more pronounced swings. This figure compares the five-year moving average in GDP growth rates for the global economy, China, the United States and 153 developing economies (excluding China) since 1963. The correlation coefficient between long-run trends in GDP growth of the United States and long-run trends in world GDP growth is 0.82 and a simple lead-lag analysis shows that the United States economy leads the global economy by one year. The Chinese economy also leads world GDP, by one or two years, but this began only after the end of the 1970s.

Figure I.9.
Growth rates of output of the global economy, China, the United States and the group of developing countries (excluding China), 1963-2005[a] *(percentages)*

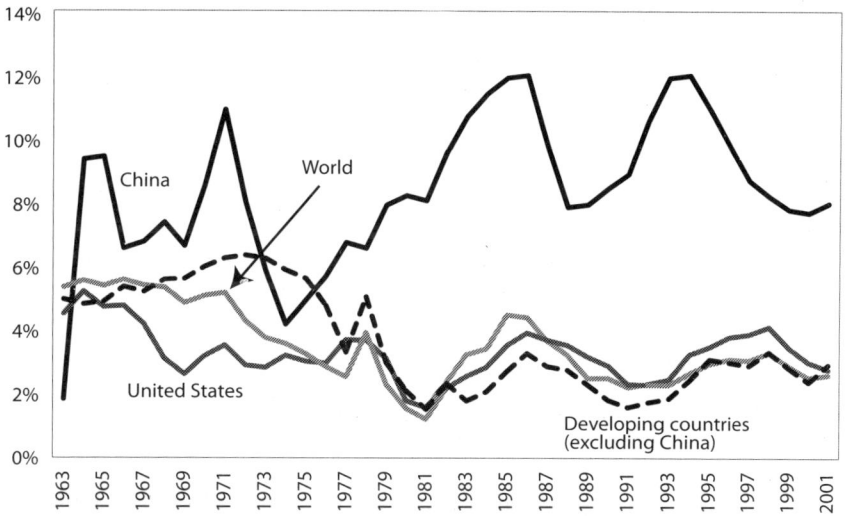

Sources: World Bank, World Development Indicators 2005 database; and UN/DESA.
[a] Five-year moving averages. The graph indicates the first year of the five-year period, that is, for instance, 2001 refers to the moving average for 2001-2005.

If the current trends are maintained, China would overtake the United States as the largest economy by the mid-2030s (or earlier, when measuring income in PPPs) but would pull up world economic growth substantially before that. But the effects of a dynamic Chinese economy are not evenly distributed. Primary exporting developing countries gain through rapidly expanding trade and improved terms of trade, but producers of low-wage manufacturing goods may lose from Chinese competition. The continuation of these patters is hard to predict, however. First of all, it is doubtful whether China can sustain its present pace of growth, at about 9-10 per cent per year over the long run. Also, as wage costs must rise with high growth, China's reliance on labour-intensive manufacturing may not be sustainable and the economy will have to undergo major structural change, which will alter the country's import structure and thereby the impact on the rest of the world. If this happens, the benefits from Chinese growth may become more evenly distributed in the rest of the developing world.

Part of the problem in analysing these and other potential scenarios is that our understanding of the determinants of economic growth is still poor. The basic outcome of the development of a very large literature on the subject over the past two decades has been that economists are rediscovering the complexities of economic growth. The new emerging consensus is that the conditions conducive to growth are many times country-specific and that the policies needed to create such conditions are not reducible to simple formulas.[9] Those who believe the determinants of economic growth need to be understood within the historical and institutional setting of a country reject the simple view of, for instance, the "Washington Consensus" that economic prosperity is a matter of getting a particular set of national policies "right", or –according to the more recent views– one of getting the institutions right. The diagnosis of growth conditions should become a search for the binding constraints, such as limitations in mobilizing sufficient finance, low levels of human capital, weak institutions and a lack of policy space for dealing with market failures and external shocks. Different country circumstances and initial conditions will point to different binding constraints, and policies targeting such constraints may be more successful than across-the-board reforms whose implementation involves political obstacles and which have often failed to achieve growth.

In the light of the previous discussion, this seems a sensible approach. However, the observed regional polarization of growth also suggests that initial conditions are not merely country-specific: they also interact with conditions specific to regional location and the dynamics of the global economy. The analysis of the role of these factors is not inconsistent with the above-mentioned approach and should complement the analysis of the specific country-level conditions. For historical reasons, countries may share similar initial conditions. During colonial and early post-colonial times, the economies of Latin America and Africa, for instance, were developed to provide raw materials and to specialize in extractive industries. Also, institutional frameworks may have similar historical roots because of a shared colonial past.

It is important to bear in mind that initial conditions are difficult to manipulate and countries with poorer endowments have greater difficulties in positioning themselves to benefit from world economic growth and make a break with the past. Hence, economies with similar backgrounds and structures will more likely move in the same direction. From this perspective, what comes to mind is Gunnar Myrdal's principle of cumulative causation, according to which poor countries continue to get poorer while the rich ones continue to get richer as long as there are no exogenous factors to force a change (Myrdal, 1957). In other words, there is no tendency towards automatic income convergence. Rather, world market imperfections compound trends towards divergence. Such global asymmetries also affect the policy space available to countries for improving growth opportunities (Ocampo and Martin, 2003).

Countries with poor and/or the "wrong" endowments tend to have greater disadvantages in respect of their benefiting from international trade and finance. It still holds that countries dependent on a few primary export commodities, be they coffee, cotton or minerals, have experienced great volatility in the world market prices of their exports; and over the past decades, they have seen their commodity prices decline relative to those of manufactured goods. This has limited available resources and weak institutions have been unable to conduct credible policies and mobilize the domestic and external financial resources for private investment and investment in human development and infrastructure that are needed to diversify. Figure I.10 suggests that there is likely a strong association between a high dependence on a few exports and lower levels of development. The group of least developed countries, comprising the poorest countries, show least export diversification; also, the regions with poorer growth performance in Latin America and Africa continue to show higher export concentration ratios than those of other regions.

Differences in initial conditions are exacerbated by the inequitable functioning of world markets. Capital flows tend to concentrate among the richer countries. Most of these flows take place among the developed economies and capital moving to developing countries tends to concentrate among those with higher incomes and better growth performance. More than two thirds of foreign direct investment (FDI) is concentrated in developed economies. Well over 80 per cent of the FDI to developing countries moves to 12 mostly middle-income countries (but including India and China), with all other developing countries receiving almost none. Only the rapidly growing Asian countries have received an increasing share of world FDI. As analysed at length in chapter IV, other forms of private capital flows to developing

Figure I.10.
Diversification of merchandise exports by region, 1980, 1990 and 2004
(export concentration index[a])

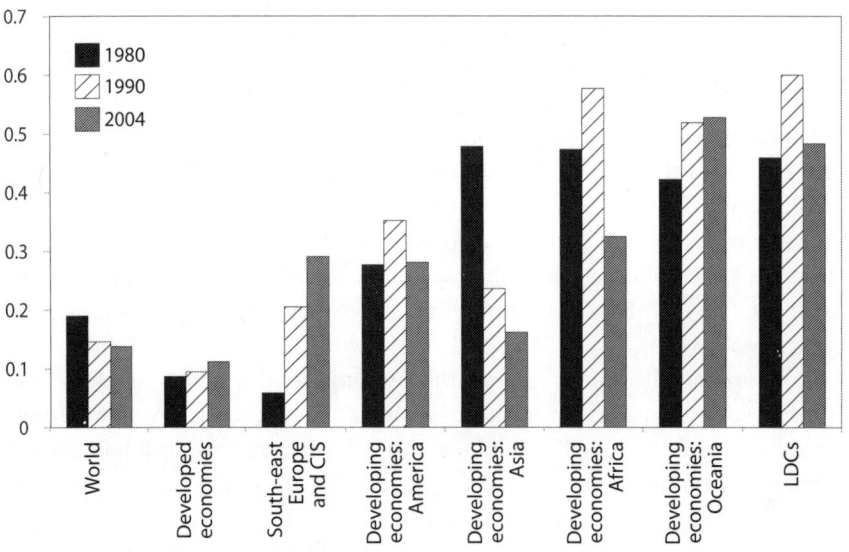

Sources: UNCTAD (2005).
Note: Country groupings are as specified in UNCTAD (2005).
[a] Measured through the Herfindahl-Hirschmann index, which has been normalized to obtain values between 0 and 1 (maximum concentration means reliance on one export product only).

countries tend to show a similar pattern of concentration and pro-cyclical behaviour. Pro-cyclical capital flows bring additional policy challenges to recipient countries, as they hamper the creation of the space required to conduct counter-cyclical macroeconomic policies and may contribute to financial instability, particularly in countries with weak financial systems.

Inequities also exist in the mobility of labour. Unskilled workers from developing countries who could earn higher wages in the developed countries encounter many obstacles when trying to migrate.

Greater global equity can be achieved by international policies that are able to improve the endowments of countries and deal with world market imperfections. Global trade negotiations include clauses giving preferential treatments to the poorest countries. Development aid has the potential of helping countries to improve their resource base and invest in improving their endowments in infrastructure, human development and other areas. Debt-relief initiatives have been undertaken to reduce the debt burden of the poorest nations and measures have been taken to promote global financial stability, such as the establishment in 1999 of the Financial Stability Forum.

However, global inequality not only reduces the opportunities of the poorest countries to gain from freer trade and financial flows, but also has a bearing on how the rules governing world markets are set. In international financial markets, no clear debt workout mechanisms have been established and the existing informal mechanisms tend to benefit international lenders, often to the detriment of developing-country investors and taxpayers. Initiatives for a better burden-sharing, inter alia, through collective action clauses, are recent and far from effective (see, for example, United Nations, 2005b). The Financial Stability Forum and the Basel Committee on Banking Supervision gather representatives from the central banks and finance ministries of the countries members of the Organization for Economic Cooperation and Development (OECD) but have no developing-country representation. The voting power in international financial institutions such as IMF and the World Bank is also skewed in favour of the more developed countries, as that power is based on the capital contributions of the member countries.

There are also important asymmetries in the policy space for conducting macroeconomic policies. Most developing countries do not have the option to issue liabilities in their own currency, and effectiveness of monetary policies is more generally limited by poorly developed financial and capital markets.[10] Such limitations severely limit the capacity of policymakers to conduct counter-cyclical macroeconomic policies. This leaves the economies vulnerable to exogenous shocks such as fluctuations in the interest rate denominated in another currency, as was the case for Latin America during financial crises and as is also the case for many African countries. Unlike East Asian countries, Latin American countries had largely pro-cyclical policies which exacerbated the magnitude of boom-and-bust cycles and deepened financial volatility and its long-lasting adverse effects on growth (see chapter IV).

Trade rules set in multilateral negotiations during the Doha Round under the World Trade Organization can result in gains also for the poorer countries. However, this impact will vary across countries and regions and, as indicated, the freer trade scenarios likely provide lesser gains for the poorer countries because of their poorer endowments. Negotiations under the World Trade Organization are equitable in the sense that each country has one vote and each country also has a veto because decision-making is by consensus. In practice, however, developing countries find it difficult to follow negotiations or invest in studies that evaluate the implications of the trade reforms for their economies, or they simply have no resources even for sending delegates to the negotiations. Poor countries can bring disputes to the World Trade Organization, but even a ruling in favour does not mean unfair protectionist measures (enacted by World Trade Organization agreement) will be redressed.

The capacity of poor countries to retaliate against powerful trading partners is low and probably ineffective: powerful countries will feel little pain from such unfavourable rulings in World Trade Organization disputes. This does not imply that all global economic governance is unfair per se; still, the role played by developing countries is limited and changing the rules of the game in their favour is hard, making asymmetries difficult to redress.

Development aid is not primarily benefiting the poorest countries. In particular, the fact that much of the provision of bilateral official development assistance (ODA) is driven by the political and economic objectives of donor countries leads to middle-income developing countries receiving an important share of the transfers. Moreover, the effectiveness of aid in stimulating growth and development has been the subject of a heated debate, analysed in chapter IV.

As a result, poorer countries have less power than richer ones to influence the institutional rules governing global markets and hence the processes that might redress the rising inequality in the world income distribution.

All of this is not to say that domestic factors, including institutions and policies, are not important. Indeed, they are crucial, though they are not simply givens or exogenous but are shaped in part through the interaction with the dynamics of global markets. The following chapters provide more extensive answers to questions like how the East Asian economies have managed to break free of their slow growth and maintain over the long run an impressive growth record, while the much richer Latin America of the 1950s has fallen behind; and why a fast-growing Botswana remains an enclave in sub-Saharan Africa, while the Republic of Korea and Taiwan Province of China manage to "export" their success to neighbouring countries. Would the presence of a Japan in Latin America or in sub-Saharan Africa be enough to induce the emergence of a first- or second-tier newly industrialized economy in these regions? In the aggregate, growth divergences among countries and regions determine global development and feed back into the patterns of divergence.

Both the experience of successful countries and that of unsuccessful ones offer lessons that are of equal importance, as they provide knowledge on how to bring about sustained growth and how to correct adverse growth trends. Chapter II investigates how structural changes in the economy are associated with patterns of long-term growth. This should inform policymakers about what kind of structural changes to aim at when designing macroeconomic policies. Chapter III presents the lessons learned from several decades of country experiences regarding the way in which growth divergences are associated with the composition of, and trends in, trade and capital flows and specialization patterns. Protection sector and trade policies have played important roles in sustaining and changing specialization patterns. In this respect, chapter III represents an attempt to learn from the successful East Asian countries and analyse the policy space left for countries in the light of multilateral trade agreements.

Chapter IV is concerned with the nature of the policy space for conducting counter-cyclical macroeconomic policies and that of the fiscal space for investing in long-term development through physical and social infrastructure; and it tries to determine whether countries that are able to conduct counter-cyclical macroeconomic policies have been more successful in achieving high long-term growth and whether those countries invest more in human development and infrastructure in order to sustain it. Chapter V explores the question which institutions and conditions for good governance matter most for long-run economic growth and hence for global divergence or convergence and further shows that growing global inequality and the underlying growth patterns also have a bearing on security and conflict. Countries specializing predominantly in extractive industries of non-renewable resources have the greatest incidence of conflicts. The results indicate that low income per capita and growth failures make countries susceptible to instability and conflict.

As argued, the growth performance of a country is determined not only by factors that come into play within its geographical boundaries, especially in today's integrated global economy. Indeed, the underlying reasons for the divergence also make it more difficult to grow out of poverty and vulnerability to global shocks. Hence, the greater likelihood of growth collapses and conflict as global inequality rises. The problem of rising global inequality thus has an important bearing on the achievement of the Millennium Development Goals and more difficult and affects global security. Failure to redress the tendency towards growing global inequality could thus have wide-ranging consequences for human development.

Notes

1. Data compare per capita incomes measured in purchasing power parities (see table I.1).
2. Income inequality between countries is sometimes referred to as "international inequality", as distinct from "global inequality" which would account for the inequality both between and within countries (see Milanovic, 2005). The latter concept would thus account for differences in income between all individual citizens of the world. As indicated, the analysis of the present study will be confined to differences between the average per capita incomes of countries.
3. Data are based on Maddison (1995; 2001).
4. The analysis here is largely based on the evidence presented in Ocampo and Parra (2005). Hausmann, Pritchett and Rodrik (2004) found a similar pattern. They searched for instances of a rapid acceleration in economic growth that had been sustained during a period of at least eight years. They supplied the initial year and the countries that had experienced those instances of an acceleration in growth in the period 1950-1998 (ibid., table 2.1). Considering an episode as belonging to a particular decade if at least four of the minimum seven years belonged to that decade, they counted 23 episodes in the 1960s, 30 in the 1970s, and only 14 in both the 1980s and 1990s.
5. See Ocampo and Parra (2005), as well as Reddy and Minoiu (2005), who reported similar results. The latter study examines real-income stagnation defined as negligible or negative per capita real-income growth for a significant and uninterrupted sequence of years. Reddy and Minoiu found that of the total number of countries for which data were available; the proportion that had experienced a stagnation spell had increased sharply and steadily between the 1960s and the 1990s, from 12 and 22 per cent in the 1960s and the 1970s, respectively, to 50 and 38 per cent in the 1980s and the 1990s, respectively.
6. Statistical Annex table A.1 provides more detailed decomposition of the Theil coefficient of international inequality, showing the contribution of each region to the overall level of inequality. The inequality estimates shown consider income differences only between countries and not within countries. The table also confirms that international income inequality is overwhelmingly explained by the differences between developed and developing countries.
7. This point is also emphasized by Ranis and Stewart (2005) on the basis of a review of the related literature.
8. The indicator used in lieu of an overall human development index is the rate of reduction of the infant mortality rate.
9. Many of these views reflect the influential work of Dani Rodrik and are well stated in Rodrik (2003), Hausmann, Rodrik and Velasco (2005), and World Bank (2005b), as well as in a special issue of *Finance & Development* (March 2006).
10. See chapter IV, Ocampo (2005a), Ocampo and Vos (2006), and FitzGerald (2008) for elaborations of this argument.

Chapter II
Structural Change and Economic Growth

An essential insight of classical development economics was that economic growth is intrinsically linked to changes in the structure of production. According to this view, industrialization is the driver of technical change, and overall productivity increases are mainly the result of the reallocation of labour from low- to high-productivity activities. The present chapter investigates to what extent this view is still relevant today and thus how the degree and nature of structural change explain the diverging growth trends between developing countries.

The first section presents alternative views of the growth process, underscoring the difference between the drivers of that process in developed countries and those in developing ones. The second section demonstrates that the fast-growing Asian regions were able to make large and speedy transitions out of agriculture and into industries and services, while economies with little structural change lagged behind. The traditional view that capital accumulation is important for growth still holds, as the subsequent section shows, although they do not stand in a one-to-one relationship. The structure of investment is also important, not only because industrialization requires more investment in the manufacturing sector, but also owing to the fact that important investments in financial and business services are needed to support industrial development. Further, low growth is associated with greater investment volatility. External shocks and erratic domestic policies are conducive to greater economic uncertainty, which hampers the long-term investment required to realize dynamic structural change, an issue that is explored in detail in chapter IV.

The final section analyses how employment and labour productivity have shifted along with patterns of growth and structural change in developing economies. Sustained increases in labour productivity and reallocation of labour from low- to high-productivity sectors are characteristics of the fast-growing economies. Yet, important employment shifts towards industrial and services sectors are also observed in those regions with low growth performance. In these cases, however, employment growth is not accompanied by higher productivity, indicating that labour is absorbed by low-productivity activities where it remains largely underutilized.

Owing to data limitations, the analysis in this chapter is restricted to a sample of 57 developing economies. They are grouped in 10 geographical country groups (with China as a single-country "group") and an analytical group made up of eight semi-industrialized countries.[1] Again owing to data problems, the information for certain variables (the structure of employment) and some groups of countries covers shorter time periods.[2]

Economic Growth requires Structural Change

Productivity growth in developed countries mainly relies on technological innovation. For developing countries, however, growth and development are much less about pushing the technology frontier and much more about changing the structure of production towards activities with higher levels of productivity. This kind of structural change can be achieved largely by adopting and adapting existing technologies, substituting imports and entering into world markets for manufacturing goods and services, and through rapid accumulation of physical and human capital. A few developing countries have been able to undertake original research and development in some fields, but technological innovation continues to be highly concentrated in the industrialized world.

These fundamental differences in the nature of the growth process between developed and developing countries remain subject to considerable debate among economists. Among the most important analytical developments in recent decades has been the explicit recognition by the "new growth theories" of the role of external economies in human capital formation and technological innovation, of dynamic economies of scale associated to learning by doing, and of institutional factors in the growth process. These new insights have moved away from the more traditional perspective that accumulation of capital was the key to economic development. They also held the promise of a better linking of policies to economic growth performance.

Nonetheless, empirical studies based on these theoretical insights, largely relying on cross-country evidence, have left many questions unanswered. In particular, the analyses failed to identify meaningful criteria for determining which of the close to 150 variables found statistically significant in various studies should be considered the core determinants of economic growth. Aside from such inconclusiveness, there was a failure by this literature to grasp the importance of context-specific factors, particularly those associated with institutional development (see chapter V). Also, it has poorly captured the fact that the growth impact of policies tends to differ across countries and time periods (an issue that is called non-linearity). The main focus has been on domestic factors, with the external factors that explain why growth successes and failures cluster in specific time periods and regions being ignored (see chapter I). Even more important for the theme of this chapter, the main emphasis of such studies has been on aggregate growth and, to a large extent, on a search for explanatory factors of technological progress, assuming that factors of production are fully utilized and use the best technology available in the country. In other words, the focus has been on the core determinants of the growth process in developed countries, rather than on such determinants in developing economies where underutilization of labour (and sometimes other factors of production) and the coexistence of modern and traditional production technologies are the rule rather than the exception.

On the other hand, economists who follow the tradition of classical development thinking have held that economic growth in developing countries is about structural change towards high-productivity sectors and that industrialization plays a key role in that process (Ros, 2000). According to this view, the development of the modern industrial sector will contribute more in dynamic terms to overall output growth, because of its higher productivity growth which results from increasing returns to scale[3] and gains from innovations and learning by doing.[4] The underemployed labour force of the rural sector, but increasingly also of the urban informal sector, provides a fairly elastic supply of labour that allows this process to take place without facing significant labour supply constraints.

Early empirical studies had already showed the importance of industrial development for higher long-term economic growth, indicating that it has indeed been an observed "regularity" in development patterns (Kuznets, 1966; Chenery and Taylor, 1968; and Chenery, 1979). Modernization of agriculture is also essential to facilitating a dynamic transformation from an agricultural to a modern industrial society (see chapter V). As economies moved up the ladder of development, services sectors would gain importance. Modern service sectors are also a source of productivity gain and are essential for the achievement of industrialization. As international trade for services grows, they also offer a new opportunity for export development (see chapter III).

Notions similar to those of classical development thinking are also embedded in the early, non-neoclassical growth theories of Verdoorn (1949) and Kaldor (1957, 1978), among others. Kaldor (1978) suggested that productivity and output growth reinforced each other. The positive effect of productivity increases on output growth has been extensively discussed in the economics literature. The reverse causality whereby productivity growth itself depends on how fast the overall economy is growing has received much less attention. In this view, productivity is determined endogenously in expanding production sectors. Learning by doing, innovations and sectoral linkages are all factors that influence productivity positively when growth accelerates. Indeed, as the economy expands, these factors become more important for productivity growth as more resources become available for investment in new technology and for the training of workers. Learning by doing and experience accumulated during the production process by both entrepreneurs and labourers are also essential for productivity growth and these factors become increasingly important when growth is dynamic.

If resources are not initially fully utilized—because of un- and underemployment—not only will growth lead to better utilization of existing resources, but productivity growth will also accelerate as resources are increasingly utilized and are shifted from low- to high-productivity activities, an idea consonant with classical development thinking. Inversely, slow economic growth will lead to increasing underutilization of resources and hence to adverse effects on productivity. In this sense, the association that is usually established between slow productivity performance and slow economic growth may have its basis not in a lack of technological change, but rather in the growing underutilization of resources that characterizes a low-growth environment, reflecting the reverse causality mentioned above. In other words, if resources are not fully utilized or are underutilized, weak productivity performance may be the result rather than a determinant of low output growth.

Building upon these foundations, one can develop a broader perspective on structural change and growth. In this view, dynamic structural change involves more than just growth of industry and modern services. It is about the ability to constantly generate new activities as well as about the capacity of the new activities to absorb surplus labour and to promote the integration of production sectors within the domestic economy (that is to say, to strengthen domestic linkages) (see, for example, Ocampo, 2005b). From this angle, the industrial sector tends to have larger potential to induce deeper domestic integration by processing raw materials and semi-industrial inputs and requiring a number of ancillary services. The degree of integration of the domestic economy further influences the size of the domestic market as well as the degree of technological and other spillover effects that exports and foreign direct investment (FDI) can create for domestic economic activity and in this way, it influences the extent to which a country is able to benefit from international trade and investment. In this sense, only when it is based on or can help create strong domestic linkages, will integration into the world economy generate rapid technological progress and contribute to high and sustained growth. These issues are dealt with more extensively in chapter III.

PATTERNS OF GROWTH AND STRUCTURAL CHANGE, 1970-2003[5]

Developing economies grow faster as the importance of the industrial and services sectors increases and that of agriculture decreases (see figures II.1 and II.2). Fast growth in China, South-East Asia and South Asia was associated with a rapid decline in the importance of agriculture and strong expansions of industry and services during 1970-2003. In contrast, sluggish long-term growth after the 1970s in the semi-industrialized countries and in Central America and the Caribbean as well as in countries in the Middle East and the Commonwealth of Independent States (CIS) was associated with a process of de-industrialization (of variable intensity). In these groups, growth was generally concentrated in the services sector with the share of agriculture in output also declining or remaining stagnant.

Clearly, also, the relationship between structural change and economic growth is not exactly the same everywhere. In particular, the dynamics of the service sectors vis-à-vis industry plays an important role in explaining performance in several regions. Thus, in recent decades, rapid economic growth in the first-tier newly industrialized economies was accompanied by much less structural change directed towards industry than in other dynamic Asian regions. This can be attributed largely to the fact that much industrialization had taken place in the first-tier newly industrialized economies prior to 1970, the starting year of the period of this analysis. Also, the expansion of services was more dynamic in South Asia relative to South-East Asia. Also, for the period from 1990 to 2003, services played the leading role in the growth experienced by Central and Eastern European countries in 1990-2003, as these countries showed (on average) some de-industrialization. On the contrary, the stagnation or contraction of the export sector explain the virtual stagnation of the economies of sub-Saharan Africa and the smaller Andean countries.

A closer look at these experiences helps to obtain a better understanding of the nature of the links between growth and structural change in different developing country regions and countries. The Asian countries followed a dynamic pattern of structural change. China is the most important case in point. Starting around 1978, it went through a gradual change from Soviet-style central planning towards greater market orientation. Despite its large population, China witnessed an impressive and rapid change in the sectoral

Figure II.1.
Economic growth and structural changes in the industrial sector, the public utilities and services sector, and agriculture, selected regions and country groups, 1970-2003

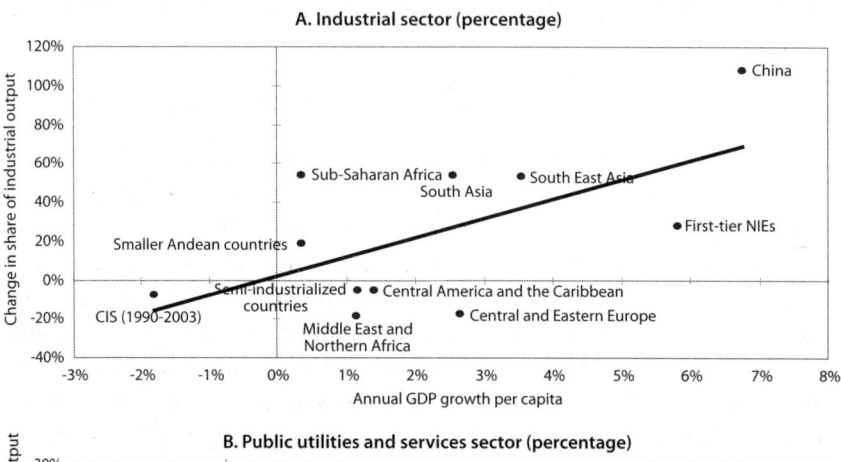

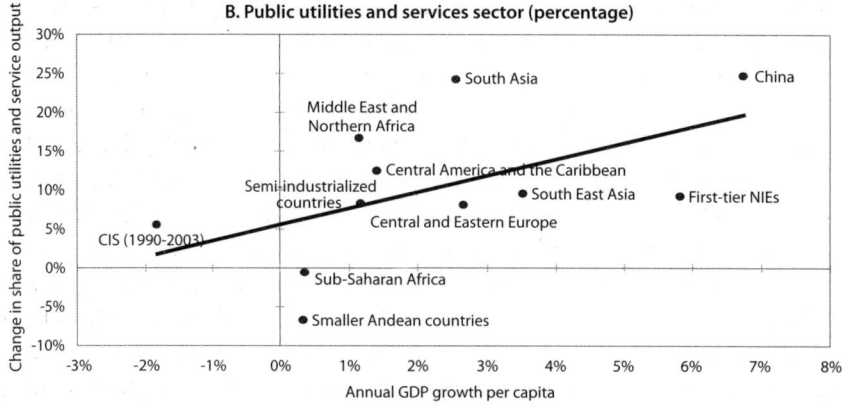

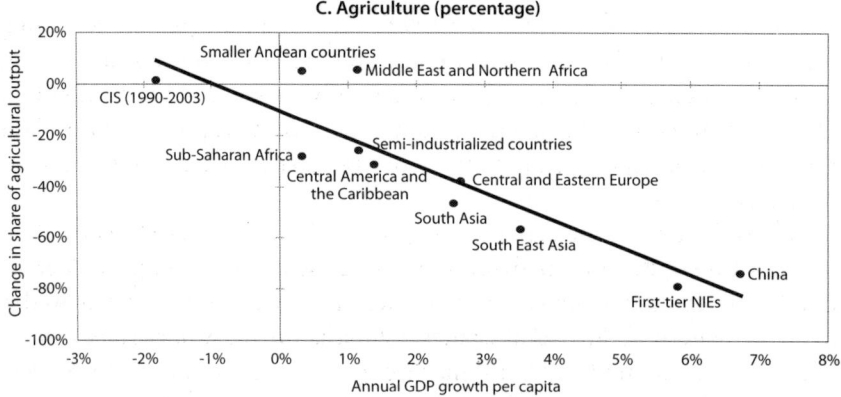

Source: UN/DESA, based on United Nations Statistics Division, National Accounts Main Aggregates database.

Figure II.2.
Annual growth rates of output per capita in agriculture, mining and manufacturing, and the public utilities and services sectors, selected regions and country groups, 1970-2003

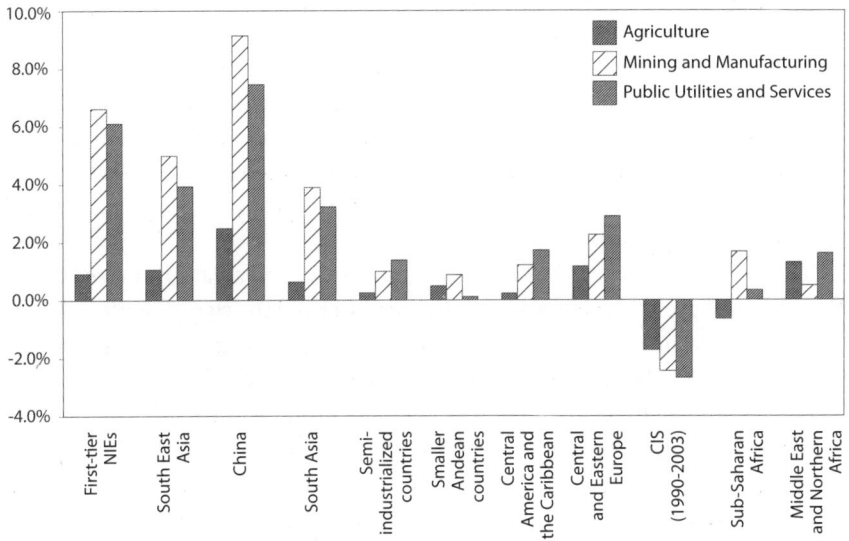

Source: UN/DESA, based on United Nations Statistics Division, National Accounts Main Aggregates database.

composition of output. Between 1970 and 2003, the share of manufacturing and mining in overall output increased from 28 per cent to 60 per cent, while the share of agriculture dropped from 49 to 12 per cent. A reform of rural institutions (see chapter V) and aggressive investment policies inducing infrastructure development in support of export industries promoted this vast transformation. The land reform and infrastructure development lifted the main binding constraints on agriculture growth and helped unleash previously untapped economic forces. Add to these trends a policy of gradual opening to world markets and one finds much similarity with the type of export-led growth strategy followed by the first tier newly industrialized economies.

The first-tier newly industrialized economies, as indicated, had witnessed substantial industrial growth in the 1960s following an initial strategy of import substitution. The industrial sector had already grown to significant proportions by the 1970s when growth became export-oriented. It should be noted, though, that import substitution policies were maintained for the development of new sectors. By the mid-1980s, these economies had switched to high-tech manufacturing production (see chapter III) and strengthened the development of modern services. The success of the first-tier newly industrialized economies in making this more recent dynamic structural change was fostered to some extent by external events. Among such events, the substantial appreciation of the yen against the United States dollar owing to the Plaza Accord of 1985 was particularly relevant to the support of export growth in these economies. As the Asian first-tier newly industrialized economies had pegged their exchange rates to the dollar, the appreciation of the yen increased their competitiveness vis-à-vis Japan in markets for technologically more advanced products and attracted Japanese investors to their export industries. This phenomenon conforms to the flying geese model created for the region.

The second-tier South-East Asian countries showed a pattern more akin to the earlier phase of development of the first-tier Asian "tigers", with industry leading economic growth. South Asia, in contrast, showed less dynamism and structural change relative to the first-tier newly industrialized economies in East Asia. The share of manufacturing and mining peaked at 22 per cent of total output in the region in the 1990s, up from 14 per cent in 1970. The pattern for the region largely reflected what had happened in India. Most recently, India's growth has been driven by a fast-growing service sector. By the traditional standards of patterns of structural change, this trend implies a premature shift into services, given the relatively low income level of the country. However, services have become increasingly tradable (that is to say, exportable) activities, building on advanced communications technology. India has been able to move into this new activity drawing on a large pool of underemployed skilled labour (see box III.2 in Chapter III).

The relatively strong growth performance of the Latin American countries up to the mid-1970s had been built on a strategy of import-substituting industrialization. The limits of this strategy, which had become visible in most countries of the region since the 1960s, led many of them to encourage, in a parallel fashion, export diversification and regional integration. Emerging balance-of-payments problems could be temporarily resolved through the easy access to low-cost commercial bank loans in the second half of the 1970s. Industrial growth, however, came to a halt in several countries since the mid-1970s. Premature trade liberalization in the Southern Cone countries led to strong declines in industrial output in the second half of the 1970s. Elsewhere, industrial development was strongly affected by the lack of foreign financing and the stabilization policies in the aftermath of the debt crisis of the early 1980s.

Subsequent trade and financial reforms turned exports into the engine of growth in most Latin American countries during the 1980s and, particularly, the 1990s. Export growth, however, was not built on dynamic industrialization. It was based instead on either a continued—and, in some cases, deepening—reliance on exports of primary products, particularly in South America, or on assembling manufacturing processes, for example, in Mexico and Central America (see chapter III; Vos and Morley, 2006; United Nations, Economic Commission for Latin America, 2004; and Ocampo, 2004). Recurrent financial crises led to more volatile growth and deficient long-term investment for dynamic structural change (see chapter IV). As a result, the share of manufacturing in total output declined in most countries during 1970-2003. The growth of the services sector in the region has been associated not so much with a dynamic transition as with the process of de-industrialization, which pushed excess workers into the (informal) low-productivity tertiary sector. The smaller Andean countries are an exception to this rule, as the share of industry increased but the service sector experienced a contraction.

The countries in Central and Eastern Europe and CIS had witnessed fast growth of gross domestic product (GDP) per capita during the 1960s and 1970s, showing average annual rates of 6.2 and 4.4 per cent, respectively. Industry was then the mainstay of economic growth. The centrally planned investment process focused in particular on the development of heavy industries which involved massive reallocations of labour from agriculture but eventually failed to produce sustained growth. A description of the case of Poland by Podkaminer (2006, p. 311) possibly applies to the entire region: "Structurally, the priorities of the development policy were grossly mistaken, as they stipulated the preferential treatment of agriculture, mining and 'heavy' branches of manufacturing (metallurgy, shipbuilding, heavy armaments such as tanks, basic chemicals such as fertilizers) at the expense of services and technologically advanced high-skill branches."

In the 1980s, all of the problems that had been accumulating over time surfaced in full force. The countries in the region were faced with huge amounts of sunk capital invested in highly inefficient industrial giants incapable of producing competitive goods that were sellable in the international markets. At the same time, the buffering effect of the Council for Mutual Economic Assistance on the oil trade was gradually phased out and Central and Eastern Europe had to pay much higher prices for oil imported from the former Soviet Union. The manufacturing, mining, construction and transportation sectors, which had been the driving forces of growth during the previous decades, shrank in absolute terms, especially during the second half of the 1980s. With the fall of the Berlin Wall in 1989, a difficult transition process to a market-based economy was initiated and led to a sharp and prolonged output decline, a phenomenon that came to be known as the "transformational recession"

(Kornai, 1993; 1994). Agriculture and manufacturing were the sectors most adversely affected by the breakdown of the central planning system. The shock of the transition was most pronounced in the Russian Federation and Ukraine owing to the output collapse in the first part of the 1990s, when the share of the manufacturing and mining sectors decreased from 35 to 30 per cent. Manufacturing and mining started to recover at the end of the century and their share reached 33 per cent by 2003; but this recovery was in part driven by rising oil and gas exploitation spurred by high energy prices.

Most countries in the Middle East and Northern Africa show continued high dependence on the extraction of oil and minerals. The regional average is strongly influenced by developments in the Islamic Republic of Iran and Saudi Arabia, as these two economies account for approximately 50 per cent of the region's GDP and 30 per cent of its population. Growth performance and patterns of structural change are largely explained by developments in the oil market. The rapid increase in the region's output during the 1970s had been caused by the two major increases in oil prices orchestrated by the Organization of the Petroleum Exporting Countries (OPEC). The 1980s, in contrast, were years of economic stagnation. The price of crude oil fell in real terms and returned to levels near those prevailing before the first oil shock. After a temporary increase in 1990, oil prices continued a declining trend up to 1999, pushing many of the oil-exporting countries of the region into deep recessions and generating high levels of unemployment. Thereafter, oil prices rose sharply again and have spurred strong economic recovery.

Structural change in the oil-exporting countries was shaped by these trends in oil markets. Extraction of hydrocarbons dominated total output but their share decreased from 35 to 22 per cent between 1970 and 2003. The share had been at an all-time low of 16 per cent in the mid-1980s as a consequence of lower oil prices. The share of the manufacturing sector had increased to 12 per cent of total output by 2003, up by 4 percentage points from a meagre 8 per cent in 1970. Tunisia was an exception in the region, as it witnessed a much stronger development of manufacturing. It is also one of the few African countries that managed to achieve sustained economic growth throughout the period.

The countries in sub-Saharan African included in the sample have not been able to break away from their low-growth development trap. This is also visible in the lack of structural change that took place in these economies. Agriculture remains the mainstay of these economies, but per capita output of the sector declined during the period 1970-2003 (figure I.2). In most countries, market-oriented structural adjustment policies adopted in the 1980s and 1990s failed to improve growth performance and, in fact, produced very little structural change. The policies insufficiently addressed the problems of poor infrastructure and human capital development, as well as the lack of well-functioning market institutions. As these binding constraints on growth were not lifted, the economies failed to diversify and continued to be highly vulnerable to external shocks, declining terms of trade and, in many instances, domestic conflict and civil strife (see chapter V). The relatively high average growth rates in manufacturing and mining recorded for the region as a whole were largely driven by Nigeria's oil sector, and had little to do with emerging manufacturing sector growth. When including Nigeria, the share of industry had reached 35 per cent by the end of the period. If Nigeria is excluded, mining and manufacturing activities generated only 17 per cent of output in the remaining countries of the region.

Investment Patterns and Structural Change

Capital accumulation is no longer viewed today—as in some of the early theories of economic development—as the only driving force of economic growth. This does not mean, however, that investment is not important. Capital investment is essential to economic development and growth, as it is a major carrier of technological change. It also plays a crucial role in the development of infrastructure and the construction of urban centres, where manufacturing and services cluster. In combination with other factors, capital accumulation also sets off structural changes. Economic transformation thus requires changes in patterns of accumulation as new resources are invested in new sectors of the economy, thus increasing their contribution to overall output.

Higher economic growth and convergence are closely associated with increases in investment per capita, although the relationship is not one-to-one. The first-tier newly industrialized economies and China, which had experienced the most dynamic structural change, as mentioned earlier, recorded the largest increases —and indeed an acceleration— in investment. In per capita terms, the volume of fixed investment multiplied, respectively, 15.6 and 12.3 times between 1970 and 2003 (see table II.1). South-East Asia followed a similar pattern, though with lower levels of investment. Investment growth has been much lower in the other regions. Investment levels doubled in South Asia, while they were virtually stagnant in Latin America, sub-Saharan Africa, Central and Eastern Europe and the CIS countries, as well as in the Middle East and Northern Africa. A high investment level thus differentiates the fastest growing East Asian regions from the rest, but it is not a distinguishing factor among the remaining growth experiences.

Table II.1.
Levels of per capita investment, selected regions and country groups, 1960-2003

	Average gross fixed capital formation per inhabitant (1990 United States dollars)				
	1960s	1970s	1980s	1990s-2003	-fold increase
First-tier NIEs[a]	218	589	1356	3392	15.6
China[a]	20	37	75	244	12.3
South East Asia[b]	103	184	174[c]	315	3.1
South Asia	36	40	53	85	2.3
Semi-industrialized countries	608	855	805	797	1.3
Smaller Andean countries	..	341	328	333	1.0
Central America and the Caribbean	171	282	249	367	1.3
Central and Eastern Europe	..	..	..	673	..
CIS	..	..	..	435	..
Sub-Sahara Africa	..	..	67	50	0.7
Middle East and Northern Africa	..	498	397	330	0.7

Source: UN/DESA, based on United Nations Statistics Division, Common Database.
[a] Data starts 1965.
[b] Excluding Indonesia for the 1960s and 1970s.
[c] Excluding Indonesia, South-East Asia's average is $ 279.

A comparison between first-tier newly industrialized economies and the group of semi-industrialized countries (mostly in Latin America) provides some further insight into the magnitude of economic divergence that occurred not only at the level of income but also in relation to a wide range of indicators. In the 1960s, the level of average investment per capita in the first-tier newly industrialized economies had been just about one third that of semi-industrialized countries. In the 1990s, the first-tier newly industrialized economies registered investment levels four times higher. Such catching up of per-capita investment (though not yet overtaking) with respect to the semi-industrialized countries is also exemplified by China, South-East Asia and South Asia.

When taken as a share of GDP, investment also showed strong and sustained increases for groups of Asian countries –and indeed, in these terms, China and South-East Asia actually overtook the semi-industrialized countries in the 1980s. This held to a lesser extent for South Asia (figure II.3). In the 1990s, gross fixed capital formation rates of the first-tier newly industrialized economies and China climbed to 34 per cent of GDP and reached 27 per cent of GDP in South-East Asia. In contrast, in the same period, the gross fixed investment rate remained practically stagnant at about 19 per cent for the semi-industrialized countries and increased only slightly (from lower levels)

Figure II.3.
Average investment rate for selected periods and regions, 1960-2003

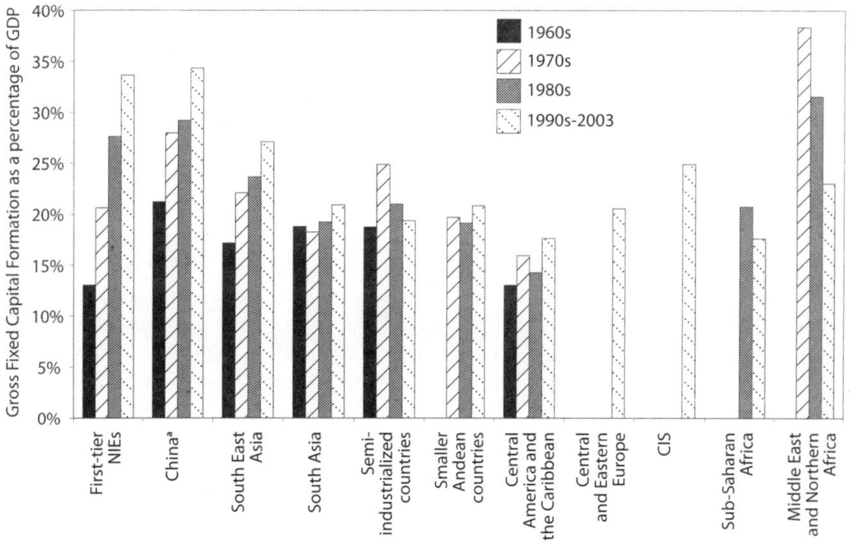

[Bar chart showing Gross Fixed Capital Formation as a percentage of GDP for 1960s, 1970s, 1980s, and 1990s-2003 across regions: First-tier NIEs, China(a), South East Asia, South Asia, Semi-industrialized countries, Smaller Andean countries, Central America and the Caribbean, Central and Eastern Europe, CIS, Sub-Saharan Africa, Middle East and Northern Africa.]

Source: UN/DESA, based on World Bank, World Development Indicators 2005 database.
a   Data for China cover the period 1965-2003.

in the rest of Latin America and the Caribbean. Investment levels decreased in sub-Saharan Africa and the region of the Middle East and Northern Africa. Investment in the economies in transition of Central and Eastern Europe and the former Soviet Union followed a somewhat different pattern as analysed in box II.1.

Poorer growth performance is associated not only with little structural change and lower investment, but also with higher investment volatility. When measured by the coefficient of variation (that is to say, the standard deviation divided by the mean for the period), investment volatility is shown to be much higher in countries with low income growth and much less pronounced in countries with a strong growth performance (see figure II.4). A simple linear regression between these two variables yields a correlation coefficient of 71 per cent. Economic instability and investment uncertainty are no doubt detrimental for long-term economic growth. Chapter IV explores the options available to Governments in developing countries for conducting macroeconomic policies that effectively reduce economic volatility and create a more conducive environment for investment in long-term development.

Capital accumulation is a catalyst of structural change. Figure II.5 shows that changes in the share of the dynamic sectors –industry and services— are strongly associated with investment growth, which is consistent with the

> Box II.1.
> **Investment growth and collapse in the economies in transition**
> Central and Eastern Europe and the Commonwealth of Independent States (CIS) are special cases in terms of investment trends because of the profound institutional changes undergone by these regions. The patterns of capital accumulation in their economies have gone through several different phases since the start of their economic and political transformation. During the early phases of transition, the dynamics of aggregate investment were marked by a combination of profound negative shocks. The deep and prolonged transformational recession experienced by all countries at the onset of transition burdened most firms with excess capacity as huge sunk capital costs surfaced in consequence of the knock-on effect of economic liberalization.
>
> The inherited structure of the centrally planned economies, which were all "over-industrialized", and the fact that the industrial structure was heavily concentrated in large State-owned firms, further compounded the problem. As production facilities were generally obsolete, active restructuring and new productive investment by firms were called for if they were to survive and grow under the new market environment. Yet, in the early phases of transition, equity and debt security markets were practically non-existent; the only available source of external funding for most firms was domestic bank lending. The emerging financial markets (markets for commercial credit were the first to emerge) were inefficient and performed under considerable uncertainty, as firms had no proper track record of creditworthiness. These market imperfections erected additional barriers to access to credit by the enterprise sector, further limiting the firms' capacity to invest. As a result, aggregate investment in virtually all transition economies experienced a prolonged downturn.
>
> Around the mid-1990s, investment rates in most countries in Central and Eastern Europe started to recover from their collapse in the initial years of transition. Investment growth was helped by a recovery in domestic saving and new inflows of foreign direct investment, largely owing to the possibility of accession to the European Union (EU). There was then no sustained recovery of investment in CIS, as investor confidence in these economies was hurt once more by the Russian financial crisis of 1998. In more recent years, growth and investment recovered on account of high oil prices.

arguments put forward in this chapter. As shown in the next section, industry and services were also the main contributors to overall labour productivity growth in these economies.

The composition of investment also matters for growth performance. A review of empirical studies by the United Nations Conference on Trade and Development (UNCTAD) (2003) suggests that investment in machinery and equipment contributes more strongly to growth than does investment in construction. Comparable data on the composition of investment by commodity—for example, machinery and buildings—are scarce and hence evidence is somewhat dispersed. Also, as argued in chapter IV, the "optimal" composition of investment also depends on the level of development of the economy, with investments in infrastructure exercising significant growth effects at relatively lower income levels. Indivisibilities in the construction

Figure II.4.
The impact of investment volatility on economic performance, 1970-2004

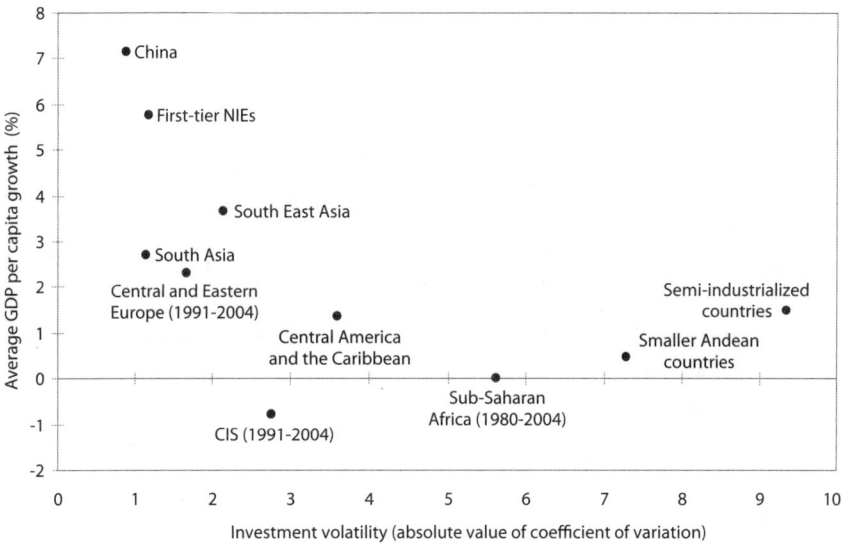

Source: UN/DESA, based on World Bank, World Development Indicators 2005 database.

Figure II.5.
Annual growth rate in investment per capita versus change in the shares of agriculture and industry in total output, selected regions and country groups, 1970-2003

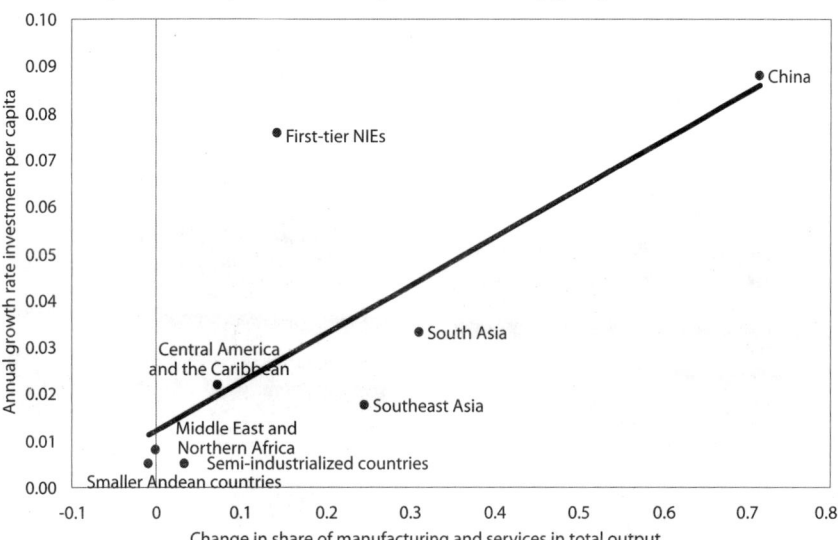

Source: UN/DESA, based on World Bank, World Development Indicators 2005 database for investment, and United Nations Statistics Division, National Accounts Main Aggregates database.

Note: For China, first-tier newly industrialized economies, Central America and the Caribbean, and Smaller Andean countries, 1970-2003; for South-East Asia, South Asia, and the Middle East and Northern Africa, 1980-2003.

48 • Uneven Economic Development

of infrastructure may require high levels of such investment, especially at low levels of development. This implies that at lower stages of development, countries should deploy relatively higher shares of construction investment.

Investment data by sector of destination are even less readily available. Yet, it is possible to argue that the anticipated structural change in developing countries implies that much of investment will initially move into the industrial sector. At higher stages of development, economies are likely to direct a higher proportion of investment to the financial and business-oriented service sectors. For instance, in developed economies, such as the United States of America and Japan, where the service sector provides over 60 per cent of output, most of investment is expected to go towards services.

Analysis of such investment patterns over time for the country groupings used in this chapter is constrained by lack of data. Data are available, however, for a few countries and those data may be illustrative of investment patterns of a larger group of countries. The Republic of Korea is a case in point. Figure II.6 shows that over time allocation of investment resources in the economy of the Republic of Korea had moved away from primary sectors, such as agriculture, towards industry and higher value added economic activities. The share of investment in agriculture had decreased from 14 per cent in total gross fixed capital formation in 1970 to 2 per cent in 2003, while the share of the industrial sector jumped from 16 per cent in 1970 to 24 per cent in 2003. Throughout

Figure II.6.
Sector investment as a percentage share of gross fixed capital formation, Republic of Korea, 1970 and 2003

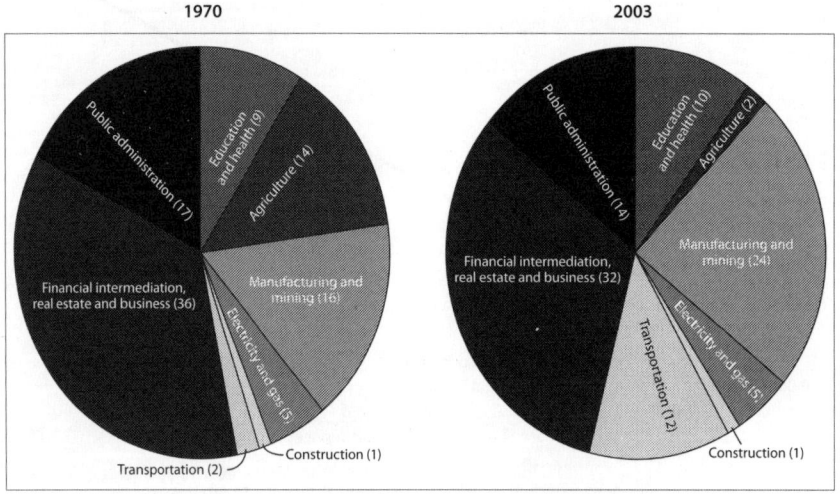

Source: UN/DESA, based on data from National Statistical Office, Republic of Korea.

the entire period, the share of other sectors in investment was relatively stable. It is worth pointing out, however, that since the early 1970s, the financial intermediation, real estate and business services sectors had been receiving a considerable share of investment. This fact signals the importance of the development of both financial and business services not only at an advanced stage, but also at the beginning of a sustainable growth process.

Employment, Productivity and Structural Change

For the economy as a whole, labour productivity growth can be achieved through technological progress and/or by moving resources from low- to higher-productivity sectors. As mentioned earlier, the type of productivity growth achieved by the latter approach tends to be more important for the developing countries. The introduction of new technology and a structural shift of the economy may, however, cause employment problems if output is not increased (since, by definition, the higher-productivity sectors use fewer workers per unit of output). Hence, sufficient dynamism (output growth) in the higher-productivity sectors will be required in the process of structural change if remunerative jobs are to be generated for all workers and the creation of unemployment is to be prevented.

According to data available in Maddison (2001), the growth process in the developed countries also entailed a dramatic change in the employment structure, involving a shift from the primary sectors into industry and, subsequently, into services. For example, the share of employment in agriculture had been 37 per cent in the United Kingdom and 70 per cent in the United States in 1820. By 1998, the share had decreased to 2 per cent and 3 per cent, respectively. However, these employment shifts lagged considerably behind the structural change in output as labour productivity in agriculture and other primary sectors tends to grow more slowly than that in industry, particularly in the early stages of development.

In countries without a labour surplus and where the agricultural sector had access to capital and technological knowledge, the lag in productivity growth between agriculture and industry was not observed. This was the case, for example, in Argentina, Canada and New Zealand, where land was not a constraint. In many other developing countries, however, a relatively slow rise in agricultural productivity might well also have reflected rapid population growth and the lack of employment opportunities elsewhere, both of which may imply growing underutilization of labour in the rural sector.

Considering these notions about the link between productivity and employment growth, the present section identifies which sectors of the

50 • Uneven Economic Development

economy have contributed the most to gains in productivity and employment. Based on a simple decomposition of economy-wide labour productivity and employment by sectors, it is possible to identify the contribution of individual sectors to overall productivity and employment growth for the countries and regions selected. In the decomposition, aggregate productivity growth equals the sum of the productivity changes in each sector of the economy, weighted by sectoral output shares, plus the reallocation of labour from low- to high-productivity sectors (see appendix to this chapter for details on the estimation method). It is important to note that the decomposition is applied to three relatively aggregate sectors: agriculture, industry (that is to say, manufacturing and mining) and services (which also include construction and public utilities). Hence, resource shifts that have taken place within these sectors are not accounted for. This is an important limitation, as high- and low-productivity units of production coexist in all of these broadly defined sectors. This is particularly important in the case of services, which is the most important generator of employment in most economies today (see figure II.7). In this sector, low-productivity activities typically comprise informal trade and domestic service and these exist next to high-productivity activities such as modern financial and business services. Also, due to data

Figure II.7.
Contribution of the agriculture, industry and service sectors to job creation, selected regions and country groups, from 1991 to 2003-2004

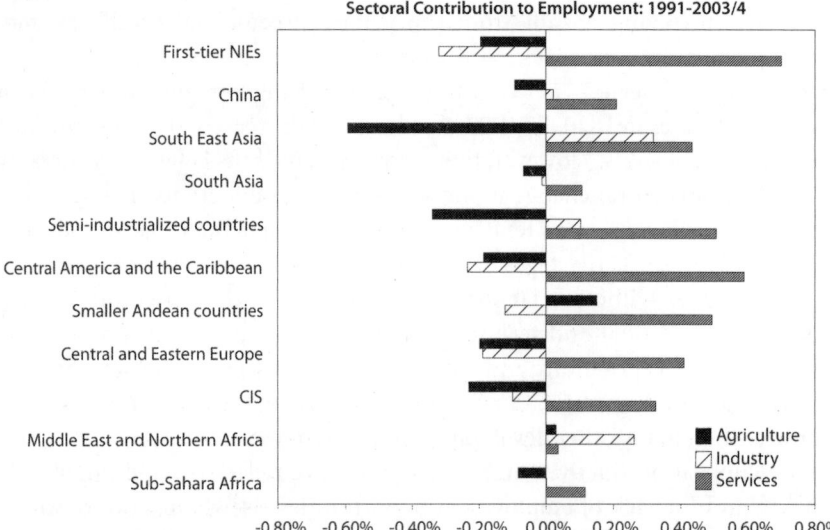

Source: UN/DESA, based on data on employment by economic activity derived from International Labour Office, Global Employment Trends Model 2005 database, and from data on sectoral output derived from the World Bank, World Development Indicators 2005 database.

Structural Change and Economic Growth • 51

limitations, much of the analysis is restricted to the patterns of change in labour productivity for the period from 1991 to 2003-2004.[6] Figure II.8 shows the results for all country groupings considered in this chapter. A longer time series, however, is available for Asian countries and is analyzed below.[7]

The most successful countries are characterized by faster productivity growth (figure II.8). In all these cases, industrial development has been a major driver of overall labour productivity growth. Labour reallocation among the broadly defined sectors, which measures the degree to which the mobility of workers directed towards higher-productivity sectors contributes to overall productivity growth, has been important in some cases (particularly in South-East Asia), but rather modest in others. This reflects the fact that in many slow-growth countries, the reallocation of labour has been dominated by employment problems in urban areas. In these countries, the insufficient dynamism of the industrial and modern services sectors pushed redundant workers into informal sector employment, slowing down productivity growth, particularly in the services sector.

This means that, in slowly growing economies, intra-sectoral allocation effects dominate inter-sectoral reallocation effects, and are reflected

Figure II.8.
Annual growth rate in labour productivity for selected country groups and regions, from 1991 to 2003-2004

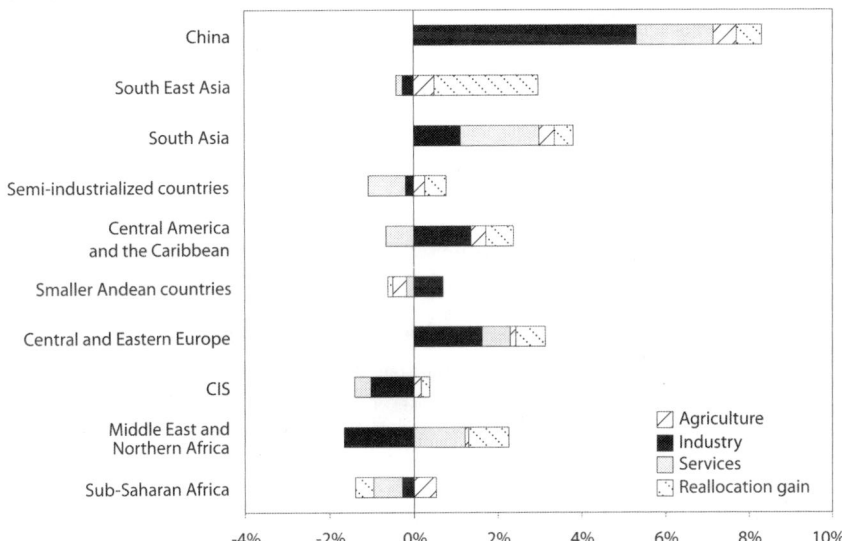

Source: UN/DESA, based on data on employment by economic activity derived from International Labour Office, Global Employment Trends Model 2005 database, and from data on sectoral output derived from the World Bank, World Development Indicators 2005 database.

particularly in the rate of productivity gains (or losses) in the services sector, which is determined by whether employment is generated in high- or low-productivity services (figure II.9). The services sector operates in these cases as the "employer of last resort" rather than as a dynamic contributor to productivity growth. Slow productivity growth in services is then the best measure of the lack of dynamism of the growth process. This is the dominant pattern. In some other cases, however, agriculture also serves as the residual employer. Under these circumstances, there is neither significant reallocation of labour nor strong productivity performance. The smaller Andean countries are the best example of such a pattern. In low-income countries, particularly in sub-Saharan Africa, very low levels of productivity in traditional agriculture are matched by significant underemployment of labour in both urban and rural areas, leading to low overall levels of productivity.

Figure II.9.
Labour productivity growth in public utilities, construction and services sector for selected country groups and regions, from 1991 to 2003-2004

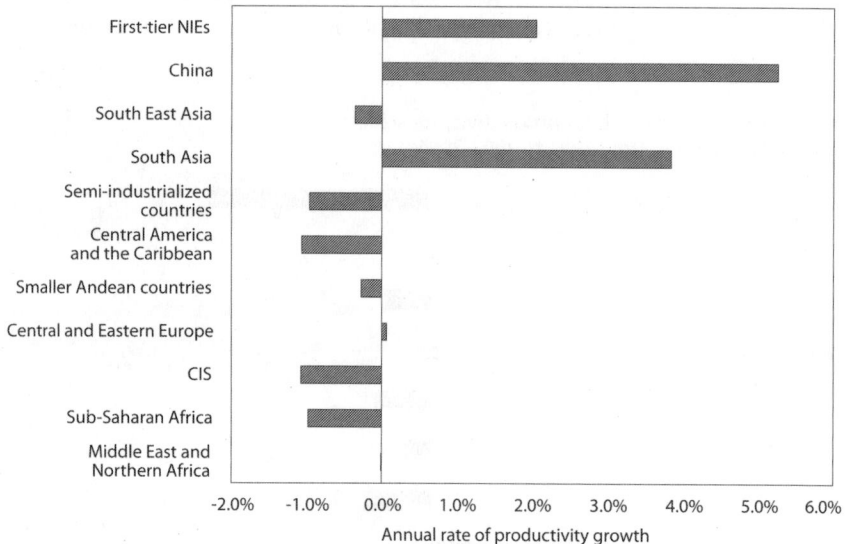

Source: UN/DESA, based on data on employment by economic activity derived from International Labour Office, Global Employment Trends Model 2005 database, and from data on sectoral output derived from the World Bank, World Development Indicators 2005 database.

Figure II.8 shows that China, the first-tier newly industrialized economies and South Asia outpaced all other regions in terms of annual labour productivity growth, experiencing high growth rates of labour productivity in all sectors together with positive reallocation effects. Strong employment growth in high-productivity sectors was thus matched by a dynamic reallocation of labour from low- to high-productivity activities. South-East Asia also experienced rapid productivity growth, but in this case it was dominated by the reallocation of labour towards higher productivity sectors. It should also be noted that the average productivity performance for the region during the 1990s had been heavily influenced by the deep recession experienced by Indonesia during the Asian crisis. China, the first-tier newly industrialized economies and South-East Asia, in contrast with other regions, combined strong productivity growth and net employment creation for the economy as a whole (figure II.10).

Figure II.10.
Annual rate of growth of labour productivity, and annual percentage change in the employment-to-population ratio, selected regions and country groups, from 1991 to 2003-2004

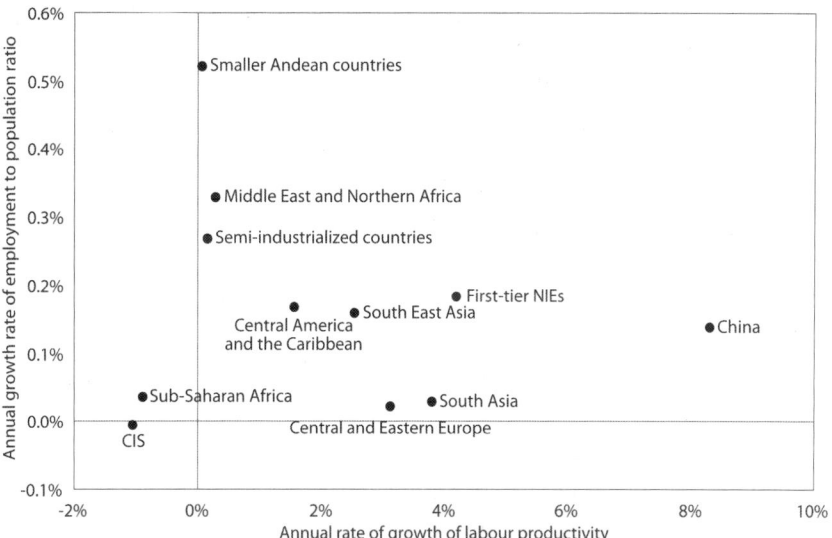

Source: UN/DESA, based on data on employment by economic activity derived from International Labour Office, Global Employment Trends Model 2005 database, and from data on sectoral output derived from the World Bank, World Development Indicators 2005 database.

Countries in Central and Eastern Europe and Central America and the Caribbean displayed patterns intermediate between those of Asia and those of regions where overall productivity performance was very poor, but hardly any net job creation. This was particularly true in Central and Eastern Europe, where economy-wide employment fell at a rate of 0.75 per cent per year during 1991-2003, mainly because of the massive layoffs and enterprise restructuring in the industrial and agricultural sectors.

With the exception of Costa Rica, the countries in Central America and the Caribbean were also unable to add many jobs in the industrial sector which, for the entire region, shed labour at an annual rate of 0.8 per cent, leading to a significant drop in the share of manufacturing in total employment. Overall, however, employment in the region increased as the service sector absorbed the unemployed workers from the rest of the economy and indeed helped to create a modest overall increase in employment. This led, however, to a reduction in the productivity in the service sector, which counteracted the rapid gains of industrial productivity.

For the smaller Andean countries, productivity growth in industry also took place to the detriment of job creation. In fact, labour productivity increased in the industrial sector essentially because employment decreased faster than output. Aggregate labour productivity growth for the region as a whole was almost nil as a result of negative productivity performance in the agriculture and service sectors, which had absorbed most of the workers shed by the industrial sectors, and indeed helped to create a net addition of employment. As indicated previously, this was the only region where agriculture played an important role in helping to absorb surplus labour displaced by the industrial sector. Overall, employment increased but was unaccompanied by productivity growth (see figures II.7 and II.8).

In the semi-industrialized countries and the economies of the Middle East and Northern Africa, the sectors absorbing most workers showed stagnant or negative productivity growth. Sectoral productivity declined in both industry and services in the semi-industrialized countries, making a negative contribution to aggregate (economy-wide) productivity growth, particularly in the service sector. Intersectoral labour reallocation compensated in part for this drop in productivity. Employment generation was dynamic overall in these two regions (see figure II.10), but most jobs were generated in the service sectors, particularly in informal activities.[8] Chile is an exception to this pattern. The Chilean economy recorded a strong labour productivity growth rate of 3.1 per cent per year, which was mainly driven by productivity improvements in both industry (1.4 per cent) and services (1.4 per cent).

The least desirable situation is one where neither net employment generation nor productivity growth takes place. In this case, both sectoral contributions to productivity growth and reallocation effects tended to be negative or nil. This situation characterizes the growth processes in CIS and sub-Saharan Africa (see figure II.10). The Russian Federation and Ukraine had suffered an acute collapse in both output and employment in the first half of the 1990s. Nevertheless, output decreased faster than employment, which led to an absolute decrease in labour productivity. Output growth recovered somewhat more recently, leading to positive labour productivity growth for the entire period.

In sub-Saharan Africa, most employment (70 per cent) remains stuck in the low-productivity agricultural sector. The labour reallocated from rural to urban activities was directed into equally relatively low-productivity services and industrial activities, giving rise to both negative productivity growth in those sectors as well as negative overall reallocation effects, Nonetheless, differences in productivity levels across sectors remain huge. Output per worker in the agricultural sector is nine times less than that in the other sectors of the economy.

The longer series available for selected Asian economies allow for a longer-run analysis of productivity growth and sectoral shifts in employment. This is particularly interesting, given the capacity of countries in this region to combine strong productivity growth and net employment creation for the economy as a whole. China recorded the strongest performance: labour productivity growth averaged 6.7 per cent annually during the period 1979-2002 (see table II.2). Labour productivity growth was strong in all sectors, especially in manufacturing. Substantial reallocation of labour from low- to high-productivity sectors—along traditional lines of development—contributed further to overall productivity growth. For the entire period 1979-2002, growth of jobs exceeded that of the workforce by 1.3 percentage points. While employment increased in all sectors, it was strongest in the service sector.

Successful growth and strong productivity performance in the first-tier-newly industrialized economies was supported by major improvements in human capital. The average years of schooling in the region increased from 6.5 years in 1975 to over 10 years in 2000. The employment rate (relative to total population) increased over the entire period despite the fact that agriculture—and in the 1990s also the manufacturing sector—contributed negatively to job creation. Workers were increasingly being pulled into the strongly expanding services sector, where the creation of many new jobs occurred simultaneously with significant gains in labour productivity.

Labour productivity growth was less spectacular–albeit still strong—in South-East Asia. The annual rate of increase of labour productivity averaged 2.6 per cent during the period 1979-2002. Job creation outpaced population growth by only 0.24 percentage points. Industrial productivity growth was higher than in other sectors, while the services sector took care of most of the job creation. As a result, the industrial sector did not play the leading role in driving aggregate productivity as it did in China. Structural change led agriculture to consistently shed labour while the other sectors created jobs.

Turning to South Asia, available data suggest that labour productivity growth picked up in the region, especially, as pointed out above, during the 1990s. This recent development was the result in part of the industrial restructuring in the first-tier newly industrialized economies as labour-intensive manufacturing, particularly textiles, moved to the region. The rapid expansion of the tradable service sector was the other major development underlying the improved productivity performance of India. At the same time, India went through a process of de-industrialization, which led some observers to question the sustainability of its growth process (see, for example, Dasgupta and Singh, 2005). In fact, available data indicate that very few jobs were being created by the economy at large throughout the 1990s, despite high levels of GDP growth. As a result, labour underutilization remains high, particularly in the case of unskilled workers, as the expanding services sector creates jobs mainly for higher-skilled workers.

Conclusions

Diverging patterns of growth among developing countries are also visible in differences in terms of structural change. An examination of the patterns of structural change over the past four decades indicates that the fast-growing East and South Asian economies were clearly characterized by dynamic transformations, characterized by a rapid decline in the importance of agriculture and strong expansions of both the industrial and modern service sectors. Economies with relatively little structural change lagged behind, particularly those in sub-Saharan Africa. Sluggish long-term growth in the middle-income countries of Latin America and the Caribbean as well as in countries in Central and Eastern Europe, the Middle East and the former Soviet Union has been associated with a process of de-industrialization. In these countries, growth—and particularly employment growth—has been concentrated in low-productivity services, with agriculture and industry remaining nearly stagnant.

The fast-growing Asian economies also show sustained increases in labour productivity and labour has moved from low- to high-productivity sectors, including modern service sectors. In the regions with low-growth performance, the employment shift to the service sector has been rather pronounced. However, in contrast with the service sectors of Asia, those of sub-Saharan Africa, Latin America and the former Soviet Union have shown declining productivity, as many workers have sought employment in services with low productivity and weak linkages with the more dynamic sectors of the economy, owing to lack of job creation in other parts of the economy.

Dynamic structural change involves productivity improvements in all major sectors and strengthening economic linkages within the economy—in other words, integrating the domestic economy. The degree of integration of the domestic economy also influences how much countries are able to gain from international trade and investment. The following chapters explore how the external environment, macroeconomic policies and governance structures have shaped these differences in patterns of structural change.

Notes

1. The ten geographical groups are the first-tier newly industrialized economies (3): Republic of Korea, Singapore and Taiwan Province of China; China (1); South-East Asia (5): Indonesia, Malaysia, Philippines, Thailand and Viet Nam; South Asia (4); Bangladesh, India, Pakistan and Sri Lanka; low-to-middle-income Latin American countries (or smaller Andean countries) (3): Bolivia, Ecuador and Peru; Central America and the Caribbean (5): Costa Rica, Dominican Republic, El Salvador, Guatemala and Jamaica; Central and Eastern Europe (6): Bulgaria, Czech Republic, Hungary, Poland, Romania, and Slovakia; Commonwealth of Independent States (2): Russian Federation and Ukraine; sub-Saharan Africa (10): Cameroon, Côte d'Ivoire, Ethiopia, Ghana, Kenya, Mozambique, Nigeria, Uganda, Tanzania and Zimbabwe; Middle East and Northern Africa (10): Algeria, Egypt, Iran, Iraq, Jordan, Morocco, Saudi Arabia, Syrian Arab Republic, Tunisia and Yemen. The group of semi-industrialized countries (8) is made up of: Argentina, Brazil, Chile, Colombia, Mexico, South Africa, Turkey and Venezuela.
2. Available international data sets (such as the United Nations Common Database, the World Bank World Development Indicators database, and the labour statistics databases of the International Labour Organization) do not provide consistent and comparable investment and employment data series prior to 1990 for a sufficiently large number of countries. Hence, part of the empirical analysis in the second and third sections had to be limited by and large to patterns observed in the 1990s and beyond.
3. Available international data sets (such as the United Nations Common Database, the World Bank World Development Indicators database, and the labour statistics databases of the International Labour Organization) do not provide consistent and comparable investment and employment data series prior to 1990 for a sufficiently large number of countries. Hence, part of the empirical analysis in the second and third sections had to be limited by and large to patterns observed in the 1990s and beyond.
4. This notion can be found in the late eighteenth century in the writings of Adam Smith and was developed further in the early twentieth century by Alwyn Young (Young, 1928).
5. The analysis in the present section is based on the evidence presented in Rada and Taylor (2008).
6. The data are derived from International Labour Office, Global Employment Trends Model 2005 database (GET).
7. Data availability allows comparison starting from 1979 for China, first-tier newly industrialized economies and South-East Asia and from 1981 for South Asia excluding India. For the latter, data are available only from 1991 onward.
8. The share in employment of the service sectors increased from 50 to 61 per cent during the first half of the 1990s. According to Stallings and Weller (2001), about 60 per cent of the new jobs created in Latin America during the 1990s were low-paid, low-productivity jobs in the informal sector. The jobs created outside the informal sector were mostly in commerce and, to a lesser extent, in financial and business.

Chapter III
Has Trade Integration Caused Greater Divergence?

It is often claimed that integration into the global economy through increased flows of goods, services, capital, technology and labour—admittedly the least mobile production factor in the group—enhances opportunities for growth and development, thus providing a powerful push towards closing the income gap between developed and developing economies. Convergence narratives that make the connection with integration usually refer to the experience of post-war Japan, to the Western European periphery since the late 1950s and to the more recent experience of the East Asian newly industrialized economies. In all these cases, a strong investment-trade nexus certainly helped to power rates of economic growth above those of the leading industrialized economies.

Yet, integration is no magic bullet for achieving rapid and sustained growth. Since the mid-1980s, most developing countries have opened up their economies to global market forces but there were a variety of outcomes, including, in some cases, a reversal of previous achievements. Most recently, developing countries, including many of the least developed countries, have exhibited a strong economic performance, reaching the fastest average rate of growth they have seen for decades. This outcome is based, among other things, on an improved policy environment, and an international context characterized by rising official development assistance (ODA), debt relief for the heavily indebted poor countries (HIPC), low interest rates worldwide, and a strong recovery of commodity prices. The last-mentioned factor, however, may not be sustainable in the longer run as commodity cycles of the past have demonstrated (United Nations, 2006).

The present chapter will focus on trade integration and the role that foreign direct investment (FDI) has played in supporting that process (financial integration will be addressed in chapter IV). It argues that the specific strategies that countries follow to integrate their economies into the global markets of goods and services indeed matter, as they largely determine the extent of the benefits those countries can derive from enhanced trade flows. The timing of integration (in terms of both the country's readiness to join

60 • Uneven Economic Development

and actively participate in global markets and the opportunities available when integration takes place) and how quickly it is implemented (gradually or through fast liberalization) are also relevant factors. However, in an interdependent world, the effectiveness of country-level strategies cannot be judged in isolation and will depend on the underlying structural characteristics of the global economy. Success in trade depends on the goods and services produced, how they are produced and whether production creates sufficient linkages with the rest of the economy so that these activities allow for a dynamic transformation of the economy while the growth stimulus coming from abroad is propagated throughout the domestic economy. FDI, when properly managed and incorporated into a strategy aiming at the continuous upgrading of the country's technological capacities, can bring lasting benefits. These factors, including policy options to enable more effective integration patterns and facilitate greater convergence, are analysed below.

The chapter is organized as follows: the first section examines the role that specialization patterns and export diversification plays in growth outcomes. It is followed by an assessment of the contribution of FDI inflows in underlying specialization patterns and in promoting faster growth in recipient countries. The analysis carried out in these two sections underscores the importance of production sector development policies in facilitating structural changes, promoting the introduction of new activities, products and processes in the economy, and upgrading local technological capacities. These issues are addressed in the subsequent section. In the context of this chapter, production sector development policies are understood as encompassing those interventions that aim at promoting structural change of the economy and shifting resources in favour of more productive activities in agriculture, manufacturing and services. The concluding section indicates some of the areas where further international cooperation is required to promote greater convergence.

The Contribution of International Trade to Growth Divergence

Faster growth of gross domestic product (GDP) is often associated with rapid export growth. Exports are connected to economic growth in several ways (United Nations Conference on Trade and Development, 1992). First, exports are a component of aggregate demand and thus have a direct and a multiplier effect on domestic production. Second, (net) export growth reduces the foreign exchange constraints faced by many developing countries and increases the pool of resources needed to finance investment and growth. Third, by removing the limits that domestic demand may impose on output expansion, exports allow for the exploitation of economies of scale in large-scale operations and increasing returns. Finally, exports, especially of manufactured goods but increasingly also of some services, can contribute through various channels to technical change, which is often associated with rapid growth.

Despite these sound theoretical arguments, the statistical evidence on the causal links between export growth and growth is mixed and seems to vary across countries and over time. Growth performance seems to be related to the particular composition of the exports that a country chooses over time. In particular, choices that involve changes in the productive structure of a country—allowing for the creation of production linkages across sectors and increased value added—and participation in growing global markets are often related to better economic performance.

Three factors need to be taken into account when analysing the links between trade and economic growth in the developing world as well as the role that international trade may play in growth divergence across countries. The first is the rate of growth of global markets for the specific exports of developing countries. Primary commodities continue to be important for many developing countries, but global demand for several of these goods grows at a relatively slow pace, particularly in the case of agricultural goods in general, and tropical agricultural goods in particular. On the contrary, fast-growing (or dynamic) export markets are generally markets for the products and services that have high income-elasticity of demand, that is to say, products and services whose demand grows faster than the increase of income in importing markets.

Developing countries can improve export opportunities in dynamic markets through economies of diversification (which create new products or services through differentiation, new designs, etc.). The globalization of production processes and the emergence of integrated production networks (IPNs) has also dynamized trade for certain products and has "creating" new markets. Several types of services with a high income elasticity and both labour-intensive (e.g. tourism) and technology-intensive (e.g. information and business services) in nature have also offered new opportunities for many developing countries. In markets for goods that face low income elasticity of demand, developing countries can still prosper by displacing production activities previously undertaken in industrialized countries, taking advantage of lower costs of production (particularly wage costs). For instance, exports of textiles and garments grew relatively fast in recent years in part because production capacity had shifted from developed to developing countries.

The second factor comprises dynamic economies of scale and thus increasing returns that characterize sectors with strong technological content. In this regard, it can be expected that specialization in sectors with greater technological content will lead to faster economic growth. This factor is linked in practice to the previous one, as products with higher technological content are often those with expanding global markets. With respect to trade in services, available data also indicates that faster-growing export markets are those that are skill- and knowledge-intensive.

The third factor relates to the multilateral trading environment, which plays an important role in helping markets to grow, or blocking their emergence. This factor is particularly important for "mature" sectors in industrial economies, in which they are losing their competitive advantages to low-cost producers. Thus, in terms of market access, agricultural products and low-skill, low-technology manufactures face relatively higher tariff and non-tariff barriers than do products with higher technological content, while the exports of services through the temporary presence of natural persons (international labour migration) are highly regulated and restricted. This limits in particular the possibilities of export growth of developing countries through displacing industrial country producers in sectors characterised by low income elasticities.

In the context of these global trends, an individual developing country can adopt either of two broadly defined export strategies. One involves increased specialization as a country boosts its market penetration ratio, that is to say, expansion of its presence in markets where it is already an established exporter. The other entails the diversification of its productive structure, so that it can participate in those markets (dynamic or otherwise) where it was not active before. In either case, the export strategy often implies wresting market shares from other participants in the market. Diversifying into products and services with greater potential for global market expansion, high value added and high productivity growth "widens the scope for the exploitation of increasing returns from larger markets and enhances the contribution of trade to growth" (Akyüz, 2003, p. 2).

In practice, these are likely to be mutually supporting rather than competing strategies. Diversification is, in any case, an essential ingredient, as there is a broad body of evidence that suggests that economic growth requires countries to move through ever more complex diversification stages up to a level of industrial maturity when service activities take on growing importance (Imbs and Wacziarg, 2003). However, diversification per se will not suffice to generate sustainable growth if the potential for productivity growth in the new sectors and the potential for linkages with the rest of the economy are limited. Accordingly, Wade (2004) distinguishes between "external integration" and "internal integration" and argues that most success cases have devised policies to ensure that these are mutually reinforcing and do not undermine each other. Thus, patterns of specialization and patterns of integration into the global economy matter for growth divergence.

Opportunities for producing and exporting primary commodities, natural resource-based and labour-intensive manufactures are more readily available for developing countries. However, the fact that the potential for expansion of global markets for these products is relatively limited may constrain long-term growth if the country does not proceed with the structural transformation of its economy beyond these sectors. Furthermore, the simultaneous entry of new participants in such markets could easily lead to saturation. In other words, what works for a country or a reduced number of countries will not necessarily bring equally positive results when several countries attempt the same trade diversification strategy at the same time. Product oversupply may lead to declining prices and deteriorating terms of trade. This "fallacy of composition" can be particularly important in commodity markets facing low income-elasticity of demand, as evidenced by the evolution of average non-fuel commodity prices, which fell by 49 per cent relative to the price of manufactures exported by developed countries during the period 1980-2000. The recent recovery in non-fuel commodity prices has not been sufficient to compensate for that loss. By the end of 2005, average non-fuel commodity prices were still below their 1980 levels in real terms (see United Nations, 2006). Additionally, commodity prices have exhibited pronounced volatility, which may undermine the effectiveness of diversification into primary product production. Such price volatility often leads to lack of stability in income and foreign exchange which is needed for long-term investment and faster growth.

Fallacy of composition may also emerge in some subsectors of manufacturing with commodity-like characteristics. In fact, exporters of some low-skill manufactures have confronted declining prices for their exports. Advances in technology and increased competition in markets for electronic and electrical goods—manufactures often associated with high-skill high-technological content—have also led to declining prices for some products (United Nations Conference on Trade and Development, 2002). Meanwhile, other countries appear to have succeeded in improving their terms of trade as their economic structure continued to diversify.

The experience of fast-growing economies shows that success depends not just on increasing exports volumes, but also on profiting from dynamic economies of scale, creating production linkages within the domestic economy and transforming production structures over time, within the context of a search for the products and services that offer potential for growth. Owing to data limitations, most of the discussion below will concentrate on specialization patterns in merchandise trade and their effects on growth; the export of services will be analysed separately.

Global markets dynamics and changes in the structure of merchandise exports

Over the past 40 years, merchandise trade grew rapidly. The value of global merchandise trade increased at an annual average rate of 10.4 per cent, and its volume by 6 per cent during the period 1962-2000. In both value and volume terms, the first half of the period witnessed relatively faster growth.[1] Although developed economies still dominate all non-oil global markets, developing countries have rapidly expanded their participation, especially since the second half of the 1980s. More importantly, there was a significant shift in the structure of exports by developing countries (as a group) away from primary products towards manufactures (see figure III.1).[2]

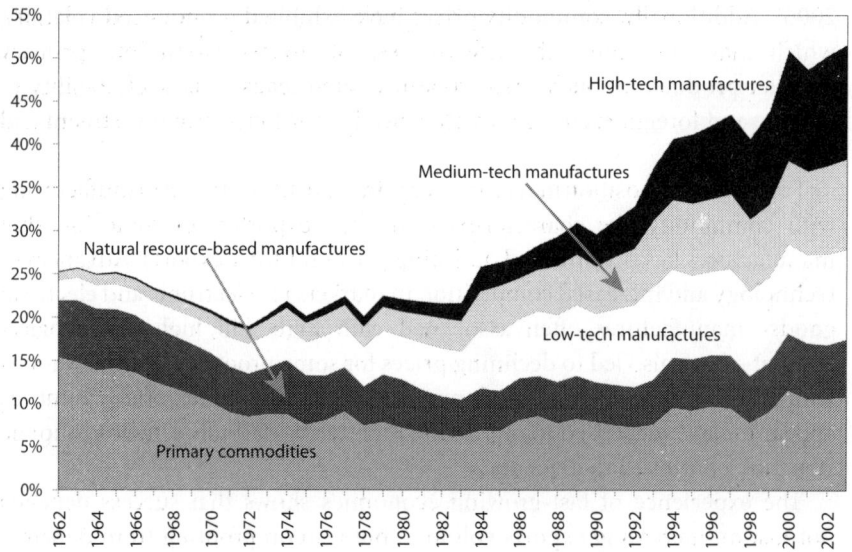

Figure III.1.
Value of exports of developing countries as a percentage of the value of exports of developed countries, by category of goods, 1962-2003

Source: UN/DESA, based on Feenstra and others (2005), database on world commodity trade.

The increased participation of developing countries in global markets has taken place in low- (LT), medium- (MT) and high-tech (HT) manufactures, whose markets have been relatively more dynamic, on average, than markets for primary products (PP) and natural resource-based (NRB) manufactures (see Appendix B for definitions, methodology and data sources). In fact, the share of the first three categories of products in global exports increased, while PP and NRB manufactures lost ground in global markets over the period 1965-2000 (see table III.1). This trend was particularly marked in PP as a result of low elasticity of income for these products, high protection and subsidies for agricultural goods, technological change and price developments (see box III.1).

Table III.1.
Share of products[a] by category in world merchandise trade, 1965-1970, 1980-1985 and 1995-2000

	1965-1970	1980-1985	1995-2000	2000-2003
Primary commodities	22.8	15.5	13.6	14.3
Natural resource-based manufactures	20.8	18.0	15.4	14.9
Low-technology manufactures	16.2	17.4	16.8	15.6
Medium-technology manufactures	31.9	36.1	32.9	31.8
High-technology manufactures	8.3	13.0	21.3	23.3

Source: UN/DESA, based on Feenstra and others (2005).
[a] Valued in current United States dollars.

Penetration by developing countries has been particularly impressive in markets for LT manufactures and by 2000 had reached 50 per cent of total world exports of this group of products. Such an outcome was largely due to the efforts of China, the first-tier newly industrialized economies and South-East Asia. Together, they supply 32 per cent of the global market of LT manufactures. Participation in markets for MT manufactures also increased and, again, the effort was concentrated in a few regions: that of the newly industrialized economies, South-East Asia and Latin America. Meanwhile, increased market share in HT manufactures was overwhelmingly due to the performance in this sector of the first-tier newly industrialized economies and South-East Asia. On the other hand, the share of developing countries in markets for PP, on average, declined as developed countries increased market penetration. As the analysis undertaken in this chapter is based on values rather than volumes (see Appendix B), divergences in price trends between commodity exports by developed and developing countries could have contributed to this outcome. Another possible factor was, as noted, the relatively high protectionism and subsidization exercised by developed

> Box III.1.
> **Can markets for primary commodities and natural resource-based manufactures be dynamic?**
>
> Despite the relatively slow overall growth in world trade of primary commodities and natural resource-based (NRB) manufactures, a number of products in these categories showed dynamism, that is to say, their exports grow faster than world exports (see annex table A.4). A proviso should be made, namely, that the export data presented here encompass values rather than volumes, which may imply that price trends could have had greater influence on export earnings than developments in export volumes.
>
> Export growth rates in the period 1962-1980, for all of the fastest-growing PP (except one) and all NRB manufactures included in annex table A.4, had been somewhat lower, however, than those for the dynamic products in other categories. In the period 1980-2000, this gap widened, while the average performance of the dynamic NRB manufactures was largely influenced by uranium-based products (see annex table A.4). Excluding these uranium-based products, the average growth rate of exports for the remaining products was lower than that in the other categories of manufactures.
>
> The above is not sufficient evidence that faster productivity growth is not possible if resources are shifted to the production of PP and NRB manufactures or that activities in these sectors are necessarily low-skill and/or have little technological content and spillover effects (see Appendix B). By the same token, participation of developing countries in exports of MT and HT manufactures does not necessarily mean that these countries have acquired the competencies needed to operate near or at the technological frontier. In these countries, with few exceptions, research and development (R&D) expenditure levels and the human resources employed in science and technology development are insufficient to match the requirements of technological content of the products they export.
>
> As discussed in chapter V, a productive agricultural sector is often essential for subsequent economic development. Moreover, several of the countries based their successful diversification on the industrial processing of their natural resources. The Chilean experience shows that it is possible to sustain high export and GDP growth rates through specializing in natural resource-based high-value exports, including mining and agricultural products. In Africa, Botswana achieved high growth rates boosted by diamond and meat exports (Acemoglu, Johnson and Robinson, 2003). Agriculture also played an important role in the industrialization processes of Malaysia and Thailand, while natural resource-based exports helped both countries cope with economic recession following the Asian financial crisis (Bonaglia and Fukasaku, 2003). Finland and Sweden, among developed economies, are other cases in point. These countries, however, did not stay specialized in the production of commodities but moved over time into other sectors that were experiencing more stable terms of trade and faster productivity growth.

countries in agricultural markets. In all, developing countries have been able to diversify their production structure and, as a result, increase their participation in the more dynamic global markets.

The structure of exports of developing countries has thus been changing rapidly over the past 40 years (see figure III.2), with some groups of countries having diversified sooner and faster than others into non-natural resource-based exports. The first-tier newly industrialized economies and South-East

Figure III.2.
Share of selected categories of non-oil exports of developing countries in total regional exports,[a] by developing-country region or country group, 1962-2000
(Percentage share in total regional exports)

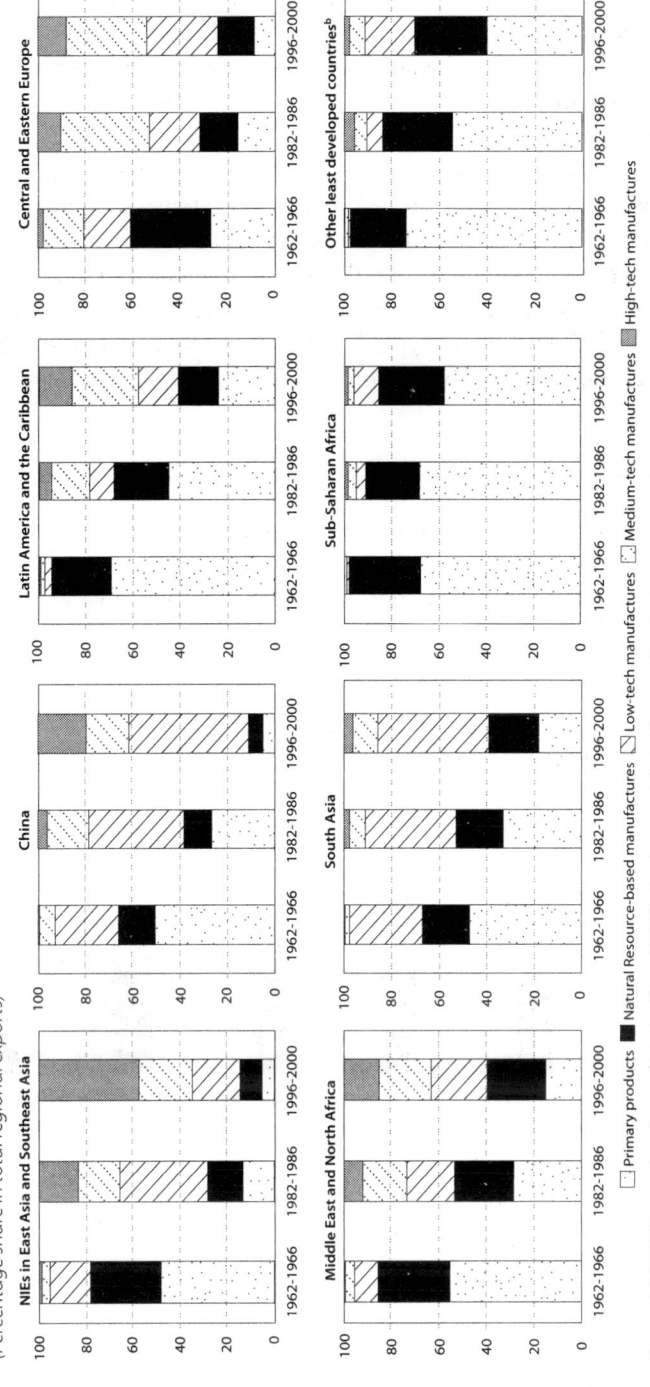

Source: UN/DESA based on Feenstra and others (2005) database on World Commodity Trade.
Note: See appendix B on definitions and methodology. See explanatory notes for country groupings.
[a] Total regional exports are a simple average for the period of the sum individual country's exports in each category.
[b] LDCs excluding Ethiopia, Mozambique, Uganda, United Republic of Tanzania and Yemen, already included in the other groups.

Asian countries are cases in point, diversifying first into LT manufactures and subsequently into HT manufactures. At the other extreme, sub-Saharan Africa has been the slowest region to diversify away from exports of primary commodities. The remaining regions lie between these two extreme cases, moving at different speeds into new export markets.

The relatively faster growth of manufactures in global trade implies that regions that had not switched rapidly or extensively enough into the production and export of these products experienced relatively slower rates of export growth and, overall, lost market shares in global markets. All regions lost market share to the first-tier newly industrialized economies, South-East Asia and China (see annex table A.3). This contributed to the growth divergence among developing countries.

Merchandise trade, specialization patterns and growth

Figure III.3 shows the divergence of per capita growth rates across groups of countries according to their dominant export structure and specialization patterns. Individual-country detail is provided in annex table A.5.

Figure III.3.
Per capita GDP growth and dominant patterns of trade specialization, 105 developing countries, 1962-2000 *(average annual rate of growth)*

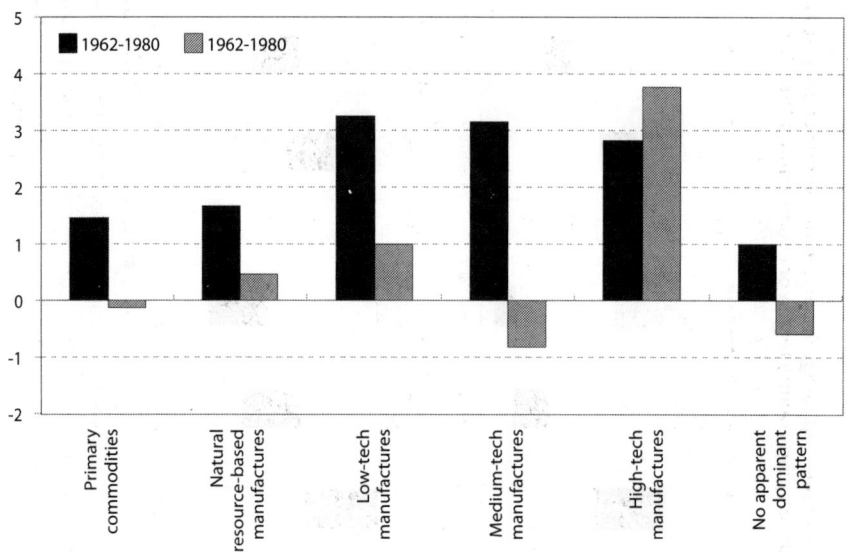

Source: Annex table A.5.

Growth divergence, albeit present, was much less marked in the period 1962-1980 than during the final two decades of the century. In the 1960s and 1970s, average rates of growth of countries specializing in PP and NRB manufactures were relatively lower, half of the rate of growth observed for other exporters. Moreover, only a few exporters of PP and NRB manufactures were able to exceed the average annual rate of growth of per capita GDP of developed countries during the period (3.1 per cent) (see table III.2).

The group of countries specializing in all groups of non-NRB manufactures grew at comparable rates. Convergence towards developed-country per capita GDP was frequent among the different groups of non-NRB exporters, as 47 per cent of them (23 out of 49 countries) were able to grow above the average rate of growth of per capita GDP in developed countries during the period. Convergence, however, was relatively faster among the group of MT exporters, as 12 out of 24 countries (50 per cent) grew at a rate above 3.1 per cent. Nonetheless, declines in per capita GDP also occurred among non-NRB exporters (Afghanistan, Liberia, Kuwait and the Niger). Other dynamics, probably idiosyncratic, were at play. Twenty-six countries did not seem to exhibit any particular diversification trend during the period. Their average per capita growth rate was the slowest among the groups of countries considered (see annex table A.5).

Divergence among developing countries seemed to have increased in the period 1980-2000. There was a marked deceleration in the rate of growth of per capita income in all groups of exporters, except for those exporting HT manufactures. None of the countries belonging to the groups of PP and MT manufacture exporters had a growth rate that exceeded the average rate of growth of per capita GDP of the developed countries (2.2 per cent), which was already lower than what had been observed in the previous sub-period. For PP exporters, increasing participation rates in slow-growing markets was not enough to offset the adverse trends, such as lower average commodity prices, that prevailed during the period. Among the NRB exporters, Equatorial Guinea had the highest average annual per capita income growth, which was largely due to the discovery and development of its oil reserves.

The majority of countries that did not show any clear diversification pattern during the period grew below the global average rate. This group was composed largely of least developed countries and/or countries that had experienced conflict and civil war during the period. Structural and institutional constraints were likely to have been among the binding factors in these cases (see chapter V).

In 1980-2000, in contrast with the previous period, growth divergence among the three groups of exporters of non-NRB manufactures was also

Table III.2.
Frequency (number of countries) of per capita GDP growth by dominant export specialization pattern, 1962-2000

	Number of countries	Growth of GDP per capita		
		Exceeding developed country average	Exceeding world average	Exceeding 3 per cent
1962-1980				
Primary commodities	12	1	6	1
Natural resouce-based manufactures	18	3	5	3
Low-tech manufactures	17	8	13	8
Medium-tech manufactures	24	12	17	16
High-tech manufactures	8	3	5	3
No apparent trend	26	2	5	3
Total	**105**	**29**	**51**	**34**
1980-2000				
Primary commodities	7	0	0	0
Natural resouce-based manufactures	21	3	4	1
Low-tech manufactures	31	8	13	4
Medium-tech manufactures	12	0	0	0
High-tech manufactures	10	7	8	7
No apparent trend	24	0	2	0
Total	**105**	**18**	**27**	**12**
Memo items:				
1962-1980				
Average annual rate of growth of per capita world gross product		2.2		
average annual rate of growth of per capita GDP of developed countries[a]		3.1		
1980-2000				
Average annual rate of growth of per capita world gross product		1.3		
Average annual rate of growth of per capita GDP of developed countries		2.2		

Source: World Bank Development Indicators database and Annex table A.5.
[a] Referring to the period 1966-1980.

marked. Newcomers to the group of LT manufacture exporters such as India, Sri Lanka and Viet Nam did particularly well during the period and grew above 3 per cent in per capita terms—the minimum rate believed necessary in order for a developing country to make a dent in poverty—while several other countries (18) grew above the average rate of growth of per capita GDP of developed countries. Growth in the majority of these countries, however, was below per capita growth of world gross product (WGP) in this subperiod. Apart from specific country conditions, it seems that the market for these products offered fewer opportunities for rapid growth perhaps owing to fallacy-of-composition effects or because of the imposition of quotas and other trade restrictions (textiles and garments are a large component of manufactures in this group) that favoured a particular group of countries to the detriment of others.

The number of countries specializing in the export of MT manufactures had shrunk by half. The newcomers were Mexico (arriving from HT manufactures), Hungary (from LT manufactures) and the United Arab Emirates (from NRB manufactures). Among the 12 countries or areas that had moved out of this group, only Costa Rica and Hong Kong Special Administrative Region (SAR) of China transferred to the group of exporters of HT manufactures; all the others diversified into sectors often perceived as having lower technology content (see table A.5).

The above suggests that, in order for a country to move into the production of HT manufactures, what appears to be necessary is a continuous effort to acquire technological capabilities and skills, but not necessarily a process of industrialization in stages, that is to say, the prior production of LT and MT manufactures. Malaysia moved into the group of exporters of HT manufactures from the group of exporters of NRB manufactures, while China, the Republic of Korea, Taiwan Province of China and Thailand moved into HT from LT manufactures.

The presence of several net fuel exporters in the group of MT manufacture exporters suggests that their overall growth was largely determined by the economics of oil—and, in the case of the Libyan Arab Jamahiriya, also by a trade embargo—, whose price was very volatile and declined during the period; but even among non-fuel exporters, economic performance was not satisfactory. In the case of Latin American and Caribbean countries, the debt crisis and its slow resolution took a toll on growth, but other forces may have been at play as well. Meanwhile, most HT manufacture exporters performed particularly well during 1980-2000, with 7 countries (out of 10) growing at above the average rate of per capita GDP growth in developed economies. Most of the economies in this group (China, Hong Kong SAR, Malaysia, the Republic of Korea, Singapore, Taiwan Province of China and Thailand) had already been participating in the fast-growing markets of the 1960s and 1970s. They successfully climbed the technological ladder and profited from continued growth, in a period when developing countries were in general stagnating. Among the other exporters, only Indonesia, Oman and Turkey were able to grow faster than developed countries in both sub-periods.

Interestingly, in recent decades, there seems to have been a significant difference in the capacity of Asian countries, vis-à-vis other countries and regions, to extract growth from exports of more technologically advanced products. For instance, the vast majority of Latin American countries, even when diversifying into the exports of manufactures, failed to attain fast growth, particularly in recent decades.

Two major factors may have contributed to such an outcome. First, the development impact of the strategy of a given country depends not only on success in entering markets, but also on the capacity to capture a share of the value added in the production chain (United Nations Conference on Trade and Development, 2002). The expansion of MT and HT manufacture exports has come intertwined with the growth of multinational firms' integrated production systems, which exhibit high import content. Therefore, the capacity to capture certain activities (such as assembly tasks) may not lead to rapid or sustained growth if these activities have limited value added and are also likely to be footloose.[3] In many instances, these outcomes are the result of the strategies countries have devised regarding FDI (discussed below).

In Mexico and Central America, for example, the relatively good export performance displayed by the maquila sector, in both garments and electronics, has been largely based on low wages, preferential access and proximity to the United States market, but this has failed to generate faster rates of aggregate output growth. In contrast, technology exports in Asia have strong linkages, which are both national and regional in nature.

Second, the impact of integration into the world economy depends not only on the type of products a country exports but also on the circumstances under which it takes place and the policies pursued during the integration phase. Faster growth in East Asian countries has been closely related to a continuous effort, both by the State and by the corporate sector, to upgrade export production capacities, and led to persistent industrialization drives. Conversely, the integration of Latin America, Africa and Central and Eastern Europe marked a sharp shift in their development strategy. It occurred in a "big bang" manner and followed a period of crisis.

Such big bang restructuring in the slow-growing regions exhibited "destructive" features, which involved the loss of previous production capacity and minimized the emergence of strong production linkages. For instance, the share of manufacturing in GDP fell in sub-Saharan Africa during the 1980s and stabilized at relatively low levels in the 1990s. A number of countries in Latin

America, including Argentina, Brazil and Mexico, experienced a particularly sharp productivity decline in traditional labour-intensive sectors, such as textiles and clothing, which shrank after trade liberalization. In contrast, productivity performance was better in medium-technology industries such as transport equipment, which continued to be heavily protected in several countries even during the recent reform period (Cimoli and Katz, 2002).

Specialization patterns in service exports and growth

While merchandise trade still constitutes the bulk of total world trade, the share of services increased over the last quarter-century, from about 17 per cent in 1980 to about 20 per cent in 2004. Services thus present an important and growing opportunity for export diversification. Nonetheless, while the export of services can be correlated with growth, this link seems to be stronger for developed countries, as they dominate the most dynamic sectors of the global export market for services.

The analysis of international trade in services is hampered by the scarcity of comprehensive and internationally comparable data. Available information based on balance-of-payments data captures only cross-border flows and may provide an imprecise idea of the actual magnitude of trade in services as defined in the General Agreement on Trade in Services, particularly trade generated through Mode 3 (commercial presence) and Mode 4 (presence of natural persons) (World Trade Organization, 2006). Furthermore, by only focusing on temporary migration, the latter does not capture all of the impact on economic growth generated by the movement of labour (an issue not analysed in this volume).[4]

Participation of developing countries in world service exports has accelerated, leading to an increase in their market penetration ratio from 19 per cent in 1980 to 23 per cent in 2004. World exports in the three major service sectors (transport, travel and other services) displayed diverging growth dynamics over the period 1980-2003 (see figure III.4).

"Other services", which includes communications, computer and information services, insurance, financial services, and other business services, was the fastest-growing sector over the entire period. The participation of developing countries in this sector increased from 14.8 per cent in 1980 to 18.3 per cent in 2003 (see annex table A.6 on service export data for all balance-of-payments subsectors).[5] Transport service exports had the slowest growth over the entire period, while exports of travel services were volatile, having grown strongly during the 1980s, but slowing down since then. Developing

Figure III.4.
World exports of services by sectors, 1980-2003
(Billions of dollars))

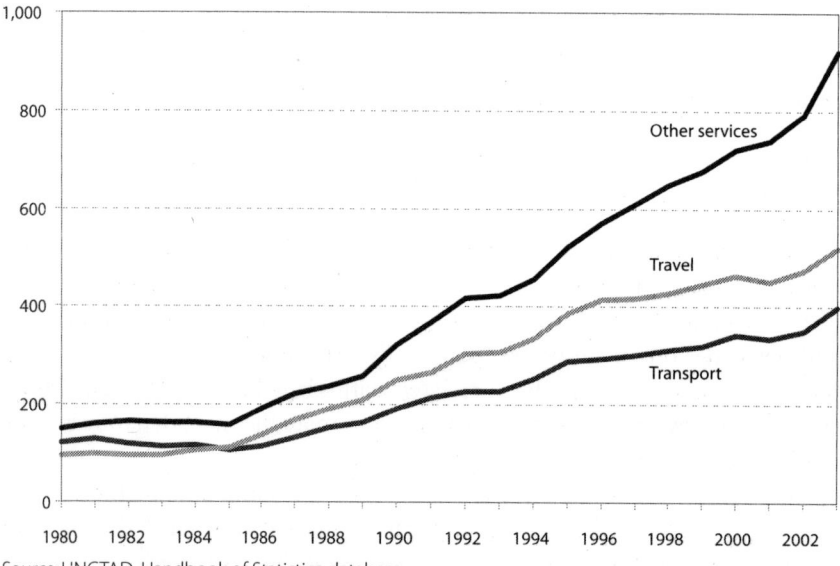

Source: UNCTAD, Handbook of Statistics database.

countries account for about 28 per cent of world exports of travel services. Tourism is an important source of foreign exchange and employment for many developing countries. For small island developing countries, as well as for a number of least developed countries, it may be "the main and sometimes only driver of economic and social development on a sustainable basis" (United Nations Conference on Trade and Development, 2006, p. 10). In addition, this sector may help reduce external vulnerability by diversifying exports away from traditional commodity exports, which face slow-growing or declining markets.

Most studies that analyse the impact of trade in services on economic growth focus on the effects of trade liberalization, and especially on the efficiency gains generated by increased service imports.[6] Empirical work on service exports has often been limited to specific service sectors or case studies (see, for example, Nielson and Taglioni, 2004; and United Nations Conference on Trade and Development, 2006). Fewer attempts have been made to estimate the existence and magnitude of the statistical relationship between the exports of services and GDP growth in both developed and developing countries.

One such analysis indicates that while there was a significant impact of services exports on growth, the impact of merchandise exports was much larger. In addition, while during the 1980s, the nexus between service export growth and GDP growth had been relatively stronger for developing countries, this trend was reversed during the 1990s, when the nexus became much weaker in developing countries but gained strength in developed economies. A possible explanation for the latter phenomenon is the effect of different export specialization patterns that had been created in the two country groups (Gabriele, 2004), with developed countries dominating in the most dynamic global markets for services.[7]

Available data on specialization patterns in service exports seem to support the hypothesis that developed countries benefited from their specialization in the booming technology- and skill-intensive services in the 1990s. In contrast, the bulk of developing countries' service exports is mostly concentrated in the relatively slowly growing transport and travel services. A more detailed analysis reveals, however, that a few major developing countries have gained significant market shares in more dynamic subsectors and have grown relatively fast. This trend may well have contributed to an increase in growth divergence across countries. To illustrate, the share of developing countries' exports of communication services is concentrated in a few major countries, with India having a strong presence. Other advanced, semi-industrialized Asian and Latin American countries also play a role.[8] Computer and information services, constituting the fastest-growing services sector, also illustrate this point: the large and growing share of developing countries in this export market (at 20 per cent in 2003) is dominated by very few players, with India—the largest exporter among non-developed countries—exporting three times as much as the runner-up, Israel (see box III.2).[9] A few other developing economies (such as Argentina, China, Costa Rica, Hong Kong SAR, Malaysia, Singapore and Taiwan Province of China) have also established their presence in this market (see annex table A.7).

Overall, as is the case for trade in goods, countries growing relatively faster have specialized in service exports with stronger growth dynamics and with greater potential spillover effects. Whereas some developing countries may be able to gradually move into more dynamic service exports, by making use of their endowments and the support of appropriate policies, others will likely find it more difficult to follow that path. While these countries are still in the early stages of building up the necessary capabilities, they can still effectively participate in other service sectors and thus promote the diversification of their economies (see chapter II). The importance of adopting sound policies both at the domestic and at the international level will be addressed in the two last sections of this chapter.

Box III.2.
Exports of Computer and Information Services: Flying Geese in South Asia?

The strong performance of some developing countries in the exports of computer and information services seems to suggest new development perspectives for these countries as well as for potential followers.

In a global ranking of export values of services in 2003, India was a close second behind Ireland, while Israel ranked sixth (see annex table A.7). These three countries stand out in that they have been able to catch up with the first tier of major software exporting nations.

The evolution of the software sector in India was heavily influenced by economic policies, past and present. Until the early 1990s, the sector had benefited from "benign neglect" by the Government, which controlled most of the economy, both directly through State-owned enterprises and via heavy regulation of the private sector (Singh, 2003, p. 18). At the same time, the Indian education system has been skewed towards tertiary education, especially in science and engineering. The resulting mismatch between the skill levels in domestic labour supply and demand contributed to an emigration push of skilled labour, largely to the United States. Surplus skilled labour was also absorbed by State-owned enterprises such as the Computer Maintenance Corporation and the Electronic Corporation of India, Ltd (ECIL). With the economic liberalization of the 1990s and the global take-off of the software industry, former employees of these enterprises had gone on to play a critical role in the establishment of the sector in Bangalore (Kochhar and others, 2006, p. 27). From this base, and with its efforts furthered by the presence of a high degree of proficiency in English, the sector was able to take advantage of strong external demand growth, fuelling the dramatic success of software and services exports since the mid-1990s. By the late 1990s, Indian firms were well positioned to take advantage of large contract volumes linked to the issue of the Y2K (or millennium) bug and the introduction of the euro.

In the 1990s, government policies continued to play an important role. The central and State Governments started targeting the growing sector, for example, by establishing export processing zones and software technology parks – allowing for duty-free hardware imports, exemptions from sales and excise taxes, and the provision of subsidized office space as well as power access. The sector also benefited from general liberalization policies, most notably in the telecommunications sector, as well as from e-governance projects, and from targeted finance. Increased FDI inflows and an "inverse brain drain" in the form of capital and expertise from Indian expatriates and returnees also helped the development of the sector.

After a decade of sustained growth, the Indian information technology (IT) sector is established as a strong and dynamic brand internationally. Domestic sales are also gaining importance, generating increasing forward linkages to other industries. Wages in the sector have increased rapidly, indicating a bottleneck in the supply of skilled labour, and calling for increased investments in education in order to maintain the country's competitive edge.

Pakistan is still a small exporter, although it shares some of the same advantages as India. Recently, the sector has witnessed strong growth, but longer-term prospects hinge on whether Pakistan will be able to overcome some key obstacles. Among the most important is the limited supply of trained professionals. Another problem stems from the latecomer status of Pakistan's IT sector, which missed the growth and learning opportunities of the late 1990s and now faces strong competition from established Indian firms. Further problems are political security concerns and the lack of an established brand identity for its software sector.

Box III.2 *(cont'd)*

Acknowledging these bottlenecks, the Government of Pakistan in its 2000 IT Policy and Action Plan adopted several measures, including increased spending on IT education, establishment of IT parks, the provision of enhanced Internet access and the enhancing of e-government. In order to increase exports by the sector, in 1996 the Government had established the Pakistan Software Export Board, with the aim of having it lead research and development activities, identify new market opportunities, and create a conducive business environment. As in India, the sector is also benefiting from the effects of reverse brain drain, albeit to a somewhat lesser extent.

In the light of these supportive policies, the strong growth rates of the sector, and the increased interest of foreign investors—not least because of emergent congestion effects in India—the future of the software and computer services sector of Pakistan looks promising. Remaining challenges are persistent adverse security perceptions and the presence of a powerful competitor and long-time regional rival, namely, India. There is room however, for learning from India's success and for attracting Indian FDI. The 2005 deal between the Indian software giant Tata Consultancy Services, Ltd., and Pakistan-based Techlogix, Inc., is a case in point. The first step in this joint venture is to be the establishment of a training centre for technology workers in Lahore, Pakistan, with Tata's ultimate goal being the creation of a software development facility in Pakistan. Assuming a successful outcome to this effort, the venture might become the harbinger in South Asia of a type of "flying geese" development pattern—a phenomenon that greatly benefited the emerging economies of East and South-East Asia.

FOREIGN DIRECT INVESTMENT AND THE CONVERGENCE-DIVERGENCE DILEMMA

Most developing countries have long accepted that FDI offers a potentially significant source of financing because, in addition to being a relatively stable source of capital, it can bring with it up-to-date technology, organizational skills and distribution networks, with possible spillover effects. On the assumption that scarce resources receive the highest returns, poorer countries—with little capital but abundant supplies of natural resources and unskilled labour—should be an attractive location for transnational corporations (TNCs), making FDI a potentially powerful force for income convergence.

Yet, for most of the period since 1960, FDI flows have not conformed to these expectations. Flows have been moving principally between capital-abundant industrialized countries. Even when they have spilled into developing countries, FDI flows have been heavily bunched both in time and in space, and along with benefits they have also generated costs. The recent surge of FDI flows does not appear to have changed this situation.

Trends in FDI

Since the early 1980s, FDI has grown at a much faster rate than both output and trade, in part facilitated by changes (discussed further below) in manufacturing production processes and in financial corporate governance, developments in equity markets, increased liberalization of FDI regimes and privatization, among other factors. As a consequence of the rapid growth in flows, the stock of world FDI has increased almost 20-fold since the early 1980s, reaching close to a quarter of world GDP. Yet, as indicated in chapter I, flows have remained highly concentrated in the developed economies (see figure III.5).

In parallel with the fast increase in global FDI flows, the developing countries had experienced a 10-fold rise in average annual inflows from the first half of the 1980s to the second half of the 1990s. FDI flows have been concentrated among a handful of countries. Since the early 1980s, the eight top recipients have absorbed three quarters of the inward flows to these countries. However, there has been a reordering among regions and countries, dominated above all by the emergence of China as a host economy: its share of FDI increased from 1.1 per cent of the global FDI inward stock in 1990 to over 6 per cent in the late 1990s.

Figure III.5.
Inward FDI inflows, developed and developing countries, 1980-2004
(Billions of dollars))

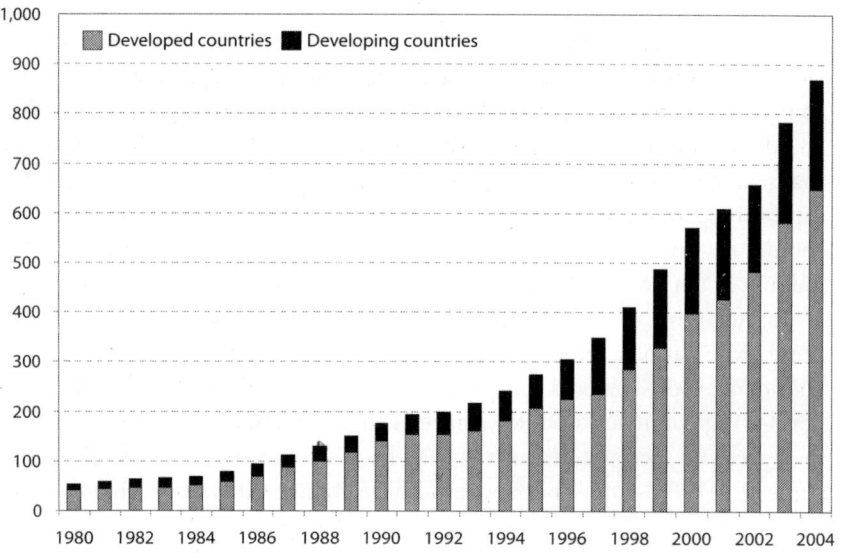

Source: UNCTAD, Handbook of Statistics database.

The sectoral composition of FDI stocks has changed in both the developing and the developed countries. Among developed countries, inward FDI flows have been increasingly directed towards services. As a result, services now account for close to three quarters of the global stock of FDI, as compared with 40 per cent in 1980. Between 1990 and 2003, the share of manufacturing in the FDI stock of the group of developing countries rose from 25 per cent to 37 per cent, while the share of developing countries in the global stock of manufacturing FDI increased from one fifth to close to one third. The tilt is particularly pronounced in some sectors, notably clothing, electronics and automobiles, which are among the most dynamic in the trading system.

Sectoral trends of FDI differ among developing countries and regions. Since the late 1980s, Latin America and the Caribbean have attracted FDI not only in large-scale natural resources and services through privatizations, but also in labour-intensive manufacturing such as textiles and clothing (notably in Central America, the Dominican Republic and Mexico). Africa has attracted FDI mainly in natural resources, particularly fuel and minerals. Some African countries have been able, however, to attract FDI in manufacturing as well: Lesotho (in textiles and garments) and the Republic of South Africa (in automobile manufacturing) are cases in point. Meanwhile, East Asia and South-East Asia have attracted more FDI in manufacturing (electronics, textiles) than have the other developing-country regions. In this respect, the concentration of the recent FDI surge in a few countries, as well as its sectoral composition, would appear to be a source of further economic divergence (Mody, 2004, pp.1201-1205).

Concentration and divergence in FDI flows

In the period up to 1980, the increasing volume of FDI flows among advanced countries had been closely connected with their fast industrialization, particularly in more capital- and technology-intensive sectors, along with rapidly growing and converging incomes (Hymer, 1976; Rowthorn, 1992). These were predominantly two-way flows, and often in the same sectors. They consisted of investment undertaken by large firms that had already established strong export ties, and for which controlling productive assets abroad offered a more assured means to appropriate or augment rents in imperfectly competitive markets. Such intra-industry FDI was principally the product of market size and technological sophistication (Driffield and Love, 2005).[10]

Most developing countries were peripheral to these trends, offering only marginal investment opportunities for transnational corporations. However, expanding local markets attracted transnational corporations to sectors relatively intensive in the use of semi-skilled labour and medium-level technology, such as chemicals and transportation, particularly in some larger developing countries and usually in cases where tariff barriers offered more secure markets.[11] Because many of the same economic forces have been behind the rapid expansion of FDI in the modern service sectors, including banking and distribution services, the bias in flows towards advanced countries has continued since 1980, including, more recently, through mergers and acquisitions (M&A).

The dominant FDI dynamics appear to be cumulative, with the size of the existing stock of FDI having a strong bearing on the size of subsequent flows. Moreover, agglomeration pressures and convergence tendencies have generated strong neighbourhood effects, that is to say, transnational corporations find a disproportionately large number of locations close to home—a trend supported by the creation of free trade areas such as European Union and the North American Free Trade Agreement (NAFTA). Similarly, in Asia, when Japan had emerged as a home country in the 1980s, it also invested heavily in some of its neighbours (United Nations Conference on Trade and Development, 1996). Since these regional blocs are very large, production facilities can be big enough to undertake most of the activities originally carried out at home by the parent company, with trade possibly being replaced. Thus, between regional blocs, direct investment and trade are more likely to constitute alternatives. Conversely, within these regional blocs, direct investment and trade are complementary. They often reflect the development of an internal division of labour within the same firm, whereby plants in different countries of the bloc collaborate in the creation of a single product. Alternatively, plants specialize to produce different goods for export to the entire bloc or beyond.

Since the early 1980s, several new trends have contributed to the boom in FDI flows globally, introducing new challenges and opportunities for policymakers in developing countries but without fundamentally changing the bias towards developed countries. First, there have been significant changes in the way Governments interact with transnational corporations owing to a rapid and widespread liberalization of FDI policy not only in developed but also in developing countries. In the latter group of countries, these changes have included reduced taxation, greater investor protection and increased incentives. Such changes have also been pushed for at the international level in multilateral forums, as well as through bilateral and regional treaties and agreements. In most cases, revisions in FDI legislation have been linked to a wider package of measures (including privatization of State-owned assets) aimed at extending the role of market forces in resource allocation. In the case of Latin America, for instance, much of the FDI inflow in services has been facilitated through privatization programmes.

Second, large corporations have introduced new practices in respect of the way they manage their assets abroad. On the one hand, there has been a shift, largely associated with manufacturing activities, from "simple" to "complex" integration strategies. Whereas, previously, a firm expanded abroad by reproducing all of its operations in a single foreign location, now the operations of separate parts of its value chain are performed in different locations and valued according to how they contribute to the objectives of the firm as a whole, rather than according to their profitability in the host country location (Hanson, Mataloni Jr., and Slaughter, 2001).[12] A great deal of FDI in manufacturing in Asia, Central America and Mexico has been undertaken as a result of such trends. By contrast, expansion along horizontal lines (where most of the output is sold in the host country) has been closely associated with the growth of FDI in the service sector.

The other development in corporate strategy is the preference for mergers and acquisitions as opposed to greenfield investments.[13] In much of the developing world, this trend has been linked to privatization programmes. However, it is also very much connected with wider changes in corporate governance associated with raising capital through the issuance of common stocks and corporate debt. And unlike the moves towards vertical disintegration—where comparative unit labour costs are a major determinant—the rise of an active equity market ties FDI more closely to short-term financial considerations, thereby adding a potentially more volatile dimension to international production relations.[14]

FDI in manufacturing: international production networks and growth

The existence of a vibrant industrial base, robust local markets and a dynamic enterprise sector are preconditions for attracting (and benefiting) from FDI in manufacturing. Countries where growth has stalled or collapsed, or where the manufacturing base has been eroded, have little chance of participating in and benefiting from the most dynamic elements of the international production system. Thus, the recent rapid expansion of export-oriented manufacturing activities linked to FDI has been heavily biased towards a handful of countries in East Asia, with China the single largest recipient of FDI in the manufacturing sector. This type of North-South FDI has been, in part, an extension of earlier flows between advanced countries, and has been triggered by the standardization of technology in some sectors, by the aggressive search for unit labour cost differentials in more competitive markets, and by the shift to a more liberal business environment in many developing countries. These same forces have also been at play in respect of the growing regional component of FDI flows in East Asia, led by emergent transnational corporations from the first-tier newly industrialized economies. And because these sectors include medium- and high-skill and technology-intensive products, the share of these products in the exports of developing countries has risen sharply.

Much of this FDI has been linked to participation in international production networks (IPNs).[15] In some cases, production is organized by large transnational corporations producing a standardized set of goods in several locations (as in the electronics and transport industries). In others, production involves groups of small and medium-sized enterprises located in different countries and linked through international subcontracting (as in clothing).

A comparison of individual-country experiences reveals how FDI and trade flows have combined in different patterns of specialization: East Asian and Central American countries have been prominent in electronic and electrical goods and these same countries along with Northern African countries have participated in clothing networks, while only the larger Latin American countries along with the Republic of Korea have been prominent in transport equipment.

A key determinant of whether or not such FDI will reduce global income inequalities is the establishment of the kind of dynamic investment-export nexus that emerged in an earlier generation of success stories in East Asia and led to a steady diversification of production away from those activities requiring only unskilled labour. A good deal depends on whether FDI organized through production networks brings increased technological and organizational spillovers to developing countries and crowds in local private investment. To date, the evidence does not support the claim that such a nexus exists in other developing economies.

IPNs are associated with increased exports and employment in host countries. Yet, the fact that parts of the same final product may cross and re-cross national boundaries more than once somewhat inflates the gross value of trade (Krugman, 1995). More importantly, there is also strong evidence suggesting an increased import content of domestic production and consumption brought about by participation in IPNs. Thus, strong increases in the manufacturing exports of developing countries—particularly those participating in IPNs—may have taken place without commensurate increases in incomes and value added. In the case of Mexico, for example, it has been estimated that over the past two decades, imports for further processing constitute as much as one half to two thirds of total sales of affiliates of United States transnational corporations in certain industries (United Nations Conference on Trade and Development, 2002). Meanwhile, growth in manufacturing valued added has been negligible in the country. Similar patterns are discernible in some Northern African economies, in Central America and in parts of Asia, including Cambodia, Hong Kong SAR and the Philippines.

The contribution to value added derived from participating in production networks is determined by the cost of the most abundant and least mobile factor, namely, labour, whereas the rewards to internationally mobile factors such as capital, management and know-how are reaped by their foreign owners. In this respect, several studies suggest that the combination of increased capital mobility and rapid entry into the global labour force of unskilled labour is likely to weaken the bargaining position of poorer countries, reinforcing highly asymmetric relations between oligopolistic market structures at the top of the value chain and competitive market structures at the bottom (United Nations Conference on Trade and Development, 2002; Milberg, 2004).

Finally, it is doubtful that IPNs are able to generate opportunities for stronger spillover effects. In the first place, participation in the labour-intensive and low-skill parts of the value chain of production networks is unlikely to attract FDI with a high level of technological sophistication. Therefore, it is not clear what kind of spillovers should be expected from these arrangements.[16] Additionally, the potential for spillovers from participating in IPNs is reduced not only because the package of technology required at any one site becomes narrower but also owing to cross-border linkages, being strengthened at the expense of domestic ones. As a result, technological upgrading can be more difficult for economies that are used by transnational corporations primarily as bases for exports to third markets than for economies where FDI is of a more traditional horizontal type that is seeking markets.[17] In either case, however, all successful cases of technological upgrading using FDI, including within the context of IPNs, demonstrate that a prominent policy component (see the section on sectoral policies below) was required to anchor FDI to the domestic economy.

Can FDI lead to faster growth in developing countries?

While there is little in the structural dimension of resurgent flows of FDI to indicate that they are a force for convergence between industrialized and developing countries, or even among developing countries, there are perceived macroeconomic advantages which may point to greater opportunities for catch-up growth. By the early 1990s, following a decade or more of macroeconomic adjustments and microeconomic reforms, it was believed that resurgent FDI flows were a sign of a more general improvement in the investment climate in many developing countries. Moreover, it was anticipated that these inflows of FDI would further reinforce that improvement through crowding in domestic investment.

FDI and domestic capital formation, however, have been moving in different directions since the early 1990s, as FDI flows increased and investment rates and volumes declined or stagnated in the major developed and developing economies (United Nations, 2006, p. 16). For instance, when measured as a share of GDP, FDI rose, while overall investment stagnated or fell in all major Latin American countries (Argentina, Brazil, Colombia and Mexico) and in some larger African economies (Côte d'Ivoire, Morocco, South Africa and Tunisia) between the 1980s and the 1990s. It is possible that the conditions that attract foreign enterprises may not be conducive to faster capital formation in the host economy, with the two sets of investment decisions driven by different motivations. Evidence on whether FDI crowds in or crowds out domestic investment is mixed and subject to country-level specificities, but several studies have suggested that the latter tendency has become more prevalent in developing countries.[18]

Evidence from the export side of the nexus is just as mixed and as contingent on the sector in which FDI is located. As noted earlier, a good deal of FDI has gone in to non-tradable sectors, services in particular. Conversely, participation in IPNs, as noted above, accelerates export growth but may also create balance-of-payments pressures owing to increased imports.

The impact of FDI on the balance of payments of the hosting country is likely to vary considerably with the sectoral pattern of FDI inflows, the share of transnational corporation profits in value added, the degree of import dependence, external debt servicing by transnational corporations and the proportion of the final goods sold in domestic markets (Akyüz, 2004). Thus, the danger is that as profit remittances and other capital outflows linked to FDI begin to accrue, the longer-term impact on the balance of payments will be negative.

Even when FDI-linked activities incur foreign-exchange deficits, such investment may still improve the balance of payments if it creates significant externalities that enhance the export potential of the overall economy. Similarly, even when FDI leads to unfavourable balance-of-payments outcomes, there may still be net benefits if there are significant technological spillovers from

FDI and the presence of transnational corporations. On balance, however, empirical evidence of positive FDI spillover effects is inconclusive (Addison, Guha-Khasnobis and Mavrotas, 2006).[19]

In order to profit from FDI, countries need to have the necessary absorptive capacity among domestic firms and institutions. Countries where an inflow of FDI has been paralleled by significant investments in building domestic capabilities (for example, Singapore and Ireland) have been the most successful in leveraging inward FDI. Conversely, when FDI is attracted in response to major tax incentives, or as a result of trade policy distortions (such as textile and clothing quotas), without a simultaneous build-up of local capabilities and without the creation of linkages between foreign affiliates and local firms, there is limited scope for long-term benefits from FDI.

It would therefore appear that FDI has been a force as much for global divergence as for convergence. On the one hand, hosting FDI, including through IPNs, can be compatible with more rewarding arrangements between national and international economic forces. On the other hand, it is also consonant with a more hierarchically differentiated division of labour in which poorer countries compete on the basis of either their abundant and inexpensive labour resources or their natural resource endowments.

Recognizing these conflicting potential outcomes still leaves unanswered the question how FDI, capital accumulation and growth might link up to form a virtuous circle in developing countries. According to some accounts, evidence of a positive correlation between lagged FDI and growth provides sufficient grounds for seeing it as an engine of growth, albeit one conditional on countries' adopting an open policy stance (Blomström, Lipsey and Zejan, 1992). Others, however, find either no evidence that FDI is an independent accelerator of growth, even under such conditions (Carkovic and Levine, 2002; Mody, 2004; Nunnenkamp and Spatz, 2004); or that the effects are very weak and disappear as more country characteristics are controlled for (Rodrik, 1999, p. 37).

All in all, the growth effects from hosting FDI seem to be highly conditional and non-linear. While FDI may affect growth, fast growth is also a determinant of FDI (Addison, Guha-Khasnobis and Mavrotas, 2006). A good deal of the evidence suggests that threshold levels, in income, human capital, technological know-how and enterprise development, must be crossed before a significant positive impact can be identified.[20] Thus, policies to attract and manage FDI should not be designed independently of the initial conditions and structural constraints facing an economy at any particular time.

Production Sector Development Policies, Diversification and Export Growth

While there has been an intense debate among economists on the rationale for and the efficacy of government intervention in the production sector, it is acknowledged that all the success cases identified in the preceding sections relied on some sort of production sector strategy to promote industrialization and/or support structural transformation of their economies. In fact, all late industrializing developing countries followed similar types of intervention, adopted comparable degrees of protection of their infant industries and attempted to promote similar types of sectors—particularly in the 1950s and 1960s but also, to some degree, in later decades (and recently, for example, in information and communication technologies (ICT)). Several of such interventions, however, are no longer possible in today's policy environment. In fact, as discussed below, the scope for production sector strategies has become very limited in the current context of worldwide trade liberalization.

Naturally, not all interventions have led to overall success. Even in successful countries, not all individual policy measures led to anticipated results. Important differences among these experiences seem to be based on how quickly inefficient policies were abandoned and how fast and how extensively countries diversified the structure of their exports and expanded into the dynamic sectors of global service and merchandise trade. Increased outward orientation in these economies, however, did not imply a laissez-faire attitude or indiscriminate liberalization. Most recently, success cases such as the Republic of Korea and Taiwan Province of China have continued to effectively promote the emergence of new sectors even in a more liberalized economic environment (Wade, 2005). Another distinctive feature of the successful interventions has been the active involvement and/or participation of the private corporate sector, which increasingly acted with greater interdependence from the Government as it acquired experience and was exposed to new technologies and competition.

It is worth viewing industrial and other production sector policies as a series of interventions in the economy that aim at enabling changes in its productive structure, while shifting resources from less to more dynamic activities, which do not necessarily need to be in the manufacturing sector. In this sense, these policies comprise economy-wide measures such as macroeconomic policies (discussed in chapter IV); horizontal or multisector policies such as investments in physical infrastructure, incentives and support for technology development, and, selective policies that target specific sectors or firms. The relevance and impact of the first two types of intervention are well recognized.

The debate has concentrated on selective interventions (Wade, 2005). Among other things, critics of this type of intervention argue that it interferes with the efficient allocation of resources dictated by well-functioning markets—a condition not necessarily present in any case in developing countries. They further indicate that Governments are prone to costly failures. Yet, eliminating distortions to markets may not suffice to generate structural change of the type required to accelerate and sustain growth (World Bank, 2005b). Slow growth in many developing countries in the 1990s, including persistent stagnation in sub-Saharan Africa, attests to this.

As discussed in chapter II, economic growth is contingent on the implementation of structural changes in the economy. Such changes are enabled by innovations in the broad sense of the term, that is to say, products, services or processes that were not produced or employed in the economy before; their diffusion throughout the economy; and the emergence of linkages among firms and sectors (Ocampo, 2005b). Without innovations, the economy remains locked in production methods that use less advanced technology, and it fails to diversify into more dynamic activities. These are the activities characterized by increasing returns and associated with new technologies and learning by doing, which, in turn, boost the profitability of capital and support higher investment and growth.

While innovations that push the world technological frontier are the clue to growth in developed countries, in developing countries innovations are often associated with the attracting activities and technologies previously developed in industrialized countries through import substitution, export promotion or a mix of both. As shown above, and in chapter II, higher rates of growth have been correlated with structural change, which was reflected in the export composition of the countries concerned. In fact, there is robust econometric evidence that countries diversify as they climb up the income ladder. Specialization or sectoral concentration takes place late in the development process (Imbs and Wacziarg, 2003). It is innovation rather than factor endowments that underlies a country's competitive advantage. Accordingly, countries with similar factor endowments can end up developing comparative advantages in distinct sectors and industries. Klinger and Lederman (2004) show that discoveries—defined as episodes during which countries start to export a new product—are not closely related to factor endowments. Moreover, developing countries are not necessarily restricted to discoveries in sectors based on their level of development. For instance, Rodrik (2006b) argues that China has an export basket that is considerably more sophisticated than the one that would normally be expected from a country at its income level.

Advances in economic theory, particularly on innovation and technical change, support the conclusion that market forces alone would not lead to optimal growth results. The acquisition of knowledge or technology, which supports growth, is a learning process subject to costs, externalities and barriers to entry. Start-up costs in the face of uncertain demand (or uncertain outcomes) and the existence of externalities—benefits that will not necessarily be appropriated by the initial investor—discourage firms from introducing new products or processes. Additionally, many projects require, in order to be profitable, complementary investments in a number of areas, often with the kind of high fixed costs that private entrepreneurs would be reluctant to bear without a sufficiently large market for their services – which it is difficult to guarantee ex ante.[21] For a producer at a particular location, building a reputation in new markets also entails start-up costs; the process may generate significant spillover effects on other firms, which will then be able to benefit from the leader's success (without having to share the costs of his or her failures).

If acquisition of knowledge is a key factor in determining a firm's competitiveness, temporary protection and granting of incentives may be warranted while the firm builds up its technological capacity and sustains the R&D costs necessary to its becoming internationally competitive (Shapiro, 2008). Similarly, public interventions may be needed to assure the entrepreneur that rents generated from risky investment in non-traditional activities will not disappear prematurely in the face of competition. Finally, public policy also has a role to play in addressing the issue of the coordination of externalities by fostering the coordination of private investment, and entry into new markets, or by providing infrastructure with high social but low private returns.

While the implementation of some policies may provide scope for rent-seeking behaviour, this should not prevent interactions between the government and the private sector. Rather, emphasis should be placed on designing a process in which public support for new activities is determined on the basis of ongoing consultations and collaboration with the private sector. These consultations should aim at identifying the binding constraints that discourage the private sector from investing in new activities. The actual policy instruments used will depend on context (Rodrik, 2004b).

From this discussion, two issues emerge: the relevance of public policies for diversification and the importance of building up technological capabilities in order to upgrade a country's economic structure. A third issue, mentioned briefly above, needs to be considered as well, namely, the quality of public intervention. An examination of these three factors will help further our understanding of divergence in countries' performance.

Creating dynamic comparative advantages: policies and outcomes

The export-led growth strategies of success cases (first-tier newly industrialized economies, for instance) often involved a preceding import substitution phase together with an active export diversification strategy. These countries used a series of interventions such as infant industry protection, export subsidies and targets, performance requirements, credit allocation, local content rules, massive investment in human capital, development of skills and build-up of local R&D capabilities, which also included slack intellectual property protection to allow for copying and reverse engineering.

While association with foreign private investors did take place, the approaches were far from uniform. In the Republic of Korea, domestic content agreements and technology screening were used extensively, with full government support. Similar measures were often used in Taiwan Province of China, which maintained, until the late 1980s, a list of industries where foreign investment was prohibited. This, despite a participation of FDI greater than in the Republic of Korea. Conversely, in Singapore, which had a weak tradition of local entrepreneurship, export-oriented industrialization relied heavily on transnational corporations. However, policies targeted specific manufacturing and service activities, through a variety of training facilities and publicly funded R&D institutions, with the aim of attracting the right kind of transnational corporation participation.[22] The approach in the second-tier newly industrialized economies has been more open to export-oriented FDI, through a series of fiscal incentives, relaxed ownership and remittance laws and the establishment of export processing zones. Costa Rica and Mexico followed similar approaches in the 1990s.

China made use of, among other things, a complex set of unorthodox polices, combining tariffs, non-tariff barriers and licensing with special economic zones, associated duty drawbacks and other incentives for export-oriented investments. Latin America also used in the past a particular series of interventions, some of them similar to those used by the first-tier newly industrialized economies, such as infant industry protection and subsidized credit allocation to priority sectors. In general, however, success was more limited. Yet, the region has successfully entered world markets for manufactures and is second to East Asia in the developing world in this regard. Such an achievement indicates that past production sector strategies adopted by Latin American countries had created industrial capabilities that allowed them to participate in and profit from the more recent phases of export development. However, as argued previously, the big bang approach to liberalization also reduced such capabilities and was biased towards sectors with weak domestic linkages (United Nations, Economic Commission for Latin America and the Caribbean, 2003 and 2004; Ocampo, 2004). It also led to the reduction of efforts in critical areas, such as R&D spending (Lall, 2003).

Efforts to promote industrial development and structural change in sub-Saharan Africa resulted in poor outcomes in the majority of cases. The technological capabilities in the region remain weak (Lall, 2000). Moreover, there has been an increasing gap in the technological capacity between East Asia and the rest of the developing countries in general, and sub-Saharan Africa in particular. If not addressed, the technological gap will likely feed into further growth divergence among developing countries.

Exogenous factors (external shocks such as natural disasters or hikes in international interest rates) and structural ones (fragmentation of local markets, a low entrepreneurial base and so on) may explain the disappointing outcomes of production sector policies in some countries, as these factors interact negatively with policy options and policy design. In the particular case of economies with small populations, there is greater difficulty in diversifying at lower costs owing to diseconomies of scale associated with the small size (Guillaumont, 2005).

In other cases, multilateral or bilateral institutional settings might have played a role in locking economies into certain specialization patterns. For instance, several countries failed to use rents obtained from preferential treatment to diversify their economies away from the sectors that had been receiving temporary benefits or to improve upon the competitiveness of such industries so as to make them viable in the absence of special concessions or arrangements. Many of the beneficiaries of the EU sugar and banana regimes or of the quotas imposed by the Multi-Fibre Agreement and its successors represent cases in point. Yet, some other countries were able to use preferences in their favour: Mauritius, for instance, upgraded and reformed its sugar sector and also successfully diversified into textiles and garments; and Caribbean countries such as Saint Lucia and Saint Vincent and the Grenadines were able to diversify their economies so as to move from the banana sector into tourism (Gillson, Hewitt and Page, 2004). Thus, policymakers' attitudes and vision as well as the quality of their policies also matter. In fact, in several instances, underlying the policy failures were lack of policy coherence and legitimacy, unclear objectives and mistaken choice of policy instruments, among other factors (see chapter V).

Outward orientation, trade liberalization and growth

The question of the impact of trade liberalization and openness on growth is the subject of intense debate. The superior growth performance and the outward orientation of East Asian economies relative to Latin America and Africa since the late 1970s have led analysts to prescribe, among other things, trade liberalization as a means to promote growth. As explained by Shapiro (2008): "The assumption was that the anti-export bias of import substitution policies, along with the lack of domestic competition, discouraged innovation and encouraged rent-seeking behaviours. These micro inefficiencies, in turn, had led to macro imbalances and slower growth rates. Exports and import competition would have dynamic effects through learning and innovation."

However, it is far from clear whether trade liberalization has helped to promote faster growth. A careful revision of econometric studies undertaken in the early 1990s that had claimed that liberalization led to faster growth revealed that the results had been based on inappropriate indicators of trade liberalization or that questionable econometric methodologies were used. The assessment of the evidence gathered in the 1990s—a period characterized by greater economic integration—did not determine that more-open economies consistently fared better than less-open ones during the period. Moreover, none of the measures linked to trade openness (tariff and non-tariff barriers, trade shares, changes in trade shares, indices or dummies for closeness and openness) were found to be significantly associated with growth (Rodriguez, 2006c).

A similar conclusion was reached by Dowrick and Golley (2004), who found that, between 1960 and 1980, increased trade had helped productivity to grow in poorer countries at double the rate attained by richer countries but that this gain was reversed in the period of more open trade between 1980 and 2000, when the marginal impact of trade on productivity growth favoured the richer countries, and indeed turned negative for poorer countries.[23] Developing countries appear to be trading more but earning less.

Another way of investigating the impact of trade liberalization on welfare is through examining whether the removal of policy-induced barriers reduces the dispersion of income levels among liberalizing countries. By using a methodology that compared the convergence pattern among liberalizing countries before and after major liberalization episodes with the pattern observed in an otherwise similar control group of countries, Slaughter (1998) found no systematic link between trade liberalization and income convergence.

Even where liberalization led to or coincided with export expansion, the impact on overall growth has been mixed across countries. Some countries seem to achieve greater GDP growth through their exports than others (Palma, 2006). This finding reinforces the thesis of this chapter, which is that integration patterns, underpinned by diversification and economic structural change, matter for growth.

Recent empirical research has indicated that the effect of trade liberalization on economic growth depends on the complementary reforms implemented by a country in order to take advantage of international trade (see also chapter V). It is also contingent upon a variety of structural characteristics (Chang, Kaltani and Loayza, 2005). Other studies show that the growth effect of trade liberalization is negligible for countries with low levels of GDP per capita but increases with the level of development, while tapering off for high levels of income (Calderón, Loayza and Schmidt-Hebbel, 2005). Based on the results of the study by Chang, Kaltani and Loayza, one can argue that trade liberalization should be perceived not as a silver bullet in the quest for growth but rather as one element in an overall development strategy (see also World Bank, 2005b). Based on the results of the research carried out by Calderón, Loayza and Schmidt-Hebbel, one might suggest that the timing of trade liberalization also seems to matter but that the causality between liberalization and growth remains ambiguous.

Many of the economies where trade liberalization was implemented rapidly (through a big bang) or prematurely have witnessed, contrary to the outcomes anticipated by the promoters of trade liberalization, a process of de-industrialization and a marked increase of imports, but not necessarily faster growth.[24] Premature liberalization compromised the process of building up industrial capabilities. On the other hand, maintaining protection for periods longer than necessary can lead to negative or perverse incentives and inefficiency. Moreover, protection alone is not sufficient and may hinder development. As stated by Wade (2004, p. xlviii): "Protection has to be made part of a larger industrial strategy to nurture the capababilities of domestic firms and raise the rate of domestic investment, always in the context of a private enterprise, market-based economy."

The phenomenon of de-industrialization was particularly noticeable in manufacturing sectors that provided intermediary inputs and components, thus contributing to the delinking of export activities from local industry and reducing the potential positive impact of exports on the overall growth of the economy. In some instances, however, timing was not the only binding factor: industries were not truly competitive owing to a misguided policy design, as mentioned above, which did not provide enough discipline while extending protection or subsidies. In other cases, trade liberalization was simply not accompanied by adequate support for firms facing new competition. Unsound macroeconomic policies, particularly an overvalued domestic currency, also played a role in eroding competitiveness (see chapter IV).

This is not to say that trade liberalization has no role in promoting competitiveness. World markets provide significant opportunities for developing countries, as many success stories in the developing world attest. Nonetheless, trade liberalization needs to be carefully incorporated into a country's production sector strategy. Interestingly, today's developed countries have used trade liberalization selectively and in combination with other policy measures.[25] Almost all of them did not practise free trade while promoting their own industrialization or, if they were late industrializers, when catching up with the lead economies of their time. Trade liberalization came only after industrial production had been well established (Chang, 2003). Even nowadays, developed countries are actively involved in the promotion of sectors of production where technological change is intensive, through support to R&D and other industrial policies. And free trade is restricted in those sectors that developed economies consider sensitive or deserving of special treatment; agriculture and labour-intensive manufactures such as garments are the most obvious examples.

The appropriate strategy is necessarily context-specific. It depends, among other factors, on the level of development, technological capacities, the size of the economies, the natural resource base, government capacities and established State-business relations. It involves not only manufacturing production but also a good exploitation of the opportunities provided by the resource endowments of a specific country and the development of modern services. Strategies can be considered successful if they promote an economy with capacity to constantly diversify its production structure, to generate strong domestic linkages, to gradually accumulate technological capacities, and to develop a vibrant private sector, including of small and medium-sized firms (United Nations, Economic Commission for Latin America and the Caribbean, 2000 and 2004).

Is there space for production sector development policies today?

The need for coherent policies in promoting a country's structural transformation has not disappeared. In the context of rapid technological change, entry costs into new productive activities are now higher than they were during the period of industrialization of the first-tier economies. This trend reinforces the need for developing countries to build up domestic capabilities to promote new sectors, either independently or in association with foreign capital. Yet, policy approaches used by successful developing countries in the past may no longer be applicable or desirable. Initial conditions may be different and opportunities available for diversification change over time. Moreover, the global and the national policy environments have evolved. The former now has jurisdiction over actions and sectors that were unregulated before. The latter went through a process of autonomous liberalization either induced by conditionalities demanded by multilateral financial organizations and bilateral donors or voluntarily embraced, for instance, through the participation in free trade agreements (FTA) whose provisions go beyond internationally agreed disciplines. Certain practices may no longer be conducted, but others are still allowed. While policy space may have become narrower, it has certainly not vanished.

The multilateral trade environment was indeed more permissible in the past. Over the years, clauses were introduced in the General Agreement on Tariffs and Trade (GATT) that accorded special prerogatives to developing countries. The original Agreement (article XXXVI, para. 8) had stated that developed countries should not expect reciprocity for commitments they made, that is to say, developing countries were not supposed to make concessions that were inconsistent with their development needs. The principle of non-reciprocity implied that developing countries could commit themselves to limited market access provisions and limited tariff binding. Moreover, agreements on non-tariff disciplines (import licensing, subsidies and countervailing measures, technical barriers to trade, etc.) applied only to signatories (exemplifying the so-called code approach used in the Tokyo Round of multilateral trade negotiations, 1973-1979). An "Enabling clause" was introduced to allow, among other things, the granting of tariff preferences to developing countries—through the Generalized System of Preferences—a clear rupture with the most favoured nation principle upon which the Agreement had been built.

In the Uruguay Round of multilateral trade negotiations (1986-1994), the "single undertaking" approach replaced the code approach. Developing countries were no longer given the choice to opt out of certain agreements. Accordingly, countries had to accept the additional disciplines brought about by, among others, the Agreement on Trade-related Investment Measures, the Agreement on Subsidies and Countervailing Measures the Agreement on Trade-related Aspects of Intellectual Property Rights and the General Agreement on Trade in Services.

The Agreement on Trade-related Aspects of Intellectual Property Rights, by establishing minimum levels of protection on intellectual property rights, prohibits or restricts practices such as copying, compulsory licensing, and reverse engineering which were widely used by some developing (and developed) countries as a means of catching up. These restrictions should be weighted against the potential benefits of the Agreement in terms of generating incentives for local innovation and the development of local brands, FDI and technology transfer. Moreover, the provisions on intellectual property in the increasingly numerous bilateral and regional free trade agreements tend to go well beyond the Agreement's commitments.[26]

The Agreement on Trade-related Investment Measures does not allow for the use of performance–related measures for foreign investors that have an effect on trade, such as local content and trade-balancing requirements. Nevertheless, export and technology transfer requirements are permitted. These have been used extensively in countries like China to build local capabilities in high-technology industries such as semiconductors and information technology (IT). It is interesting to note that, given Mexico's relatively less successful industrial performance, NAFTA rules explicitly prohibit the requirements just mentioned (Houde and Yannaca-Small, 2004). All the post-NAFTA free trade agreements signed by the United States include a similar clause. The same holds for bilateral investment treaties in general (see Cosbey and others, 2004).

The Agreement on Subsidies and Countervailing Measures, on the other hand, renders illegal subsidies, fiscal credit and incentives that require recipients to reach export targets or that are tied to actual or expected export earnings. Subsidies linked to the use of domestic products are also forbidden. In addition, subsidies targeting a specific industry or group of industries may be actionable (that is to say, contested by another country) if it is proved that they harm another party to the Agreement. Conversely, subsidies for R&D, or those that target the environment or specially disadvantaged regions are non-actionable. Countries whose per capita GDP is below $1,000 are exempt from these commitments, but differential treatment for other developing countries is limited to an extended phase-out period.

While the Agreement on Subsidies and Countervailing Measures limits government intervention in export promotion, some schemes are still World Trade Organization-consistent and are allowed. Export processing zones are no longer permitted under World Trade Organization rules, unless an extension is granted by the Committee on Subsidies and Countervailing Measures.[27] Duty-free provisions can be maintained, as well as certain forms of export assistance, including public export credits. Furthermore, certain elements of the export incentive structure may, while becoming World Trade Organization-compatible, be transformed in order to meet the same targets. For instance, one could allow firms in export processing zones to serve domestic markets as well or to extend some of the benefits enjoyed by firms in export processing zones to all domestic firms (Keck and Low, 2004). Moreover, countries may continue to subsidize specific sectors until a complaining country presents evidence of material damage (though making such a case against countries with very small market penetration would probably be difficult) (Chang, 1999).

Infant industry and balance-of-payments protection are still permitted under the World Trade Organization but are subject to additional procedural requirements. Infant industry protection provisions, however, have not been invoked by any country since 1967, most likely because they entail compensation to injured parties. As a result, developing countries extended infant industry protection through balance-of-payments provisions. With the Uruguay Round, additional disciplines were introduced:[28] countries need to consult with the International Monetary Fund (IMF) before applying measures owing to balance-of-payments considerations (Keck and Low, 2004). Although remedies are to be commensurate with balance-of-payments problems, countries can still choose the sector where measures will be imposed.

Trends in tariffs have also reduced policy space. These include the increased binding of tariffs by developing countries, their progressive decline over time and the recent modalities used and/or proposed to reduce tariffs further. Binding implies a firm commitment by a country not to raise its tariffs above the bound level. In most developing countries, there is a difference between applied and bound tariffs, with the levels of applied tariffs being lower than their respective bound levels. Yet, committing to a specific bound level reduces the flexibility available to countries in using tariffs as a tool of industrial policy: industries or sectors to be promoted change over time, while maximum tariff levels are fixed. Recent proposals emerging in the World Trade Organization Doha Round stress the desirability of full binding as one of the objectives of non-agricultural market access (NAMA) (World Trade Organization, 2005).

Another trend that will restrict policy options is reflected in the emerging consensus to adopt a non-linear formula aiming at harmonizing tariffs across countries and reduce tariff dispersion across products. This approach will weaken a country's flexibility in respect of using its tariff structure as a policy tool. Developing countries need a combination of relatively low and high tariffs applied to different sectors at different periods as they promote the structural transformation of their economies. Thus, tariff dispersion may need to be wide. Moreover, the optimal level and structure of tariffs change over time and there is a need to "reconcile multilateral discipline with policy flexibility for industrial development" (Akyüz, 2005, p. 26).

Overall, the scope for active production sector policies has been reduced, but there is still room to stimulate the "discovery" of new activities and solve coordination problems. Additional flexibility may be required, however, to promote the diversification of production and technological upgrading. In particular, more attention than in the past should probably be given to rules that support the development of infant export industries, as well as the links between the dynamic export sector and other domestic activities and thus domestic market integration. Additional space may also be needed to give a more developmental orientation to agreements on intellectual property rights. These issues should thus be the subject of greater attention in the context of the definition of special and differential treatment for developing countries in multilateral trade agreements. More broadly, as underscored in the São Paulo Consensus (document TD/412, part II), adopted by the United Nations Conference on Trade and Development (UNCTAD) at its eleventh session held in São Paulo, Brazil, from 13 to 18 June 2004, it is important to find an appropriate balance between national policy space and international disciplines and commitments.

THE ROAD TOWARDS GREATER CONVERGENCE

Increased integration into the world economy seems to have exacerbated income divergence among countries, although some developing countries have been able to grow rather quickly and reduce the income gap vis-à-vis the developed economies.

Diversifying exports

The role played by international trade in growth divergence among countries originates in differences in the types of goods and services countries produce and in the potential for export growth in international markets for these goods and services. Moreover, the way in which an economy integrates into the global economy is also relevant, as it reflects the presence (or absence) of changes in specialization patterns over time and of the linkages that the export sector generates with the rest of the economy (the internal integration referred to above).

Despite the faster growth rates of exporters of HT manufactures, diversifying into high-technology exports may not be an immediately feasible option for many developing countries. Many countries lack the required technological capacity, including a sufficiently skilled labour force, to do so. Additionally, when there is an absence of other advantageous factors at work—such as the geographical proximity and existence of transport and communications infrastructure among production units that benefit existing participants in the East Asian regional cluster—entry into this sector necessarily becomes more difficult. Fast market saturation, leading to declining prices, could also apply if several countries pursue this route simultaneously (exemplifying the so-called fallacy-of-composition effect).

Most developing countries can, however, compete in primary goods—and use them as a platform from which to move to the production of other goods—and diversify into NRB or LT manufacturing exports as the multilateral trading environment eventually becomes more welcoming. In this regard, improved market access for exports of both agricultural and LT manufactures by developing countries, reduced tariff and non-tariff protection in these sectors, and the elimination of trade-distorting domestic support and export subsidies in agriculture could enhance market opportunities for developing countries, thus contributing to faster growth and income convergence. However, in negotiating increased market access in agriculture, developing countries need also to take into account the long-term structural change of their economies. They need to anticipate moving into the production of industrial products and to avoid the stagnation often associated with commodity production and the shallow integration that may be induced by diversifying into mere assembly manufacturing. Diversifying into new activities may require some type of protection or support as capabilities are developed and firms become competitive.

Strengthening opportunities in service trade in multilateral trade negotiations

The international trade in services is also providing opportunities for several developing countries, particularly in tourism but also in transport and in some labour-intensive business services. As with trade in goods, multilateral trading negotiations also have a role to play in unlocking the benefits of trade in services. However, unlike trade in goods, trade in services often calls for the simultaneous presence of service supplier and consumer, implying that increased trade in services must be accompanied by increased factor mobility.

Trade in services via the General Agreement on Trade in Services, Mode 3 (commercial presence), is by its very nature associated with all the potential benefits –but also the limitations– of FDI. Liberalization of regulations on international labour migration (Mode 4) may be the most promising approach for increasing service exports by developing countries, as it enables them to make use of their comparative advantage of abundant labour resources. It can generate benefits similar to full-scale migration, such as the inflow of remittances, and the acquisition of technical and managerial skills, while facilitating the avoidance of some of the costs, such as sustained brain drain in the home country, or a political backlash in the receiving country. Yet, Mode 4 still faces the highest barriers, making it a priority area for developing-country interests in service negotiations during the final phase of the Doha Round of World Trade Organization trade negotiations.

Promoting participation in global markets but also domestic market integration

Market dynamics change over time and the global trends in markets for goods and services strongly influence the viability of particular strategies. Thus, countries need to be careful before trying to quickly replicate an alternative that worked in the past and need to avoid mistakes associated with some of the policies adopted before. Just as important as selecting a particular market in which to operate is choosing the strategy related to the integration pattern the country will follow. With or without the association of FDI, the creation of links with the domestic economy, through the supply not only of labour but also of goods and services, seems to be a prerequisite for achieving sustained growth. Internal integration is fundamental.

In summary, production sector strategies are important

There is very little evidence to suggest that simply by opening up and stabilizing the economy, and increasing inflows of FDI, developing countries will enter a rapid and sustainable development path. The successful post-war experiences of Eastern Asia and its integration into the global economy resulted from well-targeted trade and sectoral policies that constantly and consistently promoted the building up of technological capabilities in these countries. While the space for these interventions has been reduced over the years, there is still room for active public policies, not only in middle-income developing countries but also—and particularly—in low-income countries and in least developed countries. Yet, policy space should not be reduced further and perhaps some of the current disciplines need to be reassessed in terms of their true value for growth and development. It is thus important that the decisions to be adopted at the Doha Round of multilateral trade negotiations lead to a more conducive international policy environment in terms of facilitating dynamic structural changes in developing countries and averting further constraining economic transformation efforts by these countries. Thus, the multilateral trading regime could provide a valuable instrument for assisting countries in getting back on the road to greater convergence.

Notes

1. During the period 1962-1980, the annual average rate of growth of world merchandise trade was 15.7 per cent in value terms and 7.1 per cent in volume terms. The corresponding growth rates for the period 1981-2000 were 5.8 and 5.1 per cent.
2. Economies in transition are included in the group of developing countries in the analysis presented in this chapter.
3. In the terms used by Palma (2004), unless the industries are firmly "anchored" in the domestic economy, their growth-enhancing capacity evaporates. Ocampo (2005a) refers to these specialization patterns as "shallow".
4. The General Agreement on Trade in Services (GATS) defines four modes of supply of services: (1) cross-border supply, where the service is delivered across a national border; (2) consumption abroad, where the consumer journeys to the territory of the service supplier; (3) commercial presence, where the service provider establishes a branch or subsidiary in the territory of the consumer; and (4) presence of natural persons, where an individual service supplier moves temporarily to the consumer's territory to provide the service. Balance-of-payments data fully cover only Modes 1 and 2. Trade via Mode 3 is not covered, while Mode 4 is covered only as a rough proxy. Finally, many countries, especially developing countries, do not report detailed data beyond the three broad sectors of transport, travel, and other services.
5. For a more detailed overview, which also lists selected major developing-country exporters, see Gabriele (2004) pp. 29-40.
6. For recent literature surveys, see Nielson and Taglioni (2004), and Stiglitz and Charlton (2004).
7. This factor is not formally captured by the study, however, as it analyzes only the impact of total exports of services on growth and not the impact of individual sectors.
8. From this skill-intensive sector with potentially large spillover effects into other economic sectors good examples can also be drawn of successful intra-developing country trade. For instance, a large Mexican mobile telephone company owns licenses all over Central America, in the Andean region, and in Brazil, making it the number one provider in that region in terms of subscriber base. For a more detailed account and other case studies, see Nielson and Taglioni (2004).
9. Data on this sector, however, need to be treated with additional caution, as many countries report these exports under "other business services" (as India did up to 2000).

10 How the gains from flows among advanced countries have been distributed is still a matter of contention among researchers. For example, some studies locate most gains in the home economy (that is to say, from outward FDI) with few or mixed benefits accruing to the host (see van Pottelsberghe de la Potterie and Lichtenberg, 2001). In the context of the host economy, absorptive capacity is key to enhancing spillover effects (Blomström, Lipsey and Zejan, 1992). It should be noted that comparative unit labour costs have also continued to play a role in determining some FDI flows among advanced countries, and while such investment can bring employment gains to the host technology spillovers are less likely (see the discussion in Driffield and Taylor (2002)).

11 Up to the mid-1970s, Mexico and Brazil accounted for well over half of developing-country flows in manufacturing. For a useful discussion of the nature and impact of such investments, with reference to the Brazilian experience, see Evans (1979).

12 According to one estimate, trade based on specialization within vertical production networks accounts for up to 30 per cent of world exports, and has grown by as much as 40 per cent in the last 25 years (see Hummels, Ishii and Yi (1998)).

13 It should be noted that mergers are in reality uncommon. The United Nations Conference on Trade and Development (2000, p. 99) estimates that they had accounted for just 3 per cent of total M&As between 1987 and 1999, with full acquisitions accounting for more than half the total. Minority acquisitions (between 10 and 49 per cent ownership) appear to be more common in developing countries. On the other hand, while measurement problems preclude a precise estimate, the latter probably accounted for anywhere between one half and two thirds of global FDI flows in the 1990s.

14 On the latter trend see Kregel (1996), Plender (2001), and Kamaly (2003). The convergence in capital flows that this implies is not just a matter of M&As. As one World Bank study has noted "Because direct investors hold factories and other assets that are impossible to move, it is sometimes assumed that a direct investment inflow is more stable than other forms of capital flows. This need not be the case. While a direct investor usually has some immovable assets, there is no reason in principle why these cannot be fully offset by domestic liabilities. Clearly, a direct investor can borrow in order to export capital, and thereby generate rapid capital outflows" (Claessens and others, 1995, p. 22). However, M&As, unlike most greenfield investments, do appear to be more closely linked to boom-bust cycles, with financial crises in emerging markets creating new opportunities for acquisitions (see United Nations Conference on Trade and Development, 1999, pp. 118-119; and Mody, 2004, pp. 1209-1210).

15 Such networks are not a new development, dating back to the 1960s in parts of East Asia, and becoming a more prominent feature of the international division of labour in the 1970s (see Helleiner, 1973).

16 It is worth noting here that the evidence on FDI among advanced countries that is responding to factor cost differences does not bring spillovers to the host country (see Driffield and Love, 2005).

17 Indeed, because market-seeking FDI is more dependent on the domestic economy, it gives the Government of the host country greater bargaining power for using FDI selectively to ensure that it will create spillovers and linkages with domestic industry.

18 There is evidence for some regions and time periods that FDI can crowd out local investment. A recent study of 32 developing countries for the period 1970-1996 found that the evidence of crowding out was strongest in Latin America, whereas Asia exhibited stronger crowing in and Africa was neutral (Agosín and Mayer, 2000). In a more comprehensive study of 98 developing countries covering the period 1980-

1999, a significant relationship between FDI and domestic investment was detected in 52 countries, 29 experienced net crowding out and 23 experienced crowding in, with Latin American countries again mist vulnerable to crowding out (Khumar and Pradhan, 2002). According to Ghose (2004) the tendency of FDI to crowd out local investment rose in all developing regions, including sub-Saharan Africa, in the period 1990-1997 compared with 1983-89 which may well be due to the growing share of M&As in FDI flows. There needs to be more detailed analysis of individual-country cases; and while there are few such analyses to draw on, those that have been undertaken tend to confirm that the picture is mixed (see Harrison and Macmillan (2002) on Côte d'Ivoire; and Braunstein and Epstein (2004) on China).

19   Spillovers are essentially defined as productivity benefits accruing to domestic firms, either in the same sector or other sectors. For general reviews of the evidence, see Aitken and Harrison (1999); Gorg and Greenaway (2001); and Blomström and Kokko (2003).

20   See, inter alia, Borenszstein, De Gregorio and Lee (1995); de Mello (1997); Lim (2001). Employment figures point in much the same direction, with little evidence of positive employment effects from hosting FDI in low-income countries, but with evidence of stronger gains in higher-income countries (see Spiezia, 2004).

21   For additional analysis on building up technological capabilities for catching-up, see United Nations Industrial Development Organization (2005).

22   By contrast, Hong Kong SAR, with one of the most open FDI regimes has a poor record of upgrading in the manufacturing sector.

23   Dowrick and Golley (2004) call for further research to understand these findings. Their own tentative suggestions are that the nature of technology transfer through MNCs has changed in the latter period and that the range of complementary policies that supported successful liberalization in the earlier period are missing in the "one policy fits all" approach of the latter period. Both suggestions are in line with the arguments presented in this and subsequent chapters.

24   It should be mentioned that several of these economies that had witnessed a strong import growth in the 1990s also experienced a severe import contraction in the 1980s owing to foreign-exchange constraints, the debt crisis and resulting balance-of-payment adjustment. Growth in the 1980s was negatively affected by import compression.

25   Hong Kong SAR is the notable exception as the economy adopted a fairly liberal regime, and has also altered it is also an economy that shifted its structure and growth strategy from manufacture-based to service-based.

26   The United States in particular has pushed for greater protection to patents. It is noteworthy that, given MFN treatment obligations in the Agreement on Trade-Related Aspects of Intellectual Property Rights (TRIPS), accepting greater patent protection in agreements with the United States may force developing countries to provide similar patent protection to third countries. For instance, the United States-Morocco FTA includes provisions allowing for the protection of new uses found for existing drugs for which the original patent has expired (Cosbey and others, 2004).

27   Only certain programmes and countries qualify to be considered for extension. (See World Trade Organization, 2001).

28   Preference to price-based measures over quantitative restrictions was already introduced in the Tokyo Round.

Chapter IV
Macroeconomic Policies and Growth Divergence

A stable macroeconomic environment is commonly considered to be conducive to long-term growth. Economists disagree, however, about the degree and type of stability that should be the objective of macroeconomic policies. There is also dispute about whether economic stability should be the central objective of macroeconomic policies, or whether these should serve more directly broader development goals.

In fact, the focus of macroeconomic policies in developing countries has shifted over the past decades. Until the 1980s, they had been mostly embedded in broader, growth-oriented national development strategies. This changed in light of the paradigm shift in the mainstream approach to macroeconomic policies in the developed countries, away from a Keynesian approach of counter-cyclical demand management aiming for full employment to a more conservative, prudential monetarist view aiming at controlling inflation. In the face of the severe balance of payments crises and inflation surges that may countries faced since the mid-1970s, macroeconomic policies in developing countries also narrowed their focus to concentrate on low inflation and the avoidance of major fiscal and external imbalances. Short-term economic stabilization, in this more restrictive sense of the term, came to be seen as a key to long-term economic growth.

This new "orthodoxy" in macroeconomic policies prevailed during the 1980s and 1990s, but its effectiveness in contributing to higher economic growth is increasingly being questioned. While managing to reduce inflation and restore fiscal balances, many developing countries that applied such policies failed to achieve strong and sustained economic growth. Quite often, the stabilization policies induced a "pro-cyclical" pattern of macroeconomic policies that hurt public and private investment and thus economic growth.

Critics of the orthodox macroeconomic policy framework have argued for a return to the broader, developmental approach to macroeconomic stabilization policies based on an integration of short-term, counter-cyclical fiscal and monetary measures with long-term development policies (see, for example, Ocampo, 2005a; and Stiglitz and others, 2006). They have stressed that macroeconomic policies should be growth-centred, with full employment as the ultimate objective. Because of differences in development level and quality of institutions, the macroeconomic policy framework for developing countries should be substantially different from that in developed economies in terms of objectives, instruments, policy stance, and the criteria for macroeconomic stability.

The broader approach to macroeconomic policies is also needed because, as argued in chapter II, the growth process in developing countries is different in nature from that in developed countries. In developed countries, productivity growth mainly relies on technological innovation. In developing countries, productivity growth more typically can be achieved by successfully shifting the labour force from low- to high-productivity sectors and through the accumulation of human and physical capital. As these activities directly influence investment decisions and the process of resource allocation across sectors, the impact of macroeconomic policies on growth will be therefore be much greater in developing countries than in more developed economies. As argued in chapter III, the growth impact will further depend on how macroeconomic policies are coordinated with trade and production sector policies.

The present chapter begins with a brief discussion of some facts about macroeconomic stability in relation to the growth performance in developing countries, namely, those facts dealing with the link between inflation and growth, macro imbalance and growth, and financial development and growth. An unstable external environment may limit the effectiveness of macroeconomic policies in ensuring stability and conditions for growth. As analysed in the second section, many developing countries have faced rather strong volatility in external financing conditions since the 1970s, creating major challenges for maintaining macroeconomic stability and also influencing the way in which Governments have conducted macroeconomic policies. The pro-cyclical nature of capital flows has also made macroeconomic policies more pro-cyclical. This means that when the economy fares better, international investors are more eager to invest in the country and Governments happily spend more whereas when the economic weather deteriorates, external financiers are less willing to provide new funding precisely when it is more needed. Lacking the resources, Governments will have to reduce expenditures and central banks will have to adopt contractionary monetary policies to cool private demand, pushing the economy into a recession. The third section analyses whether pro-cyclical macroeconomic policies actually do have a negative impact on long-term economic growth and whether countries with a more successful economic growth performance achieved this in part with the support of counter-cyclical short-term macroeconomic adjustment.

The fourth section discusses the importance of public investment in infrastructure and human development for long-term economic growth and the growth divergence among developing countries. To bridge the existing large gaps, many developing countries, particularly the poorest, will have to mobilize large amounts of public resources to make the necessary investments in infrastructure and provisioning of social services. The positive impact such investments may have on productivity and economic growth typically takes some time to materialize, as infrastructure works may take several years to complete and the span between the time children are enrolled in school and the time they enter the labour market as higher-productivity workers may even be longer. The Government thus needs to mobilize substantial resources now for future economic gains and this introduces an extra, "inter-temporal" dimension to the management of the government budget. Domestic resource mobilization through taxes and more efficient allocation of existing budgetary resources may create some additional fiscal space for such expenditures, but will have to be carefully managed within a counter-cyclical macroeconomic policy framework. For the low-income countries, the scope for domestic resource mobilization will likely fall short of investment needs and an effective and sufficient allocation of official development assistance (ODA) will have to play an important role. The chapter concludes with a summary of the implications for the growth divergence and the implications for national and international policies to redress the divergence.

Macroeconomic Stability and Growth Divergence

Macroeconomic stability strongly influences the long-term growth performance of the economy. Macroeconomic stability, however, entails more than just preserving price stability and sustainable fiscal balances. It is also about avoiding large swings in economic activity and employment and, further, in particular in developing countries, about maintaining sustainable external accounts and avoiding exchange-rate overvaluation. The frequency of financial crises in developing countries indicates that macroeconomic stability is, in addition, about maintaining well-regulated domestic financial sectors, sound balance sheets of the banking system and sound external debt structures.

Macroeconomic stability and growth tend to mutually reinforce each other. Strong and sustainable growth makes it easier to achieve greater macroeconomic stability, by, inter alia, enhancing the sustainability of domestic and foreign public debt. Conversely, greater stability, in its broad sense, reduces investment uncertainty and hence is supportive of higher long-term growth.

Figure II.4 in chapter II showed that countries with less investment volatility tend to have higher long-term growth rates. Volatility in output growth was conspicuously higher in the developing world in the 1980s and 1990s and is visible in other macroeconomic indicators, such as the inflation rate (see table IV.1). However, the degree of macroeconomic instability, in these as well as other dimensions, differs strongly across groups of developing countries.

Table IV.1.
Output and inflation volatility by regions, 1960-2003
(Coefficient of variation)

	1960s	1970s	1980s	1990-2003
GDP growth				
Developed countries	0.12	0.51	0.51	0.35
Developing countries				
East Asia and the Pacific	2.03	0.41	0.20	0.32
South Asia	0.62	1.16	0.24	0.28
Middle East and Northern Africa	..	0.89	1.22	0.56
Europe and Central Asia	..	..	..	29.65
Latin America and the Caribbean	0.37	0.25	1.53	0.84
Sub-Saharan Africa	0.46	0.81	1.00	0.68
Inflation rate (CPI)				
Developed countries	0.69	0.68	1.02	0.87
Developing countries				
East Asia and the Pacific	3.70	0.82	1.00	1.25
South Asia	0.96	0.90	0.50	0.64
Middle East and Northern Africa	1.41	0.83	0.87	1.34
Europe and Central Asia	..	..	..	3.65
Latin America and the Caribbean	1.88	2.25	5.06	6.08
Sub-Saharan Africa	1.75	1.06	1.54	10.97

Source: UN/DESA based on World Bank, World Development Indicators database 2005.

Note: Volatility is measured by the coefficient of variation, which is the standard deviation divided by the mean. Output volatility is weighted for GDP of the countries in each group. Inflation volatility refers to the consumer price index and the coefficient of variation for inflation by region is unweighted.

A majority of developing countries had enjoyed robust growth and a relatively stable macroeconomic environment in the 1960s. The increase in macroeconomic volatility in the 1970s and 1980s may be attributed in part to a variety of shocks in the global economy, such as the collapse of the Bretton Woods system of international monetary arrangements in the early 1970s, the two oil crises at the beginning and the end of the decade, and the steep rise in world interest rates around 1980. The degree of vulnerability to these shocks and the capacity to cope with them differed across countries. Notably, though they were certainly not immune to crises, the fast-growing East Asian economies managed to achieve much greater macroeconomic stability, in the broad sense in which we use this term, than the slower-growing economies of Latin America and sub-Saharan Africa. Macroeconomic volatility seemed to have abated somewhat in the 1990s (at least up to 1997) in Latin America and sub-Saharan Africa, but has remained higher than in the 1960s and 1970s, albeit under conditions of much slower economic growth. A new series of financial crises in the late 1990s are part of a new wave of macroeconomic instability in many parts of the developing world, also involving some of the dynamic East Asian economies. By the mid-2000s, buoyant world trade and commodity prices were ingredients contributing to a period of both exceptionally rapid growth and macroeconomic stability in the developing world, a mix that had not been experienced since the 1960s.

Inflation and growth

Most developing countries had maintained a low and stable inflation in the 1960s (see figure IV.1). A surge in inflation rates was ubiquitous in all developing-country regions in the early 1970s. Inflation rates have been rather volatile since then, but with important differences across regions. Most Asian economies managed to keep inflation at moderate levels. Inflation in Latin America accelerated rapidly and became particularly acute during the debt crisis of the 1980s, giving rise to several episodes of hyperinflation. After having reached a peak in 1991, Latin America's rate of inflation lessened substantially thereafter. In sub-Saharan Africa, inflation increased strongly during the first half of the 1970s, but has been on the decline since, although it still shows large annual fluctuations. More generally, developing-country inflation rates started to converge downward during the 1990s as part of a worldwide trend.

For most developing-country regions with relatively low and stable inflation in the 1960s and again in recent years, since 2000, this has coincided with a solid growth performance. In contrast, most of the regions with high and volatile inflation in the 1970s and the 1980s have also shown a much poorer growth performance (see figure IV.2).

These findings seem to confirm the widely held view that high inflation is inimical to long-run growth, because it generates greater economic uncertainty, discourages long-term contracting and raises risk premiums on interest rates, thereby depressing private investment. Since high inflation also tends to be associated with large relative price variability, price signals become

108 • Uneven Economic Development

Figure IV.1.
Median inflation, selected regions, 1961-2003
(Percentage)

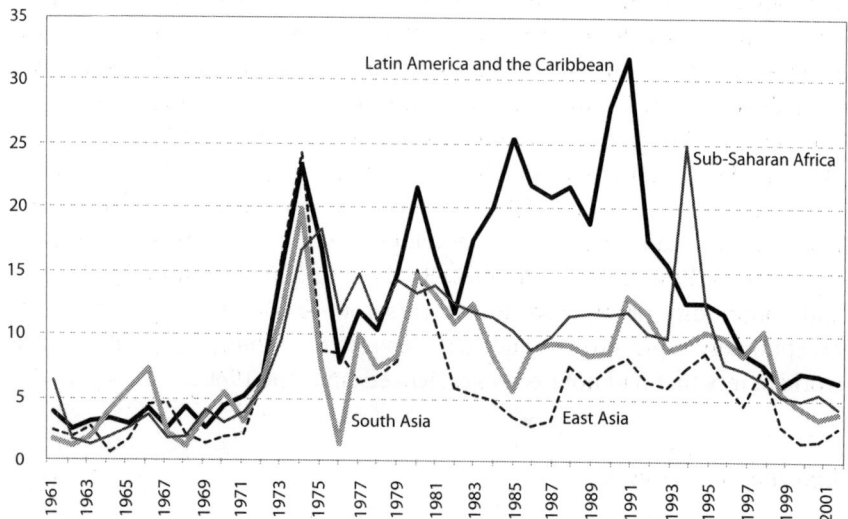

Source: UN/DESA, based on World Bank, World Development Indicators 2005 database.

Figure IV.2.
Inflation and growth performance by regions and periods 1960-2003[a]
(Percentage)

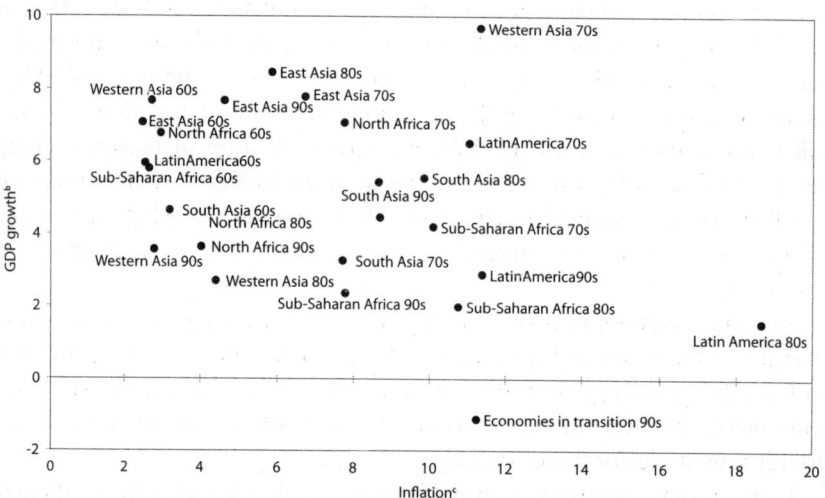

Source: UN/DESA, based on World Bank, World Development Indicators 2005 database.

[a] Period labelled "90s" refers to data from 1990 until 2003 when available.
[b] Weighted averages: Data for Western Asia in the 1960s cover only the period 1967-69; data for South Asia in the 1970s cover the period 1974-1979 and data for the 1960s do not include the Islamic Republic of Iran; data for Northern Africa in the 1960s cover the period 1961-1969.
[c] The inflation rate is estimated as the median for the region, which in turn is calculated on the basis of the median inflation rates per country for the period.

more difficult to interpret, leading to distorted allocation of resources across sectors. High inflation could further distort the inter-temporal allocation of resources via its adverse impact on interest rates and the tax system (Fischer and Modigliani, 1978; Briault, 1995).

High inflation is correlated with lower growth, but—as evidenced by econometric studies—the relationship is not robust and the causality is not definitive. In particular, moderate inflation does not necessarily lead to under-par growth. For example, between 1960 and 2000, Thailand's output growth was well below that of the Republic of Korea, even though the latter's average inflation rate was higher. Botswana has registered higher inflation than many other countries in sub-Saharan Africa but its economic growth has been notably higher. Also, many economies have experienced prolonged periods of low inflation and low growth, while others managed to combine high rates of output growth with moderate and, in some cases, even relatively high inflation rates. The latter was the case in Brazil from 1968 to 1980 and in Turkey from 1981 to 1990. Further, the experience in a number of developing countries has led some observers to hold the view that it is possible to sustain moderate inflation rates of about 15-20 per cent for longer periods without generating macroeconomic instability or harming growth (Dornbusch and Fischer, 1993). Prices should not be very volatile, however.

The weak association between low inflation rates and faster economic growth is reflected in figure IV.2, which shows that, after leaving out certain episodes (specifically, those of Latin America during the debt crisis of the 1980s and the economies of transition in the 1990s), there is no statistically significant correlation between these two variables. The upshot is that although inflation is important, it is not necessary to target a very low rate of inflation in order for macroeconomic stability to support long-term growth.

Macroeconomic imbalances and growth

Stabilization policies in many developing countries have been strongly influenced by the basic insights of the International Monetary Fund (IMF) "financial programming" model (Polak, 1957). This model served for a long time as the bedrock of the target-setting of macroeconomic policies built into almost all IMF stabilization programmes. One central principle underlying this approach is that excessive government spending and credit demand are the main factors underlying balance-of-payments problems. Hence, fiscal adjustment and measures reducing domestic credit demand would typically be called for in order to restore external deficits.

In practice, however, the macroeconomic balances of developing countries do not present any clear pattern of movement in tandem for the "twin deficits". Figures IV.3 displays the government deficit, the external balance and the private sector savings gap for four groups of developing countries, using the same country classification as that applied in chapter II. By macroeconomic accounting rules, the sum of the three balances should be equal to zero for an economy.

The four graphs show that government and external balances do not stand in a one-to-one relationship. The most frequent pattern is actually that of the co-movement of private sector deficits (savings gaps) and external balances. Although less frequent, there are several cases of negative correlation of private and government deficits. The typical association assumed in financial programming between fiscal deficits and current-account imbalances thus appears to be rather rare in practice. Fiscal austerity seems to have been more closely associated with rising private borrowing than with falling external deficits during the 1980s and 1990s.

Strong fluctuations in private and foreign net borrowing did not derail growth in the upwardly converging first-tier newly industrialized economies and (to a lesser extent) in South-East Asia. The first-tier newly industrialized economies maintained stable and nearly balanced fiscal accounts as a share of gross domestic product (GDP) during 1979-2002 (figure IV.3, part A). In consequence, the fluctuations in the macroeconomic imbalances are almost fully explained by co-movements in the external balance and private sector savings gap. The fluctuations of private and foreign sector balances were relatively large, with swings up and down exceeding 10 per cent of GDP. These fluctuations had their origin in identifiable events. For example, the private sector had swung into a savings surplus (as identified by the negative values in the graph) in the 1980s as the region accumulated foreign assets with its exports stimulated by exchange-rate realignments triggered by the 1985 Plaza Accord. This situation had been reversed in the late 1980s as private demand increased, and in the first half of the 1990s when the region's competitiveness was eroded owing to increasing competition from China. The private sector remained with small surpluses up to the 1997 crisis. The crisis led to a sharp upswing in the external balance accompanied by a sharp rise in the private surplus induced by a collapse of aggregate domestic demand. The latter, however, recovered quickly thereafter, helped to some extent by a mild counter-cyclical fiscal stance.

Private rather than public sector deficits were the characteristic of South-East Asian countries in the run up to the 1997 crisis (figure IV.3, part B). The crisis also led to a collapse of private demand in 1997 and 1998. The region,

Figure IV.3.
Macroeconomic balances: first-tier newly industrialized economies in Asia; South-East Asia; semi-industrialized countries; and sub-Saharan Africa

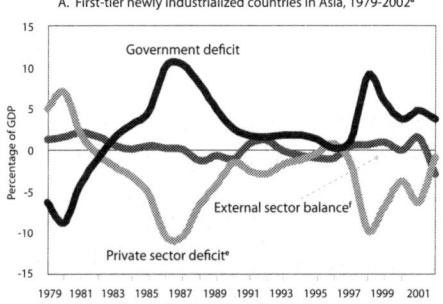

A. First-tier newly industrialized countries in Asia, 1979-2002[a]

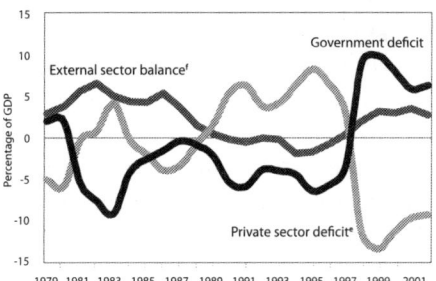

B. South-East, 1979-2002[b]

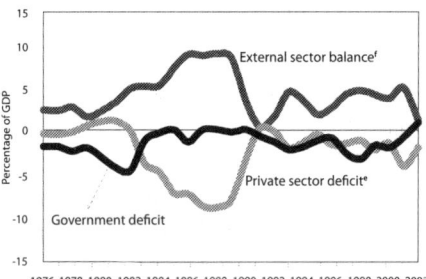

C. Semi-industrialized countries, 1976-2002[c]

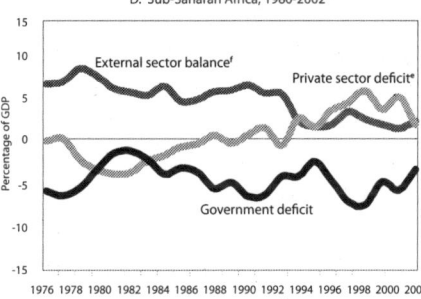

D. Sub-Saharan Africa, 1980-2002[d]

Source: UN/DESA, based on data available from http://www.icsead.or.jp/ which are derived from the United Nations Common Database, and United Nations Statistics Division, National Accounts database.

[a] Weighted averages of Singapore, Republic of Korea and Taiwan Province of China.
[b] Weighted averages of Indonesia, Malaysia, Philippines and Thailand.
[c] Weighted averages of Argentina, Brazil, Chile, Colombia, Mexico, South Africa, Turkey and Venezuela.
[d] Weighted averages of Ethiopia, Ghana, Kenya, Nigeria, Uganda, Tanzania and Zimbabwe.
[e] Calculated as a residual but standing for private investment minus savings.
[f] Equal to the current account of the balance of payments.

and particularly Indonesia, recovered much more slowly than the first-tier newly industrialized economies. Overall, as in the newly industrialized economies and China, offsetting swings in private and foreign borrowing dominated macroeconomic adjustment during the 1980s and 1990s and the level of government borrowing remained relatively stable, although with a greater frequency of periods of fiscal deficits.

In contrast, government deficits have been more prominent in the adjustment process in the semi-industrialized countries (figure IV.3, part C). During the 1980s, access to external borrowing dried up and private sector savings surpluses were needed to finance the fiscal deficit. This involved, in all cases, private demand contraction and in some, the use of the inflation tax to generate the private savings surplus. Private sector capital formation was correspondingly low owing largely to macroeconomic instability.

Fluctuations in both private and government net borrowing offset movements in the external balance in sub-Saharan Africa (figure IV.3, part D). During the 1980s, government deficits had remained rather stable, largely financed by foreign aid. When government deficits were reduced in austerity programmes, private savings surpluses fell (and private borrowing increased). Also, in this region, private sector and external deficits ended up moving in tandem, with external imbalances having failed to decline despite fiscal austerity during the 1990s.

Financial development, growth and macroeconomic stability

The growth divergence across the developing countries, as well as the different features of macroeconomic stability, has also been influenced by financial sector development over the past four decades. Financial intermediation supports the growth process by mobilizing household and foreign savings for investment by firms, ensuring that these funds are allocated to the most productive use, and spreading risk and providing liquidity so that firms can operate the new capacity efficiently. Financial development thus involves the establishment and expansion of institutions, instruments and markets that support this investment and growth process. Yet, financial intermediation has strong externalities in this context, which are generally positive (such as information and liquidity provision) but which can also be negative in the systemic financial crises that are endemic to market systems.

In the 1960s and 1970s, financial sectors in most developing countries had been characterized by bank-based systems, rules influencing the allocation of bank loans, an important role for State-owned commercial and development banks, closed capital accounts, capped interest rates, and active monetary intervention. In the decades thereafter, this traditional, "repressed" financial sector structure was dismantled during the process of financial liberalization implemented in most developing countries. Financial liberalization was expected to raise savings and investment levels, increase the rate of growth and reduce macroeconomic instability. However, in many instances, these objectives were not achieved.

This has become evident from the series of financial crises that have erupted in many developing countries since the 1980s. There is also evidence that following financial liberalization, there was a decline in funding for many large firms in productive sectors, and for small and medium-sized enterprises in general, which posed a major problem for sustainable growth (FitzGerald, 2008). For instance, evidence from four African countries (Uganda, Kenya, Malawi and Lesotho) shows that greater financial depth does not necessarily increase the volume of savings or access to credit of the commercial banks in rural areas, except for those that already have collateral (Mosley, 1999).

Conventional financial institutions, like commercial banks, also tend to be biased against small borrowers owing to the high unit costs of loan administration and lack of effective collateral, which translate into low returns and high risk. This is a major problem for all developing countries as small firms account for the bulk of production and the largest part of employment.

These "gaps" had been traditionally covered by public sector banks, but these banks were dismantled in many countries as part of financial reforms and only partly replaced by new microcredit schemes. In contrast, in the case of the fast-growing Asian economies, financial liberalization was gradual and public development banks and directed credit schemes have been sustained for prolonged periods and have supported the growth process.[1]

For such reasons, empirical studies have not been able to establish a robust causality between financial liberalization and growth performance.[2] There is also little evidence that financial deepening as such (or financial liberalization, for that matter) has resulted in higher savings rates, which were supposed to be the main contribution to higher investment and thus growth. There are two reasons for this outcome. First, financial reform has the effect of shifting savings out of assets such as property or currency into bank deposits and marketable securities. This will raise the recorded financial "depth" without raising savings rates. Second, financial liberalization expands access to consumer credit in the form of credit-card and other types of personal loans. These in turn may reduce aggregate household saving, if the lack of access to liquidity is the basic constraint that households face with respect to increasing consumer spending under a more "repressed" financial regime. Figure IV.4 demonstrates that there is no robust evidence that

Figure IV.4.
Financial market capitalization and savings rates, selected countries and regions, 2003
(Percentage of GDP)

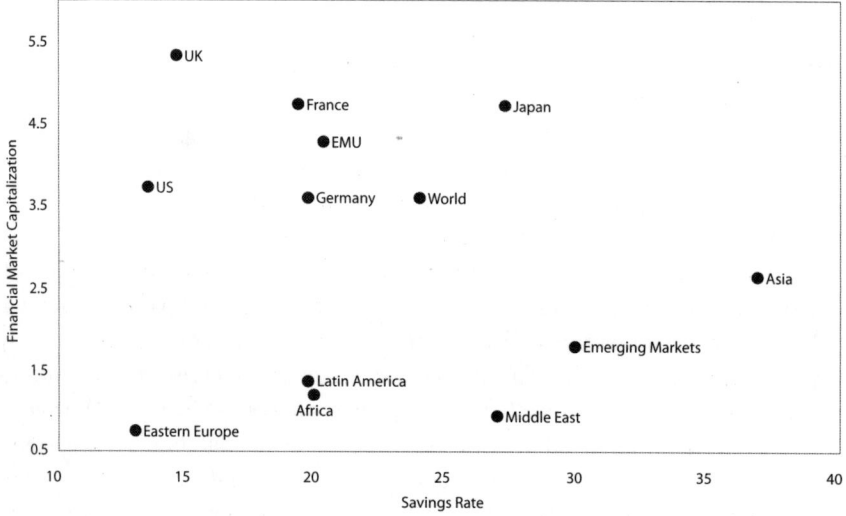

Source: International Monetary Fund (2005) Global Financial Stability Report, 2005, Washington D.C.: International Monetary Fund (April), statistical annex table 3; and IMF, World Economic Outlook database.

Note: Financial market capitalization refers to the sum of stock market capitalization, outstanding debt securities and bank assets as a share of GDP. The savings rate refers to Gross National Savings as a percentage of GDP.

financial deepening (measured by the widest possible measure, namely, total market capitalization) and the rate of saving. In fact, savings rates appear to depend on other factors such as demographic and tax influences on pension provision, funding of health and education, and the ownership structure of corporations or even family organization.

The experience of financial liberalization across countries suggests that the process of liberalization varied widely, as did the outcome. Moreover, in most developing countries where both market and non-market imperfections exist within a broader liberalized macroeconomic framework, there are a host of factors other than the volume and cost of credit that influence firms' investment decisions.

One important feature of insufficiently developed financial markets in many developing countries is the absence of a long-term domestic market for government and corporate bonds denominated in the domestic currency. This characteristic may cause problems for investment as well as for financial stability in a context of financial liberalization. The lack of a domestic bond market makes it more difficult to fund public infrastructure investment and major private modernization projects. It also forces firms to use short-term debt to finance long-term investments, thus accumulating maturity mismatches in their balance sheets, or to borrow more in international markets to finance long-term investments, leading to currency mismatches. The mix of these maturity and currency mismatches increases financial fragility in periods of exchange-rate depreciation and rising interest rates, which usually coincide owing to the pro-cyclical availability of external financing. The insufficient development of domestic bond markets and the associated financial fragility reduce in turn the scope for monetary intervention in order to counteract external shocks.

The importance of the development of domestic bond markets was made evident by the Asian crisis and led to a stronger focus of financial policies on this issue. As a result, domestic bond markets have grown rapidly since the late 1990s, not only in Asia, Latin America and emerging countries of Europe but also, to a lesser extent, in Africa (see figure IV.5).[3]

Domestic financial liberalization is frequently associated with integration into the global capital market – that is to say, with external financial liberalization. In principle, this should make an international pool of liquidity available to the domestic financial system, which should then become more stable. However, as analysed in detail in the next section, the high degree of volatility of international

Figure IV.5.
Domestic bond market growth in developing countries, 1980-2005
(Amounts outstanding, in billions of US $)

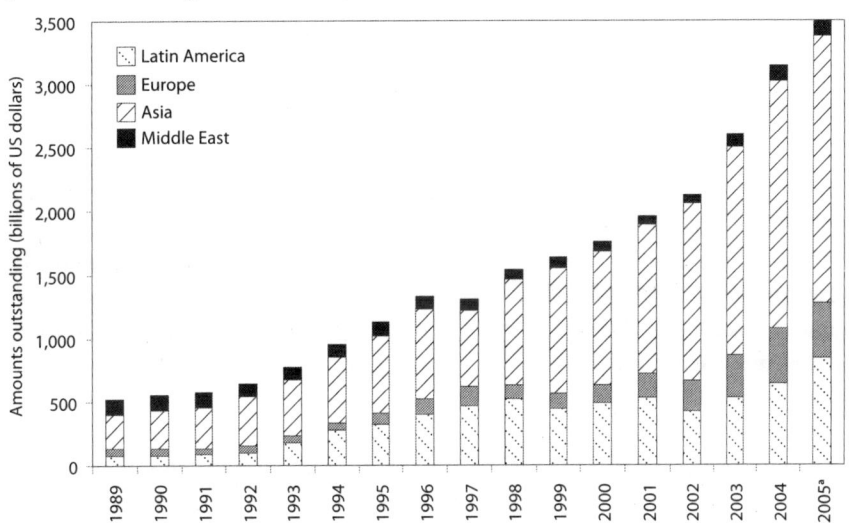

Source: Ocampo and Griffith-Jones (2006).
a   Data refer to period up to September 2005.

capital inflows combined with the maturity and currency mismatches in the portfolio of all economic agents renders the recipient countries subject to shocks and crises, which can be both large and frequent.

Macroeconomic instability increases the variance in project returns and also the adverse selection problems that banks face, thus making banks risk-averse. The real benefits of macroeconomic stability come not only from increased financial savings and greater availability of credit, but also from its favourable impact on the risk-sharing relationship between borrowers and lenders (Villanueva and Mirakhor, 1990). The pace of liberalization itself thus seems to be crucial in the sense that a sudden increase in the lending rate resulting from the freeing of the interest rate may render some firms unprofitable as they will need to pay a higher price for their funds borrowed earlier at a lower rate.

In sum, macroeconomic stability and long-term growth stand in a two-way relationship. The focus of macroeconomic policies merely on low inflation and on restoring the fiscal balance may be too narrow for the achievement of the desired growth gains, especially if the emphasis on monetary restrictions and fiscal prudence depresses economic activity in the short run and restricts broader developmental policies. Also, as shown, the role of fiscal adjustment in restoring macroeconomic imbalances seems to be limited and much depends on how such policies help promote a growth-oriented environment for the private sector. The creation of the latter depends not only on the degree of integration of macroeconomic and development policies, but also on the structure and level of development of the financial sector.

The potential contribution of financial development to economic growth is considerable and financial liberalization can help establish more efficient and liquid financial intermediation. However, these contributions to growth cannot be taken for granted and the growth impact depends on the construction of the appropriate institutional structure. Financial structures are very different across the world and there is no unique relationship between financial structure and levels of, or growth in, income per capita. What matters is that the financial sector ensure adequate finance for productive investment of enterprises, including small and micro-enterprises and farms, and for long-term investment. Depending on the stage of development, this may imply reserving an important role for public sector banks (particularly development banks) and ensuring that a domestic bond market for long-term financing in domestic currency is being established. Institutional development should also ensure adequate regulation and supervision to guarantee sound financial sector balance sheets, an issue that is considered only in passing in this report (see, however, for details, United Nations, 2005, chapter I).

Such aspects of financial development seem to have been overlooked in many programmes of financial liberalization. Growth divergence thus appears to be associated with the differences in the capacity of countries to avoid pro-cyclical stabilization policies, to link macroeconomic adjustment policies with broader development policies and to ensure that financial sector development is able to contain (rather than exacerbate) the volatility of external capital flows. The next sections address these issues in more detail.

External Constraints on Stability and Growth in Developing Countries

Economic theory suggests that private capital should flow from developed countries, where it is abundant and investment opportunities are more fully exploited, to developing countries, where it is scarce relative to ample investment opportunities. Capital inflows could supplement domestic savings in financing investment in developing countries, contributing to their growth and development. In addition, access to international capital markets would help reduce fluctuations in liquidity over the business cycle, dampening macroeconomic volatility. In practice, however, international capital flows to developing countries have been volatile and a source of macroeconomic instability.

Private capital flows to developing countries have increased but also experienced a strong cyclical pattern since the mid-1970s. In particular the developing world has experienced two full medium-term cycles in capital flows that have had a strong impact on stability and growth in many countries (Ocampo, Kregel and Griffith-Jones, 2006). A boom in international bank lending to developing countries in the 1970s ended in debt crises in the 1980s. Another boom occurred in the 1990s, which was mainly driven by portfolio investment flows and, to a lesser extent, foreign direct investment (FDI) and came to an end with a sharp decline in net flows after the Asian financial crisis. The recovery from the global slowdown in 2001, an improved international economic environment and strengthened economic conditions in developing countries provided the basis for a renewed recovery of private capital flows since 2003, indicating the beginning of a third cycle.

Commercial bank lending and portfolio investment have proved to be particularly pro-cyclical for developing countries. Both the availability and the cost of external financing ease during periods of economic expansion, and tighten and become more expensive during downswings. During the 1970s, developing countries had obtained access to commercial bank lending, after having relied mostly on ODA, multilateral development bank loans and FDI in preceding decades. The access to private financing was a result in part of the search of banks in the developed countries for new markets where their excess liquidity could be turned into profitable loans. The excess liquidity in the international banking system had originated to an important extent from the oil surpluses generated after the first oil price increase, much of which was deposited in the commercial banks. It was also the result of institutional changes in international financial markets permitting the entry of smaller and middle-sized banks which previously had not been allowed to engage in international lending. The increased competition in international lending further pushed down the cost of borrowing. At the same time, groups of banks shared risks through syndicated lending, which strengthened the concentration of loans among a few developing countries (see Vos, 1994, chapter 5). The middle-income developing countries were perceived as a good risk at the time, in part because of strong export performance, particularly in East Asia, as well as the Latin American and other middle-income primary exporters that benefited from the high commodity prices that prevailed during the 1970s.

The surge in bank lending came to a sudden halt as world interest rates rose around 1980 and the perception of risk changed with the sudden increase in the debt-servicing burden of the borrowing countries. The subsequent massive withdrawal of bank loans accelerated the debt crises that spread among developing countries. The rise in the cost of borrowing and the restriction in access came at a time when commodity prices collapsed and the need for external financing had actually increased.

The reduced access to private capital flows lasted throughout the 1980s and revived from around 1990 onward, spurred once again by the entry of new players into the market, particularly pension funds and other institutional investors that previously had been allowed to operate only in domestic financial markets. In addition, the debt restructuring under the Brady Plan in the late 1980s and the financial liberalization processes and other structural reforms in many developing countries eased the entrance of private capital flows. Much of the lending during this second cycle took the form of short-term portfolio debt and equity investment, which by their nature have proved to be much more volatile than long-term debt and FDI. Short-term bank loans proved even more volatile, as witnessed in the East Asian crisis. The Mexican peso crisis at the end of 1994 generated the first major disturbance and the 1997 East Asia crisis initiated the broad-based series of financial crises observed in the final years of the decade.

Aside from being characterized by strong pro-cyclical features, boom-bust cycles tend to spill over to other markets. Mexico's currency crisis led to capital reversals in other emerging market economies. The Asian crisis and the Russian default in 1998 caused a more general withdrawal of funds invested in developing countries. Since a country's loss of access to markets for international banks or bond markets spreads to other sources of financing (in addition to the fact that it may affect market access of other countries), an across-the-board market closure may follow. Even when countries do not fully lose market access, they tend to be subject to increases in risk premiums. The pro-cyclical downgrades by credit-rating agencies often exacerbate both reduced access to portfolio loans and the higher spreads at which bonds can be issued.

Although FDI flows were also negatively affected by the Asian crisis, they remained positive and became the dominant source of private capital flows to developing countries. It is worth noting that FDI also moves pro-cyclically, although not to the same extent as short-term lending and portfolio investment (World Bank, 1999). Therefore, FDI can also increase macroeconomic instability. This is so, in part, because an important share of FDI takes the form of mergers and acquisitions of firms in developing countries, which are pro-cyclical (see chapter III); and to the extent that FDI is geared towards the domestic market, it responds to an economic downturn in the same way that domestic investment does.

As we will se in the next section, the pro-cyclical nature of private capital flows also limits the space available to Governments in developing countries for conducting counter-cyclical macroeconomic policies. The failure to contain the impact of surges in capital inflows will lead to large macroeconomic imbalances and that will call for sizeable downward adjustment of the economy when there is a sudden stop in the access to external financing. This reduced capacity to implement counter-cyclical policies implies that access to international financial flows also has an impact on the real economy, although not by smoothing the business cycle, as anticipated by economic theory, but by magnifying it: inflows often lead to output expansion and outflows to contraction and stagnation (Kaminsky, Reinhart and Végh, 2004).

Moreover, without adequate regulatory and legal frameworks and with weak financial systems in developing countries, financial volatility is readily transmitted to the real sector (Easterly, Islam and Stiglitz, 2001; World Bank, 1999; and FitzGerald, 2008). Under weak regulation, surges in capital flows will exacerbate the tendency of excessive risk-taking and create the conditions for boom-bust cycles.

The volatility and pro-cyclical nature of private capital flows to developing countries explain in part why no evidence can be found that such capital movements in general have resulted in increased investment or higher long-term economic growth during the past three decades (Prasad and others, 2003; Ramey and Ramey, 1995; Kose, Prasad and Torrones, 2005). While capital surges stimulated aggregate demand and investment, a large part of the gains were often more than reversed in cases where the sudden stop triggered a financial crisis. Financial volatility has thus translated into increased investment uncertainty and greater output volatility, which were detrimental for long-term economic growth.

Financial crises have resulted, in particular, in slow growth for a number of years after the initial shock. Some estimates put the cumulative loss of output at as much as 25 per cent in the last 25 years (Eichengreen, 2004). Another study found an average cost of lost output (relative to trend output) of 18.8 percentage points of GDP per crisis during 26 banking and currency crisis episodes in emerging market economies in Latin America and Asia during the 1980s and 1990s (International Monetary Fund, 1998, table 15). Losses in output growth occurred in three quarters of the cases.

The pace of recovery from financial crisis since the 1990s has varied significantly among countries owing to differences in domestic policies, structural characteristics and external conditions. Crisis-afflicted Asian countries were able to emerge relatively quickly from the trough of economic growth because of relatively rapid debt restructuring and more supportive fiscal policies. The quick reversal of excessively stringent macroeconomic policies initially imposed in response to the crisis provided credit to finance export production and helped to stabilize domestic demand. Conversely, recovery from financial shocks in most Latin American countries proceeded at a slower pace in the period 1999-2003 owing to delays in debt restructuring and restrictive macroeconomic policies. Increased FDI, together the broadening of the investor base of international emerging market bonds, the growth of local bond markets in developing countries and a modest expansion of cross-border bank lending have underpinned the upward phase of the third cycle of capital flows to developing countries that has taken place in recent years (Ocampo, Kregel and Griffith-Jones, 2006).

Growth and the Cyclicality of Macroeconomic Policies in Developing Countries

The recent empirical growth literature has found some evidence that the way in which macroeconomic policies are conducted can have important implications for long-run growth. Aghion and Howitt (2005) and Aghion,

Barro and Marianescu (2006) showed that counter-cyclical policies can directly influence long-run growth. When firms are financially constrained, an economic downturn would force them to cut investment, hampering growth in the long run. If, however, the Government had the fiscal space for increasing public expenditure, reducing taxes, providing subsidies to private enterprises for long-term investment and/or relaxing the monetary stance during an economic downturn, the adverse impact on long-term investment and growth would be reduced.

In practice, however, macroeconomic policies in developing countries often tend to be pro-cyclical, exacerbating, rather than alleviating, the adverse impact of the downturns on long-run growth. This explains part of the divergence between industrialized and developing countries in recent decades. In turn, differences in the capacity of different developing-country Governments to conduct counter-cyclical policies could be a contributing factor to observed growth divergence among these countries.

As access to finance eases when the economy is in an upswing, Governments may be more inclined to allow budget deficits to widen, and/or central banks may allow interest rates to fall and credit to the private sector to expand. With open capital accounts, tighter monetary policies during booms would hardly help, as they would attract additional short-term flows. Conversely, when external financing contracts during a downswing and the cost of borrowing rises, non-interest fiscal spending may need to be retrenched severely, domestic interest rates will tend to rise and private sector credits will contract, exacerbating the domestic recession. Attempts to strengthen demand through expansionary fiscal and monetary policies could lead to capital outflows and further foreign exchange reserve losses. Volatility in public spending associated with external financing conditions may also conflict with other developmental goals, such as the need for sustained long-term investments in human resources and physical infrastructure (see below).

Kaminsky, Reinhart and Végh (2004) examined the cyclicality of monetary and fiscal policies in a sample of 104 developed and developing countries for the period 1960-2003.[4] The authors construct an index based on the weighted average of cyclicality in public expenditure and tax rates. Using that measure they study found that, in general, macroeconomic policies tended to be pro-cyclical in most developing countries and mostly counter-cyclical in developed economies. Fiscal policy in Africa and Latin America has been highly pro-cyclical, whereas in the fast-growing economies in East Asia, fiscal policies have been either neutral to the business cycle or counter-cyclical (table IV.2).

Table IV.2.
Cyclicality of fiscal policy and economic growth, selected countries and regions, 1960-2003

Region/Country	Cyclicality of fiscal policy (index)[a]	Average GDP Per Capita Growth Rate (in percentage)
Africa	0.30 (highly pro-cyclical)	1.1
Cameroon	0.51 (highly pro-cyclical)	1.0
Côte d'Ivoire	0.38 (highly pro-cyclical)	0.4
Kenya	0.26 (highly pro-cyclical)	1.2
Rwanda	0.63 (most pro-cyclical)	0.5
Latin America	0.25 (highly pro-cyclical)	1.2
Argentina	0.28 (highly pro-cyclical)	1.0
Brazil	0.22 (highly pro-cyclical)	2.4
Colombia	-0.02 (a-cyclical)	1.8
Mexico	0.19 (moderately pro-cyclical)	2.0
Peru	0.40 (highly pro-cyclical)	0.8
Venezuela	0.36 (highly pro-cyclical)	-0.3
Asia	0.16 (moderately pro-cyclical)	3.3
Fast growing Asia	0.06 (a-cyclical)	4.4
China	-0.03 (a-cyclical)	6.1
Indonesia	0.09 (pro-cyclical)	3.6
Korea, Republic of	-0.11 (counter-cyclical)	5.8
Malaysia	0.11 (pro-cyclical)	4.0
OECD	-0.11 (counter-cyclical)	2.6
Finland	-0.51 (most counter-cyclical)	2.9
France	-0.24 (highly counter-cyclical)	2.5
Germany	-0.02 (a-cyclical)	1.9
Japan	0.05 (a-cyclical)	4.0
United Kingdom	-0.37 (strongly counter-cyclical)	2.2
United States	-0.19 (moderately counter-cyclical)	2.2
High-to-Middle Income Developing Countries	0.28 (highly pro-cyclical)	2.8
Middle-to-Low Income Developing Countries	0.17 (moderately pro-cyclical)	2.0
Low-Income Countries	0.28 (highly pro-cyclical)	1.0

Source: UN/DESA based on data in Kaminsky, Reinhart and Végh, (2004).

[a] Constructed as a weighted average of indicators of fiscal policy cyclicality, which include public expenditure, a proxy for changes in tax rates and changes in expenditures over the business cycle in 104 countries. The index ranges from -0.51 to 0.63, where positive figures denote higher pro-cyclicality and negative numbers, the level of counter-cyclicality (further details may be found in Kaminsky, Reinhart and Végh, 2004).

There is a strong negative correlation between pro-cyclical fiscal behaviour and the rate of long-term growth when measured for a large sample of developing countries (see figure IV.6), although there are important outliers. The direct link between the cyclicality of monetary policy and growth is much weaker, partly because of the technical difficulty in defining a proper cyclical index for monetary policy across all countries, given the different monetary policy regimes.[5]

Figure IV.6.
Cyclicality of fiscal policy and economic growth in developing countries 1960-2003[a]
(Percentage)

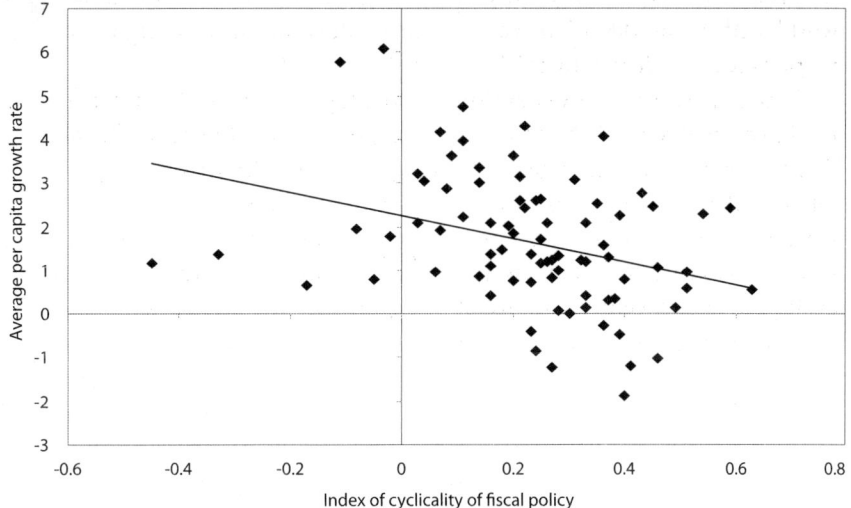

Source: UN/DESA, based on data in Kaminsky, Reinhart and Végh (2004) and World Bank, World Development Indicators 2005 database.
Note: For the definition of the index of cyclicality, see table IV.2, footnote.

In the face of volatile capital flows, exchange-rate policies generate additional complications. A stable nominal exchange rate can provide an anchor for general price stability. Particularly, in countries with a past experience of high inflation and whose central bank lacks credibility, reliance on a stable and fixed nominal exchange rate could be helpful in reducing inflation and macroeconomic instability. Nonetheless, an exchange-rate peg will limit or eliminate the room to manoeuvre for conducting counter-cyclical monetary policies. Furthermore, strong speculative pressures during periods of sudden stops of external financing have made it more difficult for developing countries to maintain a fixed exchange-rate regime, as attested by the various currency crises that occurred in countries that held on to a fixed peg.

In response, many developing countries have moved towards more flexible exchange-rate regimes. As the exchange rate provides a signal for allocating resources across countries and across sectors, a larger degree of flexibility in the exchange rate may also be needed to avoid the inefficient allocation of resources in the long run. But flexible exchange rates are no panacea. One of the major risks that they pose is that of overvaluation during periods of capital surges and/or favourable terms of trade, as well as of overshooting depreciations during crises. Flexibility may thus result in excessive exchange-rate volatility through the business cycle, which reduce the benefits from international specialization. These downsides help to explain why the move towards exchange rate flexibility has been generally mixed in the developing world with some degree of central bank intervention in foreign exchange markets (often referred to as "dirty floats").

A major reason why developing-country Governments intervene in foreign exchange markets is to promote export competitiveness. The target in this case is the real exchange rate, that is to say, the exchange rate adjusted by relative inflation rates across countries. Aside from the strictly counter-cyclical reasons for doing this, there may be long-term justifications: maintaining some level of exchange rate stability and competitiveness through the business cycle generates incentives to invest in export-oriented industries and creates more stable signals to allocate investment between tradable and non-tradable sectors.

Indeed, countries that were able to maintain a relatively stable and competitive real exchange rate seem to have fared better in terms of economic growth. Figure IV.7 shows the average degree of real exchange rate "appreciation" (or "overvaluation") measured as the deviation of the purchasing power parity (PPP) of each country's currency with respect to the United States dollar and adjusted for the difference in productivity growth of the country with respect to that of the United States. The countries in sub-Saharan Africa and Latin America are predominantly clustered in the lower-right part of the figure, indicating a combination of an appreciated real exchange rate and lower growth. East and South-East Asian countries are typically found in the upper-left quadrant, associating more competitive exchange rates with higher economic growth. Exchange-rate policies in most of these countries were in support of industrial and commercial policies to promote export-led growth. The only economy in sub-Saharan Africa in the figure to have pursued a policy of maintaining a competitive exchange rate is Uganda, which kept its currency competitive since 1986 and GDP per capita stepped up to at an average rate of 1.9 per cent per year (Rodrik 2000). A number of Latin American countries are also in the left panel, including

Figure IV.7.
Real effective exchange rate appreciation and per capita GDP growth rate, selected countries, 1970-2003

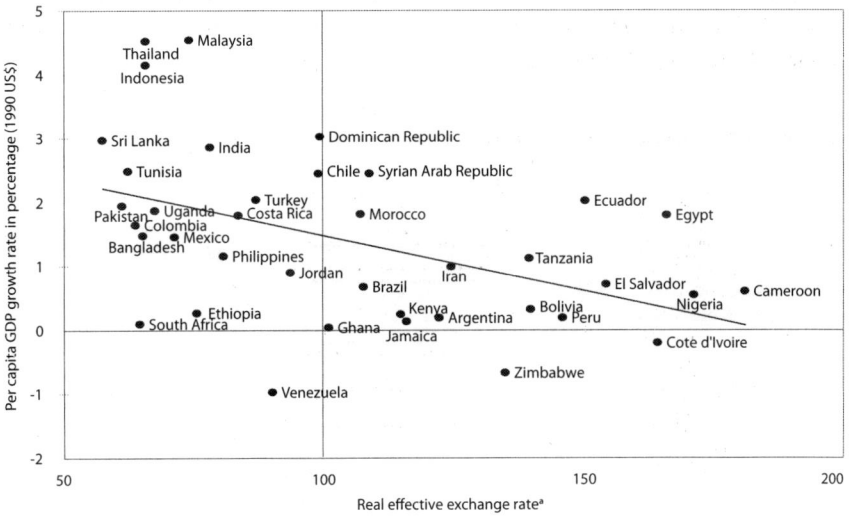

Source: GDP data from United Nations Statistics Division and exchange-rate data from Global Development Network Growth Database, Development Research Institute, New York University available from http://www.nyu.edu/fas/institute/dri/global%20development%20network%20growth%20database.htm.

[a] Values greater than 100 denote overvalued (appreciated) currencies and values less than 100, undervalued (depreciated) currencies.

Mexico, Chile, Colombia, Costa Rica and the Dominican Republic, all relatively successful exporters particularly during the 1990s. Chile stands out as the most successful Latin American economy in terms of growth. Following the currency crisis at the beginning of 1982, the fact that the Chilean economy avoided overvaluation of the peso was beneficial for both macroeconomic stability as well as growth.

Despite these benefits, currency devaluations can generate adverse short-term effects on growth, which could completely offset the gains in international competitiveness, leading to a contraction in output (see, for example, Cooper, 1971; Krugman and Taylor, 1978; Edwards, 1986; and Agénor, 1991). One of the most important contractionary effects could be caused by a currency mismatch between the assets and liabilities on the balance sheets of Governments and private companies, especially in those countries with large foreign debt. Devaluation would raise the value of foreign currency liabilities in relation to domestic assets, increasing the likelihood of bankruptcies and depressing consumption and investment. Even if a country is a net creditor overall, some firms will be net debtors, and the economic consequences of their losses might more than offset the benefits of the firms that are better off. Large-scale currency devaluations have had in practice different impacts on growth in different countries and in different periods (see figure IV.8). While about half of the selected devaluation episodes were followed by a significant contraction in GDP, the other cases involved a mild expansion.

Figure IV.8.
Expansion/contraction during selected currency crises[a], 1972-1998
(Percentage)

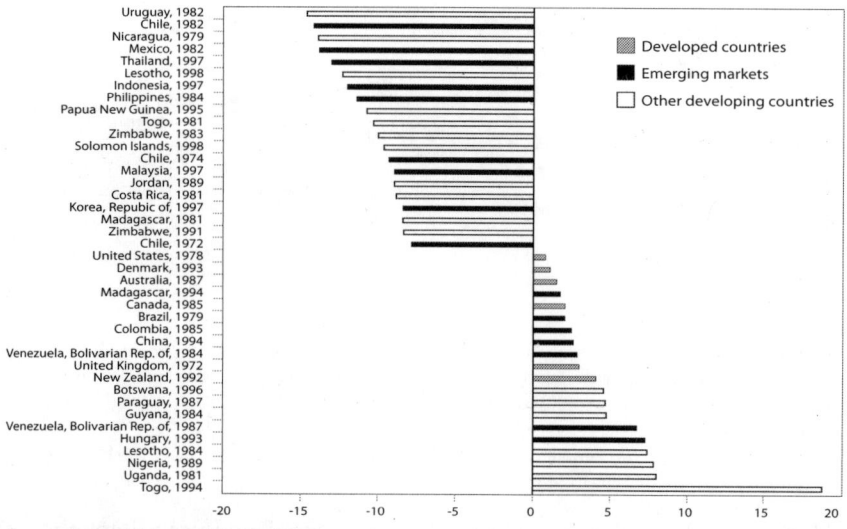

Source: Gupta, Mishra and Sahay (2003).

[a] Magnitude of contraction/expansion=g_post2-g_pre3 (tranq), where g_post2 is the average growth rate in T and T+1, T being the crisis year, and g_pre3 (tranq) is the average growth rate in T-1, T-2, and T-3 years, except when there was a crisis between T-1 and T-3, in which case the nearest three consecutive tranquil (non-crisis) periods are used instead.

The costs of pro-cyclical macroeconomic policies in developing countries are high. In the upturns, imprudent fiscal spending, could lead to inefficient resource allocation, contributing directly to the overheating of the economy and sowing the seeds for macroeconomic instability. Exchange-rate appreciation will affect export competitiveness, leading in the short-term to current account deficits and increased external indebtedness, and possibly to the dismantling of whole lines of export activities, with long-term effects. In the downturns, pro-cyclical policies, such as over-tightening monetary policy and indiscriminate fiscal adjustments, could lead to substantial losses in many valuable social projects, weakening accumulation of infrastructure and human capital and thus not only aggravating the downturn but also reducing the potential for long-run growth.

Aside from the effects of volatile capital flows on macroeconomic policies, other factors may enhance pro-cyclicality. As pointed out previously, financial liberalization, both at the national and at the international level, has contributed to volatility in many developing countries. Market agents tend to underestimate risk during booms, making loans to borrowers with lower credit quality. The rapid increase of asset prices during these periods further stimulates credit growth. The tendency for provisions to be related to the current rate of loan delinquency further increases this pro-cyclical bias. During booms, delinquencies are few and provisioning for loan losses is limited: this reduces the apparent costs of lending and thus increases credit growth. In contrast, during downturns, delinquencies increase, provisioning has to increase and lending tends to be curtailed, and may even lead to a "credit squeeze" that amplifies the economic downswing. Concern about weaknesses in the financial system during a downturn may prompt the introduction of stronger regulatory requirements, further aggravating in the short term the problem of the availability of credit (Ocampo, 2003).

Deficiencies in the domestic institutional framework provide other potentials source of pro-cyclical behaviour. Institutional strengthening is thus a key to creating policy space for counter-cyclical macroeconomic policies. As mentioned in the previous section, a major problem in many developing countries has been fragile and poorly regulated banking and financial system. Increased regulation and increased risk management in general are critical to avoid the fragility of domestic financial systems. Given the pro-cyclical effects of some regulatory practices, particularly of provisioning rules, alternative regulatory rules with clear counter-cyclical elements are essential. In this regard, one possible policy measure is forward-looking provisioning that is estimated on the basis of expected or latent losses (rather than on prevailing losses) when loans are disbursed, taking the full business cycle into account (Ocampo, 2003). This would help smooth out the cycle by increasing provisions or reserves during boom periods and thereby help to reduce the credit crunch during downturns. Along with and in parallel with this measure, regulators should encourage the adoption of risk management practices and models that would allow lending strategies that are less sensitive to short-term factors (see, for instance, Griffith-Jones, Segoviano and Spratt, 2003).

In other cases, the origin may be volatile government revenues associated with heavy dependence on primary commodities and related price fluctuations in global markets. When prices are high, and the economy is booming, Governments tend to engage in expansionary spending behaviour. When prices collapse, government revenue falls and fiscal austerity likely will need to be called for at a time when the economy is entering a recession.

Instruments such as stabilization funds can be beneficial for commodity-exporting developing countries to manage these cyclical swings. Some countries have managed commodity stabilization funds to smooth the impact of volatile commodity prices on fiscal income. These include Chile's copper compensation fund, Colombia's coffee and oil stabilization funds and Burkina Faso's cotton support fund. The performance of these funds—hence their role in mitigating the pro-cyclical nature of fiscal policy—has been variable. The institutional capacity to adequately manage these funds is an important factor in performance (Gottschalk, 2005).

Some developing countries, like Chile during the 1990s, managed to achieve broader fiscal targets that were independent of short-term fluctuations in economic growth, by designing structural budget rules. The management of this counter-cyclical policy stance was one factor accounting for Chile's much stronger growth performance and much greater macroeconomic stability compared with other Latin American countries (Fiess, 2002; Ffrench-Davis, 2006). Effectively managing such a system requires prudent and consistent policymakers and political support for upholding such rules.

More generally, since the 1980s, there has been a shift from discretionary-based macroeconomic policy arrangements to rule-based ones, based on the belief that the latter could avoid policy-generated macroeconomic instability. A rule-based system is no panacea, however. For instance, inflation targeting has recently become a much applied rules-based approach for macroeconomic policymaking. The policy rule has been adopted in about 20 economies, including a fair number of developing countries. Under this monetary regime, an independent central bank commits itself to price stability by making public a pre-fixed inflation range. There are a number of merits associated with such a policy arrangement, including its potential to enhance a central bank's policy transparency and credibility (United Nations, 2000). However, the narrow focus of monetary policy on the inflation target may generate a bias towards maintaining a strong exchange rate, may make macroeconomic adjustment pro-cyclical in response to external shocks (including shocks that affect the availability of external financing) and, more generally, may bias macroeconomic stabilization against employment and growth objectives.

In general, rule-based policies can function well under normal circumstances, but as the economic structure changes over time and different shocks may occur, the predetermined policy rules can become less relevant, or too rigid. Moreover, as the risks and uncertainties faced by an economy may be non-stationary—that is to say, they will not reproduce exactly past patterns—a certain degree of discretion in policymaking is always needed during periods of abnormalities, like crises, so as to minimize the risks for huge macroeconomic losses. The successful experience of East Asian economies and a few other developing countries has also shown the merits of balancing rules and flexibility.

In sum, pro-cyclical macroeconomic policies may be intrinsic to excessive reliance on external sources of finance and government revenues, which may be enhanced by a country's institutional framework. It is therefore important for developing countries to find ways to create more space for counter-cyclical macroeconomic policies. As it has been emphasized, pro-cyclical policies can be costly for economic growth and, especially during downturns, may affect investments in infrastructure and human development and may jeopardize long-term development prospects.

Public Investment in Infrastructure and Human Development

Part of the observed growth divergence among developing countries is attributable to the gaps in the public investment in infrastructure and spending on human development. As discussed in chapter III, public policies to promote economic structural change include multisector or horizontal policies such as investments in physical infrastructure (for example, roads, ports and telecommunications) as well as interventions aimed at increasing the quality of human capital available in the economy, that is to say, people's abilities and skills that allow them to be economically productive and to generate, adapt and use new technologies. Not all such services necessarily need to be publicly provided. However, it is mostly the public sector that needs to take a leading role, inter alia, because of the considerable amounts of funding and the high expected social returns that are usually associated with such investments.

Physical infrastructure and growth

An adequate level of infrastructure is a necessary condition for growth. By its very nature, infrastructure is characterized by indivisibilities and countries need to build up a threshold or minimum level of infrastructure (say, a minimum network of roads) to make a difference for economy-wide productivity growth. To reach a minimum level of infrastructure, countries will need to sustain substantial public investment levels over prolonged periods of time.

Their failure to do so explains partly why Latin America and sub-Saharan Africa have fallen behind the East Asian countries that have sustained infrastructural investment. East Asian economies invested more in the quality and coverage of physical infrastructure. In Africa, aid seems to have helped to sustain capital expenditures in a number of low-income countries. In sharp contrast, Latin American countries have witnessed a decline in infrastructural investment over time as a result of increased fiscal austerity since the 1980s. Public spending on infrastructural investment for a group of seven Latin American countries declined from 3 per cent of GDP in 1980 to less than 1 per cent of GDP in 2001 (see figure IV.9; and World Bank and International Monetary Fund, 2006).

Figure IV.9.
Latin America: Primary deficit (left axis) and public infrastructure investment (right axis)
(Percentage of GDP)

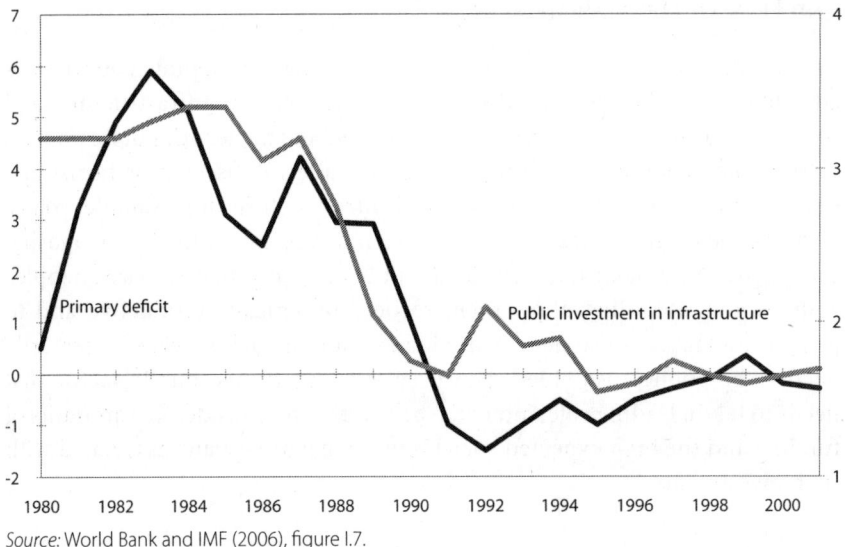

Source: World Bank and IMF (2006), figure I.7.

These have led to significant differences in the quality and availability of infrastructure. Indeed, since the 1960s, the road density in Latin America and sub-Saharan Africa has barely increased, while it has tripled in East Asia. Also, the availability of telephone lines in East Asia is twice as great as that in Latin America and 10 times greater than that in sub-Saharan Africa (see table IV.3).

Cross-national studies of infrastructure and growth often tend to find positive rates of return to investment in infrastructure. One of the first commonly cited analyses in this literature is that of Easterly and Rebelo

Table IV.3.
Telephone mainlines availability and road and railroad density: ratio of the values of two key infrastructure indicators in developing regions to values in developed countries, 1960-1995 *(Percentage)*

	1960	1965	1970	1975	1980	1985	1990	1995
Telephone Mainlines per 1,000 workers								
Developed	100.0	100.0	100.0	100.0	100.0	100.0	100.0	100.0
East Asia	7.6	10.2	14.5	18.8	24.7	29.9	35.5	41.1
Eastern Europe and Central Asia	13.2	14.9	17.8	21.1	23.7	29.4	36.8	47.0
Latin America	17.3	15.9	15.1	14.2	14.0	15.2	17.5	23.6
Middle East and Northern Africa	15.3	19.2	21.4	23.2	28.7	32.1	35.4	39.8
South Asia	0.9	0.9	0.9	0.9	1.0	1.2	1.7	3.1
Sub-Saharan Africa	3.0	2.7	2.4	2.3	2.4	2.6	3.1	4.3
Roads and railroads per square km								
Developed	100.0	100.0	100.0	100.0	100.0	100.0	100.0	100.0
East Asia	22.3	32.7	40.7	44.2	50.6	57.3	60.1	63.7
Eastern Europe and Central Asia	30.3	40.0	41.6	40.2	40.8	41.5	46.2	48.7
Latin America	2.9	3.3	3.6	3.9	4.5	4.7	4.8	5.0
Middle East and Northern Africa	8.8	10.0	11.0	11.2	12.2	13.2	12.8	13.5
South Asia	14.1	14.1	14.3	15.0	16.3	17.3	18.1	24.1
Sub-Saharan Africa	6.6	9.0	9.4	8.6	8.3	8.0	7.9	7.9

Source: Rodriguez (2006b).

(1993) who examined the relationship between economic growth and fiscal policy for a cross-section of countries during the period 1970-1988. Among other things, these authors found that public transport and communication investment was positively correlated with growth. More recent work has concentrated on the relationship between growth and stocks of infrastructure. Sanchez-Robles (1998), for instance, constructed an index of infrastructure stocks (kilometres of railways and roads, energy capacity and telephones per capita) which were found to have had a significant effect on growth. Other studies have uncovered similar effects for both developed and developing countries (Easterly, 2001; Demetriades and Mamuneas 2000; and Roller and Waverman, 2001).

While the above studies established that the provision of infrastructure contributes to growth, they did not undertake evaluations to determine whether the return from increasing public spending on infrastructure would outweigh the cost of provision. In contrast, Canning (1999) estimated that the social returns to electricity-generation and transportation routes appeared to have been no different from the private returns, although he did find that telephones per worker had a substantially higher return. He argued that this result raised doubts about the wisdom of financing infrastructure provision with distortionary taxation. Many other studies, on the other hand, did find that the contribution of infrastructure services to GDP growth tended to exceed the cost of their provision (see, for example, Rodriguez, 2006b). Moreover, public investment in transport and communications would raise private investment levels. When public and private capitals are complementary, an increase in infrastructure will raise the rate of return on private capital and thus induce an increase in the stock of private capital. This effect could be substantial, particularly in an open economy.

It could therefore be argued that lower investment in infrastructure in developing countries—caused by the retrenchment of public expenditures as a result of adjustment policies—would have contributed to increased income disparity between developed and developing countries. However, it does not appear to have been a major factor. At best, changes in public investment have been a minor contributor to the gap between rich and poor countries, accounting for no more than 12 per cent of that increase, as most developed countries also experienced a deceleration in the accumulation of their stocks of infrastructure during the 1980s and the 1990s (Rodriguez, 2006b). This allowed some developing countries to catch up and others not to fall behind.

In contrast, the increasing gap in the availability and quality of infrastructure does seem to explain an important part of the growth divergence among developing countries. According to one estimate, the diverging levels of public investment in infrastructure could explain as much as one third of the output gap between East Asia and Latin America (Calderón and Servén, 2003).

Much of the public spending decline can be traced to fiscal adjustment as implemented in stabilization programmes, which were, as indicated, largely pro-cyclical. Such spending cuts may reflect policymakers' preferences for such reductions in current expenditure, which would be more difficult to sustain politically in the short run. Yet, these cuts compromise long-term fiscal sustainability as the potential for additional fiscal revenues—at given levels of taxation—is reduced by lower growth in the future. Moreover, there are non-linear scale effects of infrastructure on growth: the incapacity to maintain infrastructure above certain minimally necessary thresholds may halt the growth process altogether. For example, the reduced infrastructure asset accumulation resulting from lower public investment was estimated to have lowered GDP growth by more than 1 percentage point in several Latin American countries during the 1980s and 1990s (Calderón, Easterly and Servén, 2003). As a result, much of the anticipated favourable effect of the infrastructure spending reduction on the fiscal position was offset by higher deficits resulting from lowered output growth in the years following the adjustment. Disregarding cases of politically motivated and inefficient or unnecessary investment, lower public spending on infrastructure will eventually weaken rather than strengthen fiscal solvency, which is contrary to the initial intention of fiscal adjustment.

Gaps in human capital investment

Fiscal policy also has an important impact on human capital formation. Human capital, in the form of a higher education level and good health, enhances people's capacities, and their creativity and productivity. Healthier and better-educated people can perform higher value added tasks more efficiently than people with low levels of human capital. They are also more likely to adopt improved technology and to innovate. Finally, workers with high levels of human capital can adapt more easily to changing job conditions and sectoral change and are more likely to have the skills needed to face international competition.

As indicated in figure IV.10, an increasing gap in education between Latin America and East Asia is discernible over the past four decades. In 1960,

Figure IV.10.
Years of schooling in 2000 and changes in education attainment between 1960 and 2000 in Latin America and East Asia

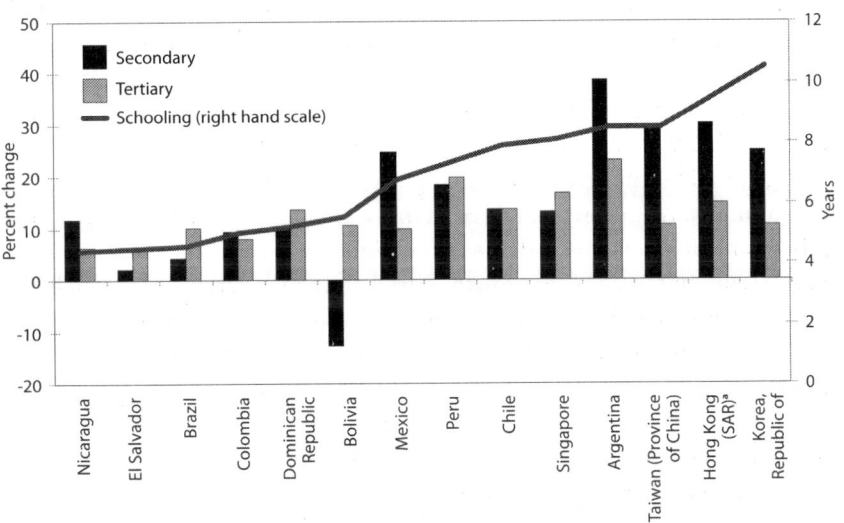

Source: UN/DESA, based on data in De Ferranti and others (2003).
a   Special Administrative Region of China.

educational attainment had been low in both Latin America and East Asia; but from 1960 to 2000, the average number of years of schooling increased by more than 4.5 years in East Asian countries, and more than doubled, to 10.5 years, in the Republic of Korea. In contrast, Latin American enrolment rates at the secondary and tertiary levels have remained low (Perry and others, 2006; De Ferranti and others, 2003). While most countries in other regions are close to achieving universal enrolment in primary education, the average primary completion rate in sub-Saharan Africa is only about 50 per cent, with marked differences between male and female attainments.

Such differences in progress in human development may thus explain part of the observed growth divergence. Early development studies had already found that investment—public or private—in health and schooling enhances the economic prospects and welfare of poor people (Schultz, 1961). Since this seminal work, the economic literature has increasingly come to recognize the importance of high initial levels of human capital as a precondition for long-run growth (Barro, 1999; Lucas, 1988; and Lee, 1997). Many of these analyses have focused on the role of education, but some have also found that better health outcomes, such as higher life expectancy, can enhance economic growth (Bloom, Canning and Sevilla, 2004).

Similarly, as discussed in chapter I, Ranis and Stewart (2005) found that economic growth was significantly associated with various measures of human capital, including the levels of literacy and life expectancy. Moreover, no country has been able to move from a situation of high economic growth and low human capital into a virtuous cycle of reinforcing high rates of human capital and growth. Several countries did, however, move from such a situation into a vicious cycle, where low human capital depressed economic growth which in turn negatively affected human capital accumulation. The authors concluded that it was not possible to reach the ideal of a virtuous cycle by first generating improved economic growth while neglecting human capital development. Any growth attained in this way would not be sustained. On the other hand, it should also be noted that higher levels of human capital do not necessarily guarantee faster growth. A well-trained, healthy and skilled labour force is a necessary but not a sufficient condition for sustained growth.

This conclusion implies that investing more in education and health may not be enough to serve the growth purpose. Other constraints on economic growth and structural change will need to be addressed simultaneously to create the employment opportunities for a better-educated and more productive population. All the same, human development remains important to growth, and, of course, is also an objective in its own right. Countries with significant gaps in education and health outcomes will have to substantially increase the fiscal space for expenditures in these areas.

This may be achieved, first, by improving the efficiency of public spending on health and education through better targeting to priority areas within the social sectors and by improving the cost-effectiveness of public programmes. Second, strengthening the tax base will be essential, particularly in countries with low government revenues. Such forms of domestic resource mobilization for human capital investment should be the core focus for the middle-income countries. For the poorest countries, this will likely not suffice and foreign aid will have to play an important role in filling the gaps (see below).

The third approach is influenced by the fact that a pro-cyclical macroeconomic policy environment makes it more difficult to reach stable and adequate levels of social expenditures and infrastructure required for enhancing long-term economic growth. Thus, while the need to maintain sustainable macroeconomic balances is recognized, new ways to balance this objective with public sector spending that is critical for economic growth and development must be explored. This includes discussing innovative approaches to adopting improved or adjusted concepts of fiscal targets, such as the exclusion of capital expenditures, as they contribute to the accumulation of assets (thereby offsetting liabilities), have counter-cyclical potential during crisis and adjustment and contribute to the sustainability of long term-growth.

Official development assistance, growth and development

In 1961, when the General Assembly proclaimed the First United Nations Development Decade, it had been understood, by rich and poor countries alike, that there would have to be an intensified effort to mobilize internal and external resources if designated growth targets were to be met. The target of 0.7 per cent of gross national income (GNI) of the developed countries for ODA emerged during the debates in the late 1960s on the Second United Nations Development Decade. The target has never been met, except by a few donor countries. In 2002, at the International Conference on Financing for Development held in Monterrey, Mexico, the international community reiterated the need for concrete efforts by the donor countries towards achieving the target of 0.7 per cent of GNI for ODA and included the Millennium Development Goals as tangible criteria against which to assess ODA effectiveness. Renewed proposals for Marshall Plans and "big pushes"—as in the early 1960s—have emerged (UN Millennium Project, 2005).

The initial logic of a big push as advocated in the 1950s and 1960s had been grounded in the concept of growth dynamics popular at the time: each dollar of additional aid would add incrementally to investment and simultaneously ease the foreign exchange constraint on imported capital goods and technology. This reasoning did not reflect a consensus, and a number of high-profile studies identified crowding out of private investment and waste as likely outcomes of increased aid flows. Much of the initial debate was hampered by missing and unreliable data.

A multitude of studies examining the effectiveness of aid have been undertaken since. These studies typically drew on a large sample of countries and looked at long periods of time. Most of these studies used econometric techniques to verify the existence of a relation between economic growth and aid commitments (or disbursements). Making sense of these studies has been complicated by familiar methodological pitfalls accompanying cross-country regressions, described by one reviewer as "an anarchy of numbers" (Roodman, 2004). As the debate on aid effectiveness progressed, it was recognized that, because aid was a multifunctional and fungible flow, its impact on growth was unlikely to be associated with a simple linear relationship (a feature of the early studies of aid's effectiveness) but likely instead to be time- and country-specific.

The growth impact of aid will depend on how it is spent and which macroeconomic economic effects it generates. The aid-growth relationship thus tends to be complex in practice. First, not all aid is meant to be used for investment purposes or spending on human development. Much of aid is allocated for emergency and humanitarian relief. Also, although this form of aid may have positive effects on growth by mitigating the negative impact of natural disasters and insecurity situations on human development, its precise contribution will be difficult to measure. Second, even if aid is allocated directly to, for instance, investment in infrastructure and human development, the growth impact will depend not only on how such investment contributes to growth, but also on other factors. Money is fungible and so is aid financing. If the Government was already intending to make such investments without the ODA resources, part of the aid might thus end up financing other expenditures or providing an incentive to a lesser effort towards tax collection. The problem of fungibility in aid spending has been extensively studied in the literature and has been found to be one reason for the reduced growth effects of aid (see, for example, White, 1998; McGillivray and Morrisey, 2001; Gupta, Powell and Yang, 2006). Nonetheless, there is recent evidence showing that—on the whole—when allocated for developmental expenditures, aid will induce higher economic growth. Minoiu and Reddy (2008) have shown that developmental aid, in contrast with geopolitically motivated aid, had a positive and significant impact on economic growth (see box IV.1).

Box IV.1.
Aid effectiveness and economic growth: the type of aid matters

In an econometric exercise based on a standard cross-country growth model, Minoiu and Reddy (2008) analysed the long-term impact of different components of aid on growth in recipient countries. The average per capita income growth in the 1990s was the dependent variable. The relevant explanatory variables included, among others, the initial level of per capita income, life expectancy, government consumption, institutional quality, geographical factors, revolutions, growth rate of terms of trade, multilateral and bilateral aid broken down by donors, and geopolitical aid as a share of GDP. These variables were averaged and the regressions were run over four different time periods: 1960-2000, 1970-2000, 1980-2000 and 1990-2000. The results indicated that lagged aid variables had been a significant factor explaining growth in the 1990s, and that an increase in aid of 1 per cent of GDP during earlier periods was associated with an average GDP per capita growth rate that was higher by as much as 0.085 percentage points in the 1990s.

The study further disaggregated total aid flows in an attempt to isolate the true effect of the developmental, growth-enhancing components of total aid from its geopolitically motivating, possibly depressing, element. Three proxies for development aid were used in alternative specifications: (a) multilateral aid; (b) bilateral aid from the Nordic countries (including Iceland); and (c) bilateral aid from a larger group of developmentally minded donor countries (Nordic countries plus Austria, Canada, Luxembourg, the Netherlands and Switzerland). The choice of proxies was based on the fact that multilateral aid is more firmly geared to developmental rather than geopolitical aims and that some donor countries were more developmentally minded than others. While this approach is not without its limitations, a recent study of Nordic aid has found clear-cut differences with respect to other bilateral donors in terms of its generosity, its bias towards democracies, its being less conditional on openness criteria but more conditional on the human rights record, and its not depending on the "friendship" of the recipient (Gates and Hoeffler, 2004). Geopolitical aid was proxied on the basis of past and present geopolitical ties (as reflected by colonial relationships, a shared language, and common membership in an entente, alliance or agreement).

The results derived from separating aid flows into these constituent components are quite striking. An increase of 1 per cent of GDP in multilateral aid receipts in the 1960s was associated with an increase by half of a percentage point of the average growth rate of per capita GDP in the 1990s, and a similar increase in the 1970s was associated with a quarter of a percentage point addition to growth two decades later. At the same time, geopolitical aid was negatively associated with growth, and in a statistically significant manner, although its marginal impact was much smaller in magnitude. A possible reason for concern about these specifications is that some bilateral aid might have been developmental in nature, yet omitted from the proxy for developmental aid in the regressions. The results obtained through including aid from the two bilateral donor groups were particularly impressive, with strong positive associations: average growth between 1980 and 2000 was higher by over 1 percentage point for countries that had received 1 additional per cent of GDP as aid transfers from the Nordic countries in the 1970s and 1980s. This result is relatively robust compared with other specifications of the regression.

Third, significant aid inflows will induce other macroeconomic adjustments as well. Some skeptics have long warned of the possibility of the so-called aid curse, much like a "natural resource curse" (see chapter V), whereby high levels of aid crowd out dynamic activities by inflating local costs or leading to appreciated exchange-rate pressures.[6] Rajan and Subramanian (2005) have reported "compelling evidence" of a real exchange-rate appreciation linked to aid flows' squeezing the dynamic labour-intensive manufacturing sector, which normally would be an engine of long-term growth in poorer countries. However, their finding is strongest for the 1980s, when the impact of aid flows on the exchange rate was weakest, suggesting specification problems. In fact, it is almost certainly the case that external shocks of the 1980s triggered additional aid flows (including debt relief) to countries whose manufacturing sectors had also been negatively impacted by those same shocks. Other studies have shown, however, that aid flows do not necessarily lead to real exchange-rate appreciation. For example, IMF (2005) found in a study of five African countries that only Ghana had observed a small real appreciation of its currency during the years in which aid flows surged and that export performance in most of these five countries had remained strong.

Such evidence on the positive long-term effects of aid on growth is certainly important in light of the renewed commitments being made by the donor community. Still, aid remains only one of the factors in the growth story. Its impact has clearly been insufficient in many cases with respect to counteracting other unfavourable influences on growth performance. Recognizing this underscores the importance of a better grasp of the possible channels of aid effectiveness. These findings, while providing a more nuanced perspective on aid flows, also offer some support to the idea of a big aid push. In this regard, the Millennium Development Goals could be understood as providing a clear set of targets that can help guide such a push towards eliminating the poverty traps existing in many countries, particularly in Africa. The underlying assumption of the big push concept is that the existing capital stock in most African economies is below a certain threshold level needed to generate a strong impact on productivity and integration of the economy. The aim is thus for the threshold to be attained through a targeted public investment drive. Once this critical level of available infrastructure and human development has been reached, the combined impact of economies of scale, complementarities and linkage effects can generate a self-sustaining process with private investment taking the lead. A well-targeted large infusion of aid—focused particularly on infrastructure, education and health projects to help raise rural productivity—could place many African economies on the path of faster growth. Naturally, minimum levels of governance must be in place if a big push is to work (UN Millennium Project, 2005).

Other findings, however, have raised serious concerns about whether the "growth-enhancing governance capabilities" needed by developing countries to manage productive assets and resources—domestically or externally created—in such a way as to ensure that cumulative income and productivity gains are generated, could be found in potential aid recipients (Khan, 2007). Similarly, Easterly (2005) and Rodrik (2006a) warned against assuming the donor community knew enough to be able to mount an ambitious drive to eradicate global poverty in the absence of domestic institutions—a drive that, through experimentation via trial and error, could discover what really worked at the local level. Certainly, as discussed in chapter V, the recent tendency to add governance conditionalities to aid and lending flows has not produced the desired outcomes in terms of better-quality public services, and thus stands as a warning against a top-down approach. Still, there are lessons to be derived from success stories that suggest that a big investment push combined with institutional learning can be undertaken in unison to establish a fast and sustainable growth trajectory (Kozul-Wright and Rayment, 2006).

Summary and Policy Implications

The growth divergence among the developing countries in the past four decades cannot be fully ascribed to differences in macroeconomic policies, but they have no doubt played a critical role. Five sets of issues seem particularly important in improving the link between macroeconomic policies and growth.

The importance of macroeconomic stability and policy flexibility for growth

Macroeconomic stability strongly influences the long-term growth performance of the economy. Macroeconomic stability should be seen in a broad sense, for it entails more than just preserving price stability and sustainable fiscal balances. It is also about avoiding large swings in economic activity and employment, about maintaining sustainable external accounts and avoiding exchange-rate overvaluation, and about maintaining well-regulated domestic financial sectors, sound private and public-sector balance sheets and sound external debt structures.

Strong and sustainable growth makes it easier to achieve greater macroeconomic stability by, inter alia, enhancing the sustainability of domestic and foreign public debt. Conversely, greater stability, in its broad sense, reduces investment uncertainty and hence is supportive of higher long-term growth.

Stabilization policies as implemented in many developing countries since the 1980s have mostly emphasized the objectives of lowering inflation and restoring fiscal balances. While moderating inflation and fiscal prudence are not in dispute as sensible macroeconomic policy objectives, there are concerns that, in practice, countries may have emphasized these objectives at the expense of considering other dimensions of macroeconomic stability. In particular, price stability often has been achieved at the cost of producing exchange-rate appreciation, low growth and unsustainable external debt burdens. Moreover, macroeconomic policies in many of the developing countries have been highly pro-cyclical over the past two decades. This has been detrimental for development, as there exists a strong negative correlation between pro-cyclical fiscal behaviour and long-term growth, and between unstable real exchange rates and economic growth. Creating space for counter-cyclical macroeconomic adjustment policies thus appears to be beneficial for growth and macroeconomic stability, in the broad sense of the term.

For many developing-country Governments, the space for conducting counter-cyclical macroeconomic policies is limited, as the available fiscal and foreign exchange resources tend to be small relative to the size of the external shocks they face. International action mitigating the impact of private capital flow volatility (see below) can further help enhance the necessary policy space. However, also at the country level, Governments can take measures to enhance the scope for counter-cyclical policies by improving the institutional framework for macroeconomic policymaking.

Macroeconomic policies and national development strategies

In the more appropriate institutional setting, fiscal policy should first of all strike a balance between fiscal prudence and fiscal flexibility in such a way as to ensure both policy credibility and fiscal sustainability. Setting fiscal targets that are independent of the short-term fluctuations in economic growth (so called structural budget rules) can be effective in forcing a counter-cyclical policy stance. Some developing countries, such as Chile, have been able to manage such fiscal rules successfully. Fiscal stabilization funds can also help smooth over time the revenues from unstable tax sources, like those based on primary export production. Although the experience with the application of such funds in different parts of the world has varied, they can form an effective instrument for resolving inter-temporal trade-offs in fiscal spending by guaranteeing long-term fiscal sustainability while protecting growth-enhancing long-term public investment in infrastructure and human development during economic downturns.

Second, a certain degree of discretionary power should be retained. Rule-based policies may be too rigid to respond to macroeconomic volatility. Some rule-based regimes, such as inflation-targeting, may bias macroeconomic stabilization towards a narrowly defined target (low inflation) and against broader employment, growth and other developmental objectives. Rule-based policies may function well for some time and when the economy is not suffering from major shocks; but as the structure of the economy changes over time, so will vulnerability to external shocks. In such a changing context, predetermined policy rules likely become less relevant or turn out to be too rigid. Moreover, as the risks and uncertainties facing an economy never present themselves in exactly the same way or with the same degree of intensity, a certain amount of space for discretionary policies will always be needed to make adjustments that minimize macroeconomic losses.

Third, macroeconomic policies should be well integrated with other areas of economic policymaking. A competitive real exchange rate seems to be critical in this regard. In the fast-growing East Asian economies, for example, macroeconomic policies were part of a broader development strategy, contributing directly to long-run growth. Fiscal policies in these economies have given priority to development spending, including investment in education, health and infrastructure, as well as subsidies and credit guarantees for export industries. Monetary policy was coordinated with financial sector and industrial policies, including directed and subsidized credit schemes and managed interest rates designed to directly influence investment and saving, whereas competitive exchange rates were considered essential to encouraging exports and export diversification. In contrast, macroeconomic policies in many Latin American and African countries since the 1980s have been focused on much more narrowly defined short-term stabilization objectives and have resulted many times in exchange-rate overvaluation.

Fourth, improved prudential regulation and supervision of domestic financial systems and enhanced risk management are essential to avoid excessive risk taking and financial crises. To reduce the pro-cyclicality brought about by the financial sector, one possible policy measure is forward-looking provisioning that is estimated on the basis of expected or latent losses (rather than on prevailing losses) when loans are disbursed, taking the full business cycle into account.

International policies to reduce financial volatility

A major challenge for the multilateral financial institutions is to help developing countries mitigate the damaging effects of volatile capital flows and provide counter-cyclical financing mechanisms to compensate for the inherent pro-cyclical movement of private capital flows. A number of options are available for dampening the pro-cyclicality of capital flows and thereby helping to create a better environment for sustainable growth (Ocampo and Griffith-Jones, 2006).

A first set of measures would include the adoption of financial instruments that reduce currency mismatches and link debt-service obligations to the capacity to pay of developing countries (for instance, through GDP- or commodity-linked bonds). This could be accompanied by public loan guarantee mechanisms with counter-cyclical features issued by the multilateral development banks and export credit agencies. A third area would involve support to developing-country Governments in strengthening regulatory frameworks that provided disincentives to short-term capital inflow volatility and sound domestic financial private and public sector structures.

In addition, multilateral surveillance—primarily by IMF—should remain at the centre of crisis prevention efforts. Enhanced provision of emergency financing at the international level in response to external shocks is considered essential to lowering unnecessary burdens of adjustment and the costs of large reserve balances. For both middle-income and low-income countries, appropriate facilities should include liquidity provision to cover fluctuations in export earnings, particularly those caused by unstable commodity prices and natural disasters. Access to official international liquidity during capital-account crises should be facilitated and made commensurate with the potentially large needs of countries that might surpass normal lending limits based on IMF quotas of members.

Despite recent progress in advancing a market-based approach to the orderly and cost-effective resolution of debt crises (through, for instance, the adoption of collective action clauses in sovereign bond contracts and the Principles for Stable Capital Flows and Fair Debt Restructuring in Emerging Markets), there is no consensus on the role to be played by multilateral institutions. The review of the effectiveness of the instruments of IMF in facilitating crisis resolution, including the "lending into arrears" policy and information dissemination, should help clarify the role the Fund could be expected to play in crisis situations, thus providing an additional instrument for assisting countries in getting back on the road to greater convergence.

Investing in infrastructure and human capital

Part of the observed growth divergence is attributable to gaps in public investment and spending on infrastructure and human development. An adequate level of infrastructure is a necessary condition for the achievement of productivity by firms. By its very nature, infrastructure is characterized by indivisibilities and countries will need to build up a threshold or minimum level of infrastructure (say, a minimum network of roads) to make a difference for economy-wide productivity growth. To reach this threshold, countries will need to sustain substantial public investment levels over prolonged periods of time. Their failure to do so explains partly why Latin America and sub-Saharan Africa have fallen behind the East Asian countries that are characterized by sustained infrastructural investment.

Empirical studies suggest that developing countries could catch up with the developed world if only they had increased levels of human development. The links between growth and human development are complex, however. The evidence presented in chapter I showed that countries with a successful economic growth performance had all had relatively high levels of human development at the beginning of the period when high and sustained growth began. Conversely, however, not all countries with relatively higher levels of human development have managed to achieve high long-term economic growth rates. Human development is a necessary but not a sufficient condition for growth. What this means is that lifting other constraints on economic growth and structural change will be necessary to create opportunities for a better-educated population.

Countries with significant gaps in infrastructure and human development will have to substantially increase the fiscal space for expenditures in these areas. In many countries, much additional space can be obtained by improving the efficiency in public spending in education and health through better targeting to priority areas within the social sectors and by improving the cost-effectiveness of public programmes. Improved financing schemes for infrastructure and the combating of corruption in contracting of infrastructural works could help reduce costs. Even with such gains in efficiency in public spending, however, resources may not be sufficient. Strengthening the tax base will be essential, particularly in countries with low government revenues. For the poorest countries, it is clear that substantial additional resources will be required for the necessary investments. More development aid will be required and will need to be allocated in support of investments in infrastructure and human development.

Counter-cyclical fiscal policies, as discussed above, can also help smooth the way towards maintaining adequate levels of current government spending and public investment and help ensure that spending on education, health and infrastructure is not unduly curtailed during economic downswings.

Increasing aid and its effectiveness

The contribution of ODA to economic growth has been the subject of considerable debate. The analysis in this chapter concludes that the weight of the evidence supports the view that aid has been positive for long-term development. Accordingly, ODA has partly countered the tendencies leading to the income divergence witnessed during the past 40 years. However, since the magnitude of aid transfers has remained limited, the impact of ODA on reducing international income disparities has been weak at best.

This finding provides some support for the revived idea of a big push for developing countries fuelled by aid. Well-targeted programmes supported by aid could put the poorest nations on a path of faster growth. Such an approach assumes not only that enough is known on how to channel such resources efficiently in specific country contexts but also that Governments in the recipient countries have the administrative capacity to manage the resource flows in such a way as to ensure that cumulative income and productivity gains are generated. A consideration of the conditions for improvements in the governance structure—particularly in such areas as transparency in budgetary processes, building a quality civil service and improving social service delivery—thus have to be part of the assessment of additional needs for development assistance. What really works at the local level, however, varies from country to country, hence adding externally defined governance conditionalities to aid and lending flows, which has been a recent practice of donor agencies, may not produce the desired outcomes in terms of better-quality public services.

Notes

1   See, for example, World Bank (1993) on the role of public interventions in financial markets in the "Asian miracle" and United Nations (2005b, chap. I, sect. entitled "Long-term financing") on the role of development banks in providing long-term finance in developing economies.
2   See, for instance, King and Levine (1993) and Prasad and others (2003) for oft-cited studies and FitzGerald (2008) for a critical survey of the literature.
3   The growth of the domestic bond market has also been substantial when expressed as a percentage of GDP, having increased by 13-16 percentage points in Asia, Europe and Latin America. Only for Africa has there been a decline, when expressed in these terms, of 0.5 percentage points.
4   Policy cyclicality is defined as the correlation between the cyclical measure of a specific policy stance and the cyclical measure of GDP growth. The Hedrick-Prescott filter approach is commonly used to isolate the cyclical from the "structural" component of the trends in output growth, fiscal spending, taxation and monetary variables.
5   It is more difficult to find a common measurement for all countries of the monetary policy stance compared with fiscal policy, as some countries target the aggregate money supply, others target the interest rate and still others target the exchange rate.
6   In the economics literature this type of effect is often referred to as a "Dutch disease". For a discussion of why this does not adequately describe the experience with aid flows, see, among others, Gupta, Mishra and Sahay (2003, pp. 21-22); and International Monetary Fund (2005b).

Chapter V
Governance, Institutions and Growth Divergence

This final chapter examines how institutional and governance factors can help account for the divergence in economic growth among countries. As shown in chapter I, a fairly small group of countries—those in Western Europe and its offshoots—had increased their growth rates in the period after 1820 and enjoyed sustained growth and they have remained the richest countries in the world. This was a unique achievement in historical terms. Moreover, the example of Japan appeared to indicate that other countries would "catch up" by enjoying faster rates of growth than those of the first industrialized countries, and would thus achieve comparable standards of living. Yet, as chapter I also showed, this has not happened because most other countries failed to achieve faster rates of growth than those of the developed countries. After 1980, there was a dual divergence, involving lower growth rates of developing countries as a group vis-à-vis the industrialized countries and strikingly different growth experiences among the developing countries themselves.

This chapter argues that the quality of institutions and governance structures matters for the growth of a country and for growth divergence among countries. Ideally, governance promotes the public interest by, inter alia, promoting social cohesion, making the society more fair and stable, guaranteeing an adequate provision of public goods, ensuring the functioning of markets, and encouraging risk-taking behaviour by individuals and businesses leading to innovations. The experience of some successful countries indicates that building higher quality institutions in specific areas where constraints on growth are most stringent (but without necessarily overhauling the entire governance structure) can lift the economy to a higher growth path. Furthermore, they show that these institutional changes are based on country-specific practices and organizations and thus that there is no unique way to achieve the goal. These experiences demonstrate, therefore, the effectiveness of adopting a gradualist or, in a sense, experimental approach (as opposed to a big-bang approach) to institutional reform. Furthermore, they support the argument that successful economic transformations depends on creating institutions that guarantee not just the better functioning of markets, but also social cohesion.

The chapter begins with a consideration of the relationship between institutions and economic divergence. It then examines two dominant theories concerning the importance of governance structures in economic growth/development and their relevance to policymaking in the developing world. The third section analyses several country cases in which transformation of the governance structure successfully lifted binding constraints on growth and led to sustained economic growth thereafter. The following section examines institutional and governance aspects of countries which have experienced long periods of economic decline. The chapter concludes with a few policy recommendations.

INSTITUTIONS, GOVERNANCE AND ECONOMIC GROWTH

It is difficult to pin down exactly what institutional "quality" and what forms of good governance should be pursued in order to support sustained growth processes. Such features appear to be inherently country- and context-specific. Looking at economic history, it appears that building better institutional frameworks in specific areas can be sufficient to lift binding constraints on growth and initiate a sustained growth process. In the seventeenth century, protecting a broad group of trade merchants in the Netherlands and Great Britain from arbitrary interference in the exercise of their property rights and building an effective and extensive legal system to safeguard those rights constituted one of the foundation for the sustained growth process of these countries (see box V.1). More recently, China's reform of rural and agricultural institutions that began in the late 1970s laid the groundwork for its current economic success (see below).

Furthermore, successful economic performance within the context of a market system depends on creating institutions that guarantee not just the better functioning of markets but also social cohesion. Growth that is achieved at the expense of the latter is not likely to be sustainable over the long term, while improvements in the functioning of markets and greater social cohesion are mutually reinforcing.

No rigid distinction can be drawn between "governance" and "institutional" factors. Institutions correspond generally to a somewhat broader concept, as they encompass formal and informal rules and regulations that not only dictate the functions of the State, but also govern those of private entities (see United Nations, 2000, chapter VIII).

While there is some overlap between the two sets of institutional factors—those creating and guaranteeing the proper functioning of markets, and

> Box V.1.
> **The first great divergence and the importance of the Atlantic trade**
>
> The importance of the Atlantic trade to the first great divergence in economic growth can be judged from the fact that those Western European countries that engaged in that trade had faster rates of urbanization and growth in gross domestic product (GDP) than the Western and Eastern European countries that did not (see Acemoglu, Johnson and Robinson, 2005).
>
> The profits from the Atlantic trade, colonialism and slavery were one factor that directly accounted for their faster growth. However, another factor, indirect but equally significant, was the shift in the balance of power within the trading countries themselves away from the narrow royal circle to a broader group of merchants, slave traders and colonial planters who profited from this trade and who demanded—and obtained—significant institutional reforms protecting their property rights. In those two countries where there were already constraints on the monarch, namely, England and the Netherlands, the members of this group were successful in securing added protection for their property rights.
>
> In Britain, where the majority of commercial interests had been alienated as a result of the grants by James II of various monopoly privileges and had supported the invasion of William, the Dutch stadtholder, the outcome of the Glorious Revolution of 1688 was the acceptance by the new monarch of the principles of constitutional monarchy and the supremacy of Parliament, as affirmed in the Bill of Rights of 1689. The Glorious Revolution was a revolution in the sense not of having overturned existing institutions, but rather of having restored those "laws and liberties" that were thought to have been endangered by the absolutist tendencies of the Stuart monarchy.
>
> Similarly, the merchants in the Netherlands constituted a major group pressing for independence from Hapsburg rule and for greater protection for their property rights. Dutch institutions favoured economic growth. Religious tolerance encouraged skilled immigration. Property rights were clear and transfers encouraged by cadastral registers. An efficient legal system and sound banking favoured economic enterprise. High taxes were levied on expenditure, but this encouraged savings, frugality and hard work.
>
> Political institutions in Spain and Portugal, in contrast with the Netherlands and Britain, were more absolutist. As groups allied to the crown were granted monopolies over the Atlantic trade and were the main beneficiaries of transoceanic trade and plunder, they did not press for institutional changes. With institutional atrophy came considerably slower economic growth: by 1700, incomes per head in the Netherlands and Britain had reached $2,110 and $1,405 respectively, as against $854 and $900 in Portugal and Spain (Maddison, 2001, p. 90, table 2-22a).

those strengthening social cohesion—they can be usefully subdivided along the lines suggested by Ocampo (2006). The first group of institutions can be classified as those that: (a) help create markets, by reducing transaction costs and granting and protecting property rights; (b) provide public goods (non-rival and non-excludable goods) as well as those that generate positive externalities, and reduce the supply of the ones that generate negative externalities; (c) help in regulation at the industry level, particularly to avoid non-competitive market practices; and (d) provide for regulation that avoids short-run macroeconomic imbalances, and design structural strategies and policies that create conditions for long-term growth by extending adequate incentives and helping finance innovation, human capital accumulation and investment.

The other set of institutions that make the workings of the market consonant with social cohesion are those that: (a) guarantee adequate provision of the goods and services that a particular society considers to be those that should be provided to all its members; (b) through redistributive policies, change the structure of wealth ownership and income distribution so as to achieve levels of redistribution considered desirable or at least tolerable by society; (c) manage conflicts that can be generated by the functioning of markets; and (d) determine participation in decision-making processes, relating not only to distributive outcomes, but also to the very functioning of markets, as it is not possible to achieve the desired distributive results without influencing how markets function.

These institutions very much reflect the views within society at a particular time as to what is just and fair with regard to the appropriate level of redistribution of wealth and income within society, the appropriate role of the Government in the provision of public goods, and the goods and services that should be guaranteed to citizens. Even among the developed countries, there is considerable difference of opinion as to what the institutions should achieve, with the Scandinavian countries, for instance, using the taxation system to achieve a redistribution of income and benefits greater than that in the United States. Moreover, historical experience has shown that successful societies have made progress on both fronts, namely, in perfecting the workings of the market economy and in achieving social cohesion, and have not just single-mindedly pursued one particular abstract notion such as "the defence of property rights" or the "unfettered workings of the market". As was pointed out by Karl Polanyi in 1944, the pursuit of a pure self-regulating market without any government or societal involvement reflects a dangerous illusion (Polanyi, 1944). Success has generally come from extending the scope for participation and by making continuous changes so that the changing relationships within society are managed in a stable manner.

The resulting institutional arrangements affect the incentives of people to invest, work, learn and conduct research and development. The effectiveness of the system is determined, to a large extent, by its ability to promote growth and rising levels of income and overall well-being and to achieve social cohesion and, in general, to produce a society that is perceived by its citizens as being just and fair (Rawls, 1999). As will be argued below, the success of countries in East Asia and of African high achievers such as Botswana and

Mauritius was largely based on a widespread sharing of the benefits of growth which created a sense, among the population, of justice and fairness.

CHANGES IN GOVERNANCE STRUCTURE AND GROWTH

The shifts in paradigm in development policies over the past decades brought vast changes to the institutional frameworks within which economic policies are conducted. Following the poor growth experience that started around 1980, development policies have predominantly focused on reducing government interference in the economy by freeing domestic markets of price controls, lifting trade barriers, liberalizing financial markets and privatizing State-owned enterprises. Rolling back the State, so the logic went, would lead developing countries to higher and more sustained growth. As noted above, the growth performances since the initiation of these widely implemented reforms have differed among developing countries: some (particularly in East and South Asia) have continued to outperform all others and have been rapidly catching up with the rich countries; others have had poor to very poor growth performance either on a more or less sustained basis (in many parts of sub-Saharan Africa, for example) or as a result of boom-bust cycles (as in Latin America).

Two approaches to unravelling the importance of the governance structure as a determinant of growth and development have emerged in the recent literature: (a) new comparative economics, where the rights of the individual in law (including property rights) and other governance-related factors are considered to be the key factors, with the significance of these key factors often being estimated by cross-country analyses; and (b) the varieties of governance systems approach, which recognizes differences in institutions over time and across space and examines how economic agents respond in different contexts to the specific set of rules and regulations governing markets.

The cross-country analysis approach seeks to establish a positive and causal correlation between the quality of governance and growth. However, as will be argued below, attempts to measure the quality of governance face serious conceptual and empirical challenges. Recognition of to what extent governance systems can vary, on the other hand, gives rise to the possibility of explaining in part the formation of both the regional "convergence clubs" and the divergence patterns examined in chapter I. If a country has developed its own unique governance system, it will be difficult (if not impossible) to transplant the system to another country; however, a unique system may be adopted, with slight modifications, by neighbouring countries with similar socio-economic conditions.

New comparative economics

Cross-country growth regressions have been the favourite tool among some economists for assessing the significance of the governance system in economic development. Income per capita or the growth rate is regressed on several governance quality indicators—such as the rule of law, (anti-) corruption, political stability and government effectiveness. Other non-governance-related variables, such as geographical and historical characteristics, are also used in such regressions.

Cross-country regression analyses typically use the correlation between income per capita and measures of the quality of governance, such as the rule of law, to claim that good governance exerts a positive influence on economic performance. Take, for example, the indicator for the rule of law which measures the extent to which citizens have confidence in and abide by the rules of society and includes their perceptions on the incidence of crime, the effectiveness of the judiciary and the enforceability of contracts (Kaufmann, Kraay and Mastruzzi, 2004, p. 4). It presents a strong association between the quality of governance—the fairness and predictability of rules in this case—and the income level. To capture the multifaceted aspects of the governance system, a composite index consisting of several governance indicators—such as government effectiveness, regulatory quality and anti-corruption measures—can be constructed and applied in a similar cross-country framework. Many studies have also attempted to identify factors influencing the quality of governance, and have used ecological, geographical, geologic and historic data.[1]

The literature has shown that governance has a strong influence on incomes even after the non-economic reasons have been factored out. Developed countries enjoy high living standards because the rule of law prevails, contracts are enforceable, corrupt officials are likely to be caught and punished according to the law, the barriers to entry into a new business are low, monetary and fiscal policies are prudent and appropriate social safety nets are in place to mitigate unforeseeable risks. Above all, when conflicts arise over issues such as the distribution of income or wealth, and the provision of public goods, these countries have a governance system by which the State is able to arrive at a different arrangement through democratic processes. A deficient governance system, on the other hand, discourages productive activities and long-term investment, thus depressing potential growth opportunities. It also discourages investments in human capital through education and thus further reduces the chances for sustained growth. Weak governance has often failed to prevent social unrest or, once it has emerged, to mitigate its adverse impacts on the society.

However, there is a message carried by these findings that is both pessimistic and deterministic (Dixit, 2005, p. 5). The message is pessimistic because it implies that if a country does not possess the right governance system at the start of development then that country is doomed to failure. And, if it is indeed the case that geographical and geologic factors and history have a strong influence on governance or on the income level, and that there is therefore little that can be done, as these factors are predetermined, then the message is also deterministic. The thrust of the theory of the natural resource curse (discussed below)—that a country endowed with abundant natural resources is unfortunate—is a well-known expression of such pessimism and determinism.

However, some developing countries, particularly in East Asia, managed to undergo major economic transformations in tandem with changes in their governance structures, thereby casting doubt upon the pessimistic and deterministic predictions of cross-countries regression studies. Because such studies look only at the outcome of economic and governance development, they are silent on the subject of how better governance systems have been built in these countries. They are thus unable to explain the reason for the success of these countries. Instead, their framework could be better employed to show how improvements in governance systems may lead to better economic performance.

Critiques of governance measures and cross-country analysis

Strictly speaking, the evidence provided by cross-country analyses identifies the correlation between growth and the quality of governance as measured by indicators whose interpretation is largely based on the subjective judgement of researchers or of those who were asked to complete survey questionnaires. Because of the subjective character of these evaluations, the difficulties in finding objective indicators of the quality of governance and the complex nature of governance itself, studies linking economic performance to the governance structure are subject to severe criticisms. Moreover, when aid allocation to developing countries is decided on the basis of such subjective, clouded measures, it may not produce the intended outcomes.

The first critique is based on the fact there is a two-way relationship between economic performance and the governance system: economic performance and the quality of governance exert an influence upon each other and thus are determined jointly. This being the case, the results of cross-country regression analyses are biased.[2] Neither governance nor its quality is directly observable. People's perception of the quality of governance is strongly influenced by the economic performance of a country; when a country faces an economic or financial crisis, people are likely to perceive the quality of the country's governance as deteriorating. The rule-of-law indicator widely used in the literature can again be taken as an example. After Argentina had abandoned its currency board in January 2002, the value of this indicator assigned to the country sharply declined from the level comparable to that for a typical middle-income country, such as Egypt or Turkey in 2000, to one for a low-income country, such as Bangladesh or Guinea in 2002.[3] Yet, it is not conceivable that a country could lose the effectiveness of its judiciary to such an extent within only two years. What was being estimated, in fact, was not the quality of the rule of law itself, but the perceived quality of the rule of law, which in turn had been largely influenced by the vicissitudes of economic performance.[4].

The second critique focuses on the usefulness of the conclusions drawn from such analyses for actual policymaking. A technique called the "instrumental variable" estimation is a common method used to clarify the issue of causality with respect to governance quality (or perceived quality) and economic performance. Some of the instruments that have been found to be useful are the colonial history of countries (see, for example, Acemoglu, Johnson and Robinson, 2001), geography (see, for example, Gallup, Sachs and Mellinger, 1998) and natural resources (see Sachs and Warner, 1995). While they are technically appropriate, they do not provide insights that are very useful for policymaking.

The history-based approach, for example, argues that those parts of the world where European colonizers confronted great health hazards—and thus high settler mortality rates—were less likely to build a European-based governance system, including the protection of property rights against arbitrary interference (measured in these studies by investors' perceptions with regard to the risk of expropriation by the State), and more likely to put in place institutions designed to plunder the area's resources in the shortest period of time. The prime example of the kind of "extractive State" characterized by such institutions is probably the tragically misnamed Congo Free State under King Leopold II of Belgium (Ascherson, 1963; Hochschild, 1999). Thus, settlers' mortality rates centuries ago are used to identify which countries acquired "high-quality" governance and to determine to what extent the rates help predict today's income levels. Countries in Northern America, Australia and New Zealand, where the mortality rates were low, enjoyed high income per capita, while European colonizers experienced higher mortality rates in much of Africa and, to a lesser extent, Latin America and the Caribbean, and so were deterred from building high-quality governance structures which over time would have enabled the countries to achieve high incomes per capita.

However, this result should not be interpreted as meaning that colonialism—as captured by settlers' mortality rates—was the root cause of the great divergence of economic performances. The divergence in the past two or three centuries among countries that were never colonized has been as great as among colonized countries. The former group includes Afghanistan, Ethiopia, Japan, Thailand and Turkey. The mortality rates proved to be capable of capturing the forces underlying economic divergence, but they do not provide a convincing explanation. Finding an appropriate instrument to measure the quality of governance at the present time is thus a different matter from providing an adequate explanation for economic divergence. The geography- and natural resource-based approaches employ similar lines of analysis, using ecologic or geologic variables.

The third criticism of cross-country regression studies is that the measures of governance and its quality used in these studies does not correspond to what governance is thought to be. Governance is supposed to constitute one of the more durable elements of any economic system but, as argued previously, Argentina's rule-of-law indicator before and after the collapse of the currency board showed a sharp change. Glaeser and others (2004) demonstrate that this lack of stability is exhibited by most measures of institutional quality used in the literature—and that those measures that exhibit more stable features show no significant relation with economic performance. These experts, along with others, question the relevance of the governance indices, arguing instead that human capital is the basic determinant of economic development and indeed of institutional quality and that the settlers brought not so much their institutions as they themselves, with their existing educational and technical attainments and their desire to improve through further learning. In this respect, it has been noted that, of all the New World colonies, Canada and the United States of America, were the ones to put the most emphasis on education and that, by 1800, the latter had probably the most literate population in the world (Sokoloff and Engerman, 2000).

The final critique focuses on the use of the outcomes of such cross-country analysis for actual aid allocation by donor countries and international financial institutions (Herman, 2005). Because of the apparent high correlation between the quality of governance and growth, donors maintain that if aid-recipient countries "get their governance right", they will have created an environment that is conducive for development. Recipients should be able as a result to use the aid disbursed more effectively and efficiently.

There is indeed considerable debate on the use of governance-based conditionality. As examined above, the indicators currently used to measure the institutional quality or governance of the recipient country should claim to be no more than "windows into a partial and clouded picture of development" (Herman, 2005, p. 282). One should be modest when assessing the extent to which such measures and analysis can effectively capture the quality of governance and its significance in development. This is especially important if such indicators are considered comparable across countries and, in this sense, to be global measures of governance. Recent analyses by the World Bank seem to agree with this evaluation and claim that these indicators at best signal longer-run trends (World Bank and International Monetary Fund, 2006, p. 14).

Varieties of governance structures

Another approach to examining the linkage between governance and economic performance is to analyse the functioning of economic systems on a country-by-country basis. The distinctive nature of this approach lies in its explicit acceptance of the fact that countries have developed their own particular institutional structures within which government, firms and households achieve their individual or societal goals. Existing governance structures are the cumulative result of the interaction with one another of many agents over long periods of time during which the existing structure is continuously being reshaped (Young, 1998).

The upshot is that there is no one set of governance elements that are the "best" for all countries and for all times.[5] Each country is required to find, by trial and error, its own governance system—the one that works best in its existing context. This approach also implies that there will be multiple governance structures that are able to tackle the problems that constitute barriers to growth (Haggard, 2004). Because the functioning of one governance element depends on other elements of the governance system or non-governance factors—such as "common sense", social norms, intra-company labour relations and even culture—a governance system cannot be easily transplanted from one country to another.

The fact that there exists an interdependency—in the form of what are often called complementarities—among governance elements also casts some doubt on the effectiveness of policy recommendations urging the improvement of only those governance capacities that are necessary for ensuring the efficiency of markets. These recommendations often assume that if a Government ensures market efficiency by enforcing property rights and the rule of law, reducing corruption and committing itself not to expropriate, private sector activities will then drive development. Market functioning, however, needs to be complemented by the governance capacities of the State in order to ensure productivity growth[6] and to make the workings of the market consonant with social cohesion.

Significant complementarities also exist across different areas of policy reforms and they help create either a vicious or a virtuous circle. The presence of suboptimal governance makes it difficult for a Government to initiate a change without creating complementary changes in other governance elements. The lack of human and financial capacities in the Governments of many developing countries always constitutes a barrier to undertaking such multifaceted reforms or, if they do manage to be initiated, prevents relevant efforts from being sustained for the sufficiently long period of time required for those reforms to become fully effective. The mere introduction of a market-enhancing institution that should reduce transaction costs does not ignite economic activity unless there is also a functioning legal system that can be trusted with enforcement. Similarly, coordinating trade and industrial polices often becomes a challenge for developing countries (see the discussion in chapter III).

The complementarities existing among various governance elements seem to explain at least some of the dynamics of the divergence patterns and of the emergence of regional convergence clubs identified in chapter I. These can create a virtuous circle once a Government establishes its credibility with its citizens in respect of planning and implementing reforms. By the same token, the Government can gain credibility only if the promise that its citizens will share in the benefits of growth is kept over a considerable period of time. This shared growth, which fostered social cohesion, was one of the results of the policies pursued in East Asia. While not all the countries in the region offered equal access to the political system to all members of their population, the fact that leaders could build on a fair amount of social cohesion, based on shared values and relatively low economic inequality, established the legitimacy of their reform policies. The development success of Botswana can also be understood in this framework: the country created a shared-growth path through its traditional consensus-building democratic process.

Countries with Successful Governance Transformations

Some developing countries achieved sustained growth over the past three to four decades and narrowed the income gap existing between them and developed countries. Their success in governance transformation is illuminating in two respects. First, it demonstrated the importance of addressing the binding constraints on growth being faced and of creating a sense of priority in governance transformation. The success of such transformation therefore does not depend on the comprehensiveness of reforms in governance structure. Rather, a step-by-step, or gradual approach to removing such constraints can be very effective. Second, their experiences demonstrated that when a governance reform (such as a trade reform) induces large shifts of income from one group to another, it was important to make the workings of the market consonant with social cohesion. These success stories show the importance of addressing the issues of complementarity not only between economic reforms, but also between economic and social management.

The cases of land reform and trade and financial reforms analysed below, and the gradual reform process in China, highlight these points. They show that step-by-step changes to governance structures can be sufficient to trigger growth. At the same time, the experiences examined demonstrate that governance changes can take different forms across countries. This is particularly the case for land reforms in Asia. China's growth success is shown to have been based on gradualist governance reform and to have been achieved through a process quite different from any that might have been developed according to the policy prescriptions emanating from the Washington Consensus.

Land reforms

For countries with the majority of their population engaged in subsistence farming, increasing productivity in the agricultural sector is critical to initiating sustained long-term growth. Higher agricultural productivity not only leads to lower food prices, but also improves the nutrition of the population (thus increasing labour productivity in the economy as a whole) and creates demands for manufactured goods and services that contribute to the development of non-agricultural sectors.

In many contexts, low agricultural productivity constitutes a major binding constraint on sustained growth. Land reform is an effective means of easing this constraint by transferring ownership to farmers who operate the land or, more generally, by securing for farmers the right to share an appropriate return from their activity on the land. The Republic of Korea and Taiwan Province of China, two of the first-tier newly industrialized economies, implemented the redistribution of land from landlords to smallholders or tenants and secured the private property rights of landholding (United Nations, 2000, chapter V).

Such outright transfers of ownership do not represent the only way to undertake land reform. In fact, they were possible and successful only in the context of the socio-economic conditions prevailing in these economies at that time. The Governments of both economies distributed land previously owned by Japanese persons or companies to farmers who were tenants on the land. Large inflows of migrants from the mainland to Taiwan Province of China further necessitated comprehensive land reform.

When outright transfers of landownership are not feasible for political or socio-economic reasons, higher agricultural productivity can be achieved by merely enforcing tenancy law or by guaranteeing a return to farmers' activities on the land. In fact, the reforms of China, India and Viet Nam did not involve the full-fledged transfer of ownership to farmers. Different forms of governance changes can ease one of the major constraints on the sustained growth process of many low-income developing countries—low agricultural productivity.

In 1978, China initiated one of many major reforms, the household responsibility system, under which households were provided with use rights to collectively owned land under long-term leases (initially 5 years, but later extended to 30 years). In exchange, farmers were obliged to supply a pre-fixed share of output to the collectives' production quotas, but could sell the remaining output on the free market or to the Government at negotiated prices.[7] The reform was complemented by the relaxation of restrictions on private market transactions in rural areas and on non-agricultural activities by farmers.

In Viet Nam, collective farming was replaced with family farming during the period of "doi moi" (the policy of renovation) in the 1980s. Under the new system, farmers were allowed to sign contracts with the Government on parcels of land for up to 15 years—in effect, they leased the land—and were given the freedom to sell their products as they wished. As in the case of China, other reforms proceeded at the same time, including the introduction of market-based transactions in agricultural and non-agricultural products and liberalization of trade-related activities and foreign direct investment (FDI).

In the case of India, on the other hand, effective land reform involved only stricter enforcement of the existing tenancy law. The country had enacted a land-reform act in 1955 but did not enforce the law largely because of the lack of administrative and legal resources. During the 1970s, however, the State of West Bengal launched a new programme, called Operation Barga, which was designed to enforce tenancy laws that regulated rents and accorded security of tenure to sharecroppers (Banerjee, Gertler and Ghatak, 2002).

The Land Reforms Act of 1955 and its successive amendments have guaranteed to sharecroppers permanent and inheritable incumbency rights to land that is registered, as long as they pay the legally stipulated share. Because of loopholes in the law and little administrative support for poor and often illiterate sharecroppers, very few of them had actually registered with the State. Under the Operation Barga project, those sharecroppers were encouraged to register with the Department of Land Revenue and supported by the State in doing so. The State would entitle them, when registered, to permanent and inheritable tenure on the land they sharecropped as long as they paid the landlord at least 25 per cent of output as rent. Owing to the success of Operation Barga, 65 cent of share tenants in the State had been registered by 1993, as compared with 15 per cent before the project began.[8]

As a result, the State of West Bengal had experienced a significant jump in the growth rate of production of rice, its major food crop, from 1.8 per cent during the period 1960–1980 to 4.7 per cent during the period 1977-1994 (Raychaudhuri, 2004). This growth experience is in fact comparable with that of Taiwan Province of China whose agricultural production after land reform had grown by about 4.2 per cent per year during the 1950s and 1960s (United Nations, 2000, chapter V). Between 1973 and 1999, for which comparable data are available, the rural poverty rate—defined as the proportion of people in rural areas below the poverty line of 49 rupees per capita per month in 1973-1974 prices—fell from 73.2 to 31.7 per cent.

What was common to these reforms was a limited transfer of property rights to tenants (as opposed to a full transfer of landownership, as in the cases of the Republic of Korea and Taiwan Province of China) as a means of easing the constraint on agricultural productivity. The transfer gave the farmer the right to claim a certain share of output and long-term (or permanent) use rights. Despite the limited transfer of rights, there were significant increases in agricultural output, which led to economy-wide sustained growth some years later. The land reforms—constituting a change in the governance system—clearly influenced the incentives of farmers to work harder, to improve the soil and to invest in new equipment, new seeds and new techniques.

What was not common, though, was the design of the policies adopted by these Governments. Reform policies were based on the prevailing socio-economic systems in each economy. Several forms of governance restructuring can therefore lead to the same outcome—in this case, a rise in agricultural productivity.[9]

Trade-policy reforms

Difficulties in undertaking a trade policy reform lie in the fact that it constitutes only a small part of an economy-wide reform package. As argued in chapter III, trade reform can be complemented by production sector policies to promote the emergence of new economic activities. By the same token, a shrinking tax base, as a result of lower tariffs, should be complemented either by increasing the existing taxes rates, or by creating new tax bases (Aizenman and Jinjarak, 2006). Furthermore, conflict management institutions, including social insurance or a safety net, should be in place to shelter at least temporarily those who are affected adversely by the new trade regime. At the same time, new institutions or rules for macroeconomic stability have to be established to stave off external shocks once the economy becomes more exposed to developments in the global economy.

Countries that successfully integrated trade policy reforms into their overall development strategies adopted gradual or dual-track approaches, which shielded protected sectors from competition during a period of time, and/or included some active production sector policies. While the scope for undertaking such production sector policies has increasingly been limited (see chapter III), the well-known successes of China, Mauritius and East Asian countries point to the necessity of allotting some policy space to developing countries for finding new activities through which to take advantage of a more liberalized trade regime.

The trade reform in Mauritius had been launched in 1970 with the creation of free trade in an export processing zone (EPZ). Until the mid-1980s, the domestic sector outside the EPZ was highly protected in order to maintain social cohesion because of the fragile social and ethnic fabric of the country. The EPZ provided a means to expand opportunities for external trade and employment creation, especially for women, without the country's running the risk of igniting social unrest (United Nations, 2000, chapter VIII). The country thus established a system for maintaining social cohesion and a shared growth pattern.

The success of Mauritius was not repeated in sub-Saharan African countries. Although the reasons for this appear to be numerous (Subramanian and Roy, 2001), two governance-related factors are especially relevant in this context. First, macroeconomic adjustment and stabilization were pursued consistently in Mauritius under three different democratically elected Governments with divergent political ideologies; and within the context of the democratic political system, the transparent decision-making process enabled economic problems to emerge and be tackled early. Second, the competent and (equally important) well-paid civil service managed to minimize rent-seeking.[10] Export processing zones have failed in many other countries in the region because their governance systems were not able to combat rent-seeking and the other types of inefficiencies that need to be controlled by selective interventions.[11]

Economies in East Asia, on the other hand, employed the network of interactions between the bureaucracy and segments of the public sector to achieve export-led growth. As in the case of Japan, which provided the "model" of export-led growth to neighbouring countries, the interaction was a means to overcome the lack of information flows about market conditions—prices, quantities produced and sold, bottlenecks in production and shortages of input materials—and to manage the large differences in income being generated by the various industries. This interaction greatly reduced the chances of "coordination failure" and contributed to these economies' setting appropriate national priorities for the development of new sectors, which figured prominently in their development strategies. The underdevelopment of the domestic financial market also necessitated direct involvement of the Government in channelling finance to the priority industries.

Coordination efforts at the central government level on the allocation of goods, services and finance ensured that the benefits of the success were shared among the population. Such efforts also contributed to building up a consistent set of trade and industrial policies in East Asia. Heavy market interventions by the Governments may have distorted resource allocation and thus created "static" inefficiency in markets, but there is little dispute that those interventions accelerated the pace of development. In other words, they turned out to be efficient in a dynamic sense. As the shared-growth path was seen to be successful, this reinforced the credibility of the Governments' policies.

At a more practical level, what is common among these examples are the proper recognition by the economies concerned of the constraints that they faced and the creativity they employed to remove or soften them (Hausmann, Rodrik and Velasco, 2005). The success of these countries lies in the fact that they practised the step-by-step approach to undertaking complementary policies, according to constantly evolving domestic and external situations. In fact, they were among the first developing countries, between the mid-1960s and the early 1970s, to reorient their policies towards exports and away from import substitution in order to deal with the lack of domestic demand and to force companies to be competitive in global markets. Export orientation was not though, however, as inconsistent with active industrial policies and gradual reduction of protection of domestic markets. As noted in chapter III, the rules of the General Agreement on Tariffs and Trade (GATT) prevailing at that time allowed countries more freedom than would have been available under the current World Trade Organization rules to achieve this policy mix.

The gradualist approach: China

China can be taken as an example of successful ongoing institutional change. The Chinese economy has been growing at a rapid pace since the initiation of its reform policies in the late 1970s. Its economic achievement has lifted tens of millions of people out of abject poverty in the last two decades. The sustained growth of the Chinese economy has confounded the pessimists and disproved much conventional wisdom, particularly that the major institutions of the market economy must be in place before any major reforms can be expected to lead to positive results. Instead, the gradualist approach China adopted in its reforms presents a sharp contrast with what occurred in many transition economies. The gradual reform process endowed the economy with great resilience which it needed in order to confront an unfavourable world economic environment or the constraints arising from a rigid bureaucracy and the absence of a sound market infrastructure.

As described by Deng Xiaoping, Chinese economic reform has been a process of "crossing the river by groping for the stepping stones" and one where no stereotypic reform package was adopted in advance. Designed with a pragmatic vision, institutional reform has been immune to ideological considerations and economic development has been laid down as the ultimate goal (Qian and Wu, 2000; Qian, 2003).

The institutional reform process has been guided in the general direction of improving overall economic efficiency by providing individuals with incentives, by fostering competition among different categories of market players and by ensuring that the resulting economic affluence is shared by a growing number of recipients. This in turn has elicited broader support for the reform process. The reform experiments have ranged from providing incentives to the agricultural sector and encouraging the formation of township-village enterprises to reforming the fiscal sector and, more recently, State-owned enterprises and the banking sector. In general, China's transition to a market economy has been a gradual process of economic reform which can be characterized as having taken place in three stages.

In the first stage, which spanned the period from 1978 to 1993, reform had been carried out incrementally to improve incentives and to expand the scope of the market for resource allocation. The second stage began in 1994 at which time the Chinese Government decided to set the eventual establishment of a modern market system as the goal of reform. The most recent stage has put a stronger emphasis on the need to deal with the growing regional and income disparities generated by the accelerated growth process.

The first stage had been characterized by successful agricultural reform and the dual-track price-setting scheme described above. Implementing the reform was relatively easy, as most peasants, benefiting greatly, embraced the scheme. Some enterprises and bureaucrats also enjoyed its benefits. Nevertheless, the dual-track price-setting scheme, like any scheme involving two prices for the same product, nurtured a degree of corruption, especially in relation to the allocation of key productive materials, and created much resentment among the general public.

In the second stage, the task of reform had been more challenging, as it would impinge upon the fundamentals of the central planning system. The dual-track price-setting scheme was phased out, with market forces coming into full play with respect to allocation of resources, and the administrative power of various key sectoral departments was dismantled. From 1994 to 2000, several radical reforms were implemented, namely, the unification of official and swap exchange rates, the reform of taxation and fiscal systems, the full recognition of the functions of the central bank in maintaining price stability and promoting economic growth, the experimental privatization of small-scale State-owned enterprises and the establishment of a social safety net.

The third stage has put a stronger emphasis on the need to spread the benefits of economic growth more equitably among all social groups and all regions of the country. The country's Gini coefficient—a measure of income equality with zero signifying greatest equitability and 1 greatest inequality—has been on the rise in recent decades and is currently expected to increase further in the next decade and a half (World Bank, 2003). Regional income disparities, particularly between urban and rural areas, are a major cause of this rising inequality. Owing to the success of the first-stage reform, rural incomes had increased to 55 per cent of those of urban areas by 1984, but declined to a level of about 40 per cent in the 1990s. To address these inequalities, the Government announced in 2006 its plans for implementing four types of reforms that should raise rural incomes: a reform of rural taxes and administrative fees; water conservation projects and technological support to enhance agricultural productivity; increases in public investments in education and other social infrastructure for the rural population; and political reforms providing self-governance to villagers.

In addition to the question how to distribute benefits from economic growth, other challenges remain, in particular the reform of the large State-owned enterprises. Currently, the greatest success in the reform process has been limited to the privatization of small State-owned enterprises in the mid-1990s which resulted in the layoff of redundant employees. The large-scale State-owned enterprises still pose a major problem, particularly as they threaten the quality of the portfolio of large State-owned commercial banks and impose a potentially large fiscal burden on the State. The future of large State-owned enterprises will ultimately depend on the improvement of corporate governance, which will first entail the severance of the government-business relationship and the establishment of a free and competitive enterprise system. Furthermore, China's entry into the World Trade Organization commits it to fully observing the rules of a market economy, including the protection of intellectual property rights, which will entail the need to undertake further reforms.

China's experience has shown that it is not indispensable to set up the institutions regarded by some analysts as "best practice" in order to initiate a process of reform. Even with institutions that these same analysts might consider "imperfect", a reform package that conforms to the existing economic and political realities can still achieve a favourable outcome. China's experience underlines the importance of viewing institutional reform as a process, rather than as a one-off event, and of ensuring progress both in the reform effort and in economic development.

China's experiences illustrate the broader lesson for all countries that there are different types of obstacles to growth and equally many ways to remove (or minimize) such obstacles. Countries that achieved success had been likely to initiate their reform processes with a careful evaluation of the existing obstacles and then remove them step by step. As the above analysis of the varieties of governance systems suggest, a country's success cannot be directly exported to other countries. Policymakers can combine their knowledge of their own countries with the lessons learned from other countries that had successful institutional reforms in order to start their own reform processes. This approach differs significantly from the application of the across-the-board reform packages that was recommended in the past.[12]

The cases examined should provide a message of some optimism, as their experiences make clear that it is not necessary to have all the required elements of good governance in place before sustained growth can be initiated. Countries need not first go through a long process of institutional reform before growth results may become visible. The reforms need not even be comprehensive, but they do need to be able to unlock economic potential previously blocked by inadequate rules and regulations.

Sources of Growth Failures

Growth failures in the past 50 years: an overview

While other chapters in this publication have analysed some of the macroeconomic and structural characteristics of economies that can account for their slow growth, the emphasis in the present section will be on the role of governance and institutions in explaining growth failures. To illustrate the extent of the failure of societies to grow, table V.1 gives data for those countries that saw a long-term slide in living standards, as measured by a fall in real income per head over seven consecutive years or more.

The table shows that countries that suffered from such growth failures were at all levels of development, some of them being oil producers with relatively high levels of income. Many fuel- and mineral-rich countries had failed to turn this wealth into assets, including human capital, that would have provided a supplementary or alternative long-term source of growth. However, on the whole, countries that faced growth failures tended to be poor, to be located in certain regions of the world (in particular sub-Saharan Africa and Latin America), to be conflict-ridden and/or to be dependent on primary commodity exports.[13] Growth collapses also occurred elsewhere, but those with more diversified economies did not usually end up having become full-fledged growth failures (see the discussion in chapters I and III). It should be noted in this respect that several economies with a heavy dependence on commodities can still be highly diversified and less liable to a growth collapse. Examples are Brazil, Chile, Indonesia and Malaysia which have important mineral as well as agricultural sectors.

The growth collapses in many countries that are highly dependent on commodities have given rise to a belief in the "natural resource curse", according to which countries that are heavily reliant on resources are likely to grow more slowly than other countries. Several reasons have been advanced for this phenomenon—the deterioration in the terms of trade of commodities as against manufactures; the volatility of commodity prices which makes investment planning difficult and discourages investment because of the risk and sunk costs; the Dutch disease, whereby a boom in a resource sector renders other industries unprofitable; and rent-seeking, whereby economic agents pursue short-term objectives to extract monopoly profits, rather than attempt to invest in the long-term future of the industry. Such rent-seeking is made easier in cases where the commodity is a "point resource", that is to say, one (like a mine or oil well) located in a specific area, rather than a "diffuse resource" (like wheat), which is one produced over a large area.

Table V.1.
Countries with at least seven consecutive years of decline in real per capita income, 1950-2003

	Real GDP per capita[a]				
	Period of decline	Initial	Final	Percentage decline	Number of years of negative growth[b]
Africa					
Cameroon	1986-1994	1,695	978	42.3%	11
Côte d'Ivoire	1985-1994	1,798	1,214	32.5%	23
Democratic Republic of Congo	1974-1983	842	587	30.3%	32
	1986-2001	598	202	66.2%	
Djibouti	1984-1998	1,802	1,092	39.4%	29
Kenya	1997-2003	1,064	998	6.2%	21
Liberia	1979-1989	1,230	889	27.7%	26
Lybian Arab Jamahiriya	1979-1995	7,565	2,321	69.3%	25
Madagascar	1971-1978	1,246	1,007	19.2%	26
	1979-1988	1,076	784	27.1%	
Namibia	1981-1988	4,159	3,478	16.4%	14
Sao Tome and Principe	1985-2000	1,486	1,226	17.5%	25
United Republic of Tanzania	1976-1985	620	519	16.3%	24
Uganda	1971-1980	871	577	33.8%	21
Latin America and Caribbean					
Bolivia	1978-1986	2,715	2,074	23.6%	17
Cuba	1957-1965	2,406	1,988	17.4%	20
Haiti	1980-1994	1,304	753	42.3%	29
Jamaica	1973-1980	4,130	3,121	24.4%	17
Nicaragua	1983-1993	2,169	1,308	39.7%	22
Paraguay	1996-2002	3,282	2,919	11.1%	18
Venezuela	1977-1985	11,251	8,521	24.3%	23
Western Asia					
Iraq	1979-1986	6,756	3,759	44.4%	22
Qatar	1980-1991	29,552	6,467	78.1%	30
Saudi Arabia	1992-1999	9,498	7,502	21.0%	20
United Arab Emirates	1981-1988	25,894	11,189	56.8%	17
Afghanistan	1987-1994	726	426	41.3%	25
Korea, Democratic Republic of	1991-1997	2,841	1,170	58.8%	22

Source: UN/DESA, based on Maddison (2001) and UN Statistical database.
[a] Measured in 1990 Geary-Khamis dollars.
[b] Meaning the total number of years in which income per head was less than in the previous years, which therefore do not necessarily represent a period of uninterrupted decline.

As the recent surge in demand for commodities, in particular to fuel China's economic expansion, could have major benefits for commodity producers (see chapter I), it is particularly important to judge whether the natural resource curse can be avoided by appropriate policies and institutional changes, enabling natural resource-rich countries to attain fast and sustainable growth. That the curse could be avoided was the opinion of the report of the Commission for Africa (2005).

Slow growth is, however, not an unavoidable outcome for developing countries with abundant natural resources. The experiences of Botswana and South Africa show that, when the right set of policies is in place, natural resources can be a source of prosperity, not necessarily a 'curse'. Other resource-rich countries in Africa could achieve similar success if they pursue prudent management of the resource flows from their wealth The experiences of South Asian and Latin American countries suggest that, given the right set of policies, commodity-dependent African countries have, like them, the potential to diversify and upgrade their agriculture to achieve rapid growth. One possibility for these countries is to move towards commodity-based export-oriented industrialization (as in the case of Indonesia or Malaysia) or diversify within the primary sector itself (such as in Chile, Costa Rica or Colombia).

In the nineteenth century, resource-rich countries such as the United States and Australia, as well as the Scandinavian countries, were also able to achieve sustained growth and large increases in living standards.

Institutional aspects of natural resource abundance

One of the most important ways to avert the realization of the natural resource curse is to prevent rent-seeking behaviour, by ensuring that the resources in question are produced by efficient and reputable operators and turned into wealth that accrues both to the producers and to the Government in the form of taxes and (if the Government has a stake in the operations) of dividends. Furthermore, the revenues accruing to the Government should be monitored in a transparent fashion and used wisely in the country's long-run interest. In this connection, the Extractive Industries Transparency Initiative and the "Publish What You Pay" campaign are designed to inform debate and to lead to a better distribution of the wealth generated by the mineral industry in such a way as to foster social cohesion and avoid possible conflicts.

Under efficient producers, exploitation of a natural resource can be highly profitable, yielding a large difference between its price and the cost of production (see United Nations Conference on Trade and Development,

2005a, pp. 124-126). It is therefore in the Government's interest to establish mutually beneficial relationships with commercially-driven enterprises that can exploit the country's resources profitably and efficiently. This can be a painstaking and difficult process, often requiring considerable administrative capabilities on the part of the Government, but the results can be highly beneficial to both parties, as attested by the relationship between De Beers and the Government of Botswana.

Many countries prefer to maintain a strong presence of State-owned enterprises, sometimes associated or coexisting with private firms, in the exploitation of their mineral or oil and gas resources. These include countries that are widely believed to have highly liberalized economies, such as Chile, where CODELCO, the highly efficient State-owned copper company and a world leader, coexists with private sector copper enterprises. It is then crucial to establish institutional rules that allow these firms to operate with high technical standards and administrative independence.

In other commodity industries, particularly agriculture, the need is not so much to attract new entrants as to provide sufficient incentives and support to existing producers. Much of the failure of poor countries to grow, especially in Africa, was due to the direction of insufficient attention to the development of their agricultural resources (Collier and Gunning, 1999). Often it was thought that industrialization could be facilitated by using the funds available from the agricultural marketing boards that had survived independence and whose proceeds were not ploughed back into increased earnings for farmers or the improvement of the agricultural sector, particularly through research and development. To pay insufficient attention to agriculture was to ignore the fact that the industrialization of many of the existing developed countries and of the earlier globalizers (examined above) had been possible only because of their firm agricultural base.

Even with the most efficient producers' being engaged in developing a country's natural resources and being provided with the appropriate incentives for doing so, there is one feature of mineral and agricultural commodity price markets alike that can hardly be eliminated: their extreme volatility, with price variations of over 30 per cent a year. Inasmuch as the mineral industry, especially mineral fuels, is highly capital-intensive, relying on immovable assets for its profitability and employing relatively few people, it can provide the bulk of a nation's taxable income. Whereas in a diversified economy the mineral industry will supply only a relatively small part of government revenues, in some of the developing countries over 50 to as much as 90 per cent of government revenue can come from extractive industries (United Nations Conference on Trade and Development, 2005a, table 3.5).

With government and export revenues highly reliant on the proceeds from one industry, effective planning of government expenditures becomes a key to mitigating the consequences of fluctuations, as described in chapter IV. Moreover, stabilization funds can be used to smooth government revenue flows: funds can accumulate during the boom periods to be drawn down to support government programmes during the period of low prices. However, the pursuit of such counter-cyclical policies is difficult in poor countries with limited administrative abilities. Indeed, the success of stabilization funds requires strong governance and institutional arrangements (Davis and Tilton, 2005, p. 238). Such funds have proved successful in a country like Botswana (see chapter IV) which generally is considered to have well-functioning institutions and where the authorities are able to set aside funds during boom years. In countries with weak institutions, the tendency will be to spend the revenues coming in from a boom and to borrow to maintain expenditures after the boom has ended, often resulting in debts that are difficult to repay (for a fuller discussion of counter-cyclical policies, see chapter IV).

Governance, civil strife and conflict management

The failure of institutions to function properly and to resolve the many internal non-violent conflicts to which all societies are subject is most evident in those countries where conflict has erupted into civil war. In this context, the institutions that failed were more those promoting social cohesion than the ones established for the purpose of guaranteeing the functioning of markets.

After the Second World War and its aftermath, the peak in the number of armed conflicts was reached in 1991-1992, after which there has been a decline, with many long-running conflicts coming to an end. However, since the end of the cold war in 1989, there have been 118 conflicts in 80 locations, and so conflict continues to exert a major influence on country and regional economic performance (Murshed, 2008). Most wars are now internal conflicts taking place in poor countries. These conflicts, which can extend over long periods of time, have heavy immediate and long-term economic costs. For instance, during a war, the growth rate is typically reduced by about 2 per cent. Losses can continue after the war, as people continue to move their money out of the country owing to perceived high risks of future conflict (Collier, 2006, p. 10). Conflict is also recurrent: after the end of a war, about half of the conflicts are renewed during the following five years. During a conflict, much of the infrastructure, including roads, railways, schools, hospitals and power plants, is destroyed, either through direct military action or through lack of maintenance. The number of lives lost during a conflict is typically much greater than the number of direct military casualties and includes lives cut short because of famine or the failure to deliver medical services. Moreover, warfare destroys social capital, which is much harder to rebuild than physical capital. Warfare also diverts efforts from productive economic activity to rent-seeking, violence and illegal activity, including illicit drugs, which have been used to help finance some conflicts. Normal economic activity also breaks down during a conflict, and often the situation is not even secure enough to permit planting for the next year's harvest. The educated class will leave their homeland and many children will not go to school. Indeed, the subsequent further impoverishment of the country due to conflict helps breed ready recruits, even among children, for those benefiting from the conflict, the so-called conflict entrepreneurs.

In addition, warfare in one country inevitably has repercussions on other countries, through the displacement of refugees, through the destruction of infrastructure needed for domestic production and for export (for example, during the conflict in Angola, the Benguela railway which had served the mining industry of Central Africa, was closed) and through the deterring of domestic and foreign investors who judge the overall climate of a region to be unfavourable for making commitments. These regional effects will cause growth rates to converge downward. All regions, including Europe, have witnessed conflicts, but recently the regional dimension is perhaps most apparent in Africa, which until recently has seen declining growth rates and a lack of interest by foreign investors, as attested by the continent's small share in global FDI flows and by the fact that about 40 per cent of African savings are kept outside the continent, as compared with just 6 per cent for East Asia and 3 per cent for South Asia (Commission for Africa, 2005, p. 26). For these reasons, the full economic effects of civil wars are difficult to assess, but can hardly be overestimated (Murshed, 2002, p. 388).

One measure of the results of conflict—and also of domestic human rights violations—is the number of internally displaced persons. In December 2005, it was estimated that the global total of such persons amounted to 23.7 million (Norwegian Refugee Council, 2006). Some 50 countries across Africa, the Americas, Asia, Europe and the Middle East were affected by conflict-induced internal displacement in 2005. The human suffering caused by such displacement is incalculable as are the pure economic losses (arising from the fact that the victims are not as gainfully employed as they would be if they were able to enjoy stable, secure and settled lives).

In a sample of 17 countries that had been subject to internal conflict, those with a manufacturing or diffuse commodity base tended to maintain positive growth over time, while those with point source resources, such as alluvial diamonds or timber, tended to show a decline in output (Murshed, 2008). Declines in output, leading to increases in poverty, heighten the inequalities within society, breed grievances and enhance horizontal inequality. As horizontal inequalities within society have been found to constitute a fertile breeding ground for conflicts, there is a linkage among growth failures, conflict and resources. This linkage can be broken by governance and institutional arrangements that help turn natural resource endowments into a source of long-term growth.

The steady building of institutions for conflict management strengthens what may be described as the social contract, will serve to diminish the risk of conflict and will help pave the way towards more sustained growth. Violent conflict is unlikely to take hold if a country has a framework of widely agreed rules, both formal and informal, that govern the allocation of resources, including resource rents, and the peaceful settlement of grievances. Such a viable social contract can be sufficient to restrain, if not eliminate, opportunistic behaviour such as large-scale theft of resource rents, and the violent expression of grievances.

The principles that apply in a post-conflict situation are similar to those that apply in peaceful conflict resolution. There is a need to build those institutions and governance practices that will convince the population that the benefits of growth and wealth creation will be fairly shared and thus that long-term investment is viable. Reducing poverty is one of the essential tasks in any post-conflict situation; and in many poor countries, this can be most effectively accomplished by the revitalization of the agricultural sector. Selective policies of subsidies to productive sectors might have to be instituted to encourage long-term investment and thereby reignite the growth process (Murshed 2001).

Economic growth helps reduce conflict risk in several ways. By decreasing poverty and providing employment opportunities, it breeds fewer ready recruits for conflict entrepreneurs. It can reduce horizontal inequality, which is a major source of conflict in many countries. By creating denser sets of interactions between economic agents, economic growth produces a situation where there is more to lose from engaging in conflict. This can help improve institutional functioning and may even lead to the emergence of democracy. These benefits of growth have been particularly noted in African countries that have emerged from conflict and are progressing towards sustained growth and building democratic institutions.

Growth itself is not enough, however, for there should be an active policy to promote social cohesion among all groups and, in particular, to lessen inequality, especially horizontal inequality. Investment should also be directed towards human capital and infrastructure in order to make the growth sustainable. In countries where much of government revenue comes from natural resource rents, fiscal and budgetary institutions that are open and transparent should be put in place to ensure that there is no siphoning off of revenues and windfalls by ruling elites. In sum, it is through improvements in institutions and governance that the resource curse can be averted and resources turned, instead, into a vehicle for growth, poverty reduction and conflict prevention.

Conclusions

Good governance and sound institutions can provide the environment in which decisions on long-term investment in both human and physical capital, essential for economic growth, can be made. The advanced countries have developed, over time, an intricate governance and institutional structure to assist in achieving economic growth and have used it to build strong and cohesive societies. As described in this chapter, the foundation of such a system must be rooted in a shared concept of justice: citizens must believe that they are being treated fairly, that changes would be made to the laws and regulations to remove any perceived injustices, and that the country is moving in the right direction. With such confidence, economic activity and especially investment will be encouraged.

The sense that the changes being made constitute steps in the right direction can sometimes be created by fairly minor changes in existing governance structures. This can have profound results as long as the perception exists that there will be further changes and that those changes will be steps in the same direction, as was best shown in the case of China. Having established the perception that they are moving in the right direction, countries can also initiate numerous changes in governance structure.

There is, therefore, no justification for the pessimistic belief that certain countries will remain mired in low growth and shackled with institutions that impede their growth. Sustained growth is indeed possible with initially imperfect institutions; what is important is that the Government itself be credible in its commitment to making the changes that will remove institutional obstacles to growth (Johnson, Ostry and Subramanian, 2006).

The description of the origins of growth failures in many poorer countries, particularly in Africa, has stressed the role of institutional factors, thereby providing not only an explanation of what caused economic decline, but also guidelines on how to achieve sustained growth. Sustained growth is achievable through a careful reform of institutions so that what may be considered to be a just society can be created—one in which the benefits of growth are felt to be shared justly and where the incentives for legitimate economic activity are encouraged and those for rent-seeking are removed. This is a complex and difficult undertaking: although some general principles can be laid down, there is no one set of institutions that can be readily adopted to ensure this outcome. What is required is that all sectors of society be involved in the effort to build new and vigorous institutions. That such a task is too complicated and wide-ranging to be undertaken by one single authority is a fact that is widely appreciated at the present time.

The challenge for many developing countries is to put in place those participatory institutions that will allow all segments of society to feel that the fruits of the nation's wealth and the industry of its citizens are being put to good use and that the benefits of this wealth are being distributed appropriately.

This challenge is doubly important for poor countries with weak institutions in which significant fuel and mineral deposits are found. The very wealth that can be produced in a short period of time by their exploitation can exacerbate social conflicts, as its distribution—particularly between the central authorities and the local interests where the deposit is located—can be a source of contention. If strong institutions are not in place to resolve these issues right at the start of exploitation, separatist violence can erupt and, in general, existing differences within society can be heightened if it is felt that the wealth is not being distributed justly. One of the major research findings has been that this particular manifestation of the resource curse can be averted if countries have strong institutions.

For the international community, this finding has particular relevance to countries that are emerging from conflict or have become "failed States". In most cases, the most important consideration is to foster the resumption of economic activity, which usually means first the revival of the agricultural sector. As demonstrated throughout the chapter, a solid agriculture sector is usually essential for subsequent economic development, as it will encourage further investment in that sector and raise farmers' incomes so that their own demand as directed towards the rest of the economy will increase. A prosperous agricultural sector can show that growth is indeed shared and so can help create a stable and just society. With economic growth comes the opportunity to adjust institutions and improve governance so that a virtuous circle is created.

The international community has also assigned a central importance to improving governance in its efforts to achieve the Millennium Development Goals. Governance issues are assuming an increasing weight in bilateral and multilateral lending programmes. In this process, efforts should be made to improve governance through actions aimed at remedying specific deficiencies rather than through the attachment of conditions to aid that are based upon global measures of governance which, as analysed earlier, are highly subjective and riddled with serious conceptual problems. International support in this area should be directed towards improving specific areas of governance weaknesses, such as public budget and administrative management systems (World Bank and International Monetary Fund, 2006, p. 21). Help should also be given in supporting or developing institutions that create and support fair markets, that enhance growth, that manage conflicts over the distribution of the benefits of growth, especially in the case of natural resources, and that in general promote social cohesion. Imposing on aid-recipient countries wide-ranging conditionality based on global measures of the quality of governance should be avoided, as these measures have serious limitations.

Notes

1. Perhaps the most influential article in this field is Acemoglu, Johnson and Robinson (2001).
2. For technical discussions, see Brock and Durlauf (2001). Some say that if institutions (including governance) are endogenous to a particular outcome (say, economic performance), then institutions cannot matter for growth, because they are not the sort of factors that may infl uence the outcome (Przeworski, 2003).
3. For the interpretation of differences in governance indicators across countries and over time, see Kaufmann, Kraay and Mastruzzi (2005).
4. Rodrik (2005) argues that a similar linkage exists between growth and economic policies.
5. Analysis is here based on United Nations (2000), chap. VIII.
6. Khan (2007) distinguishes between two types of governance capacities necessary to achieve sustained growth: market-enhancing governance and growth-enhancing governance. The former encompasses governance factors, such as the protection of property rights and the enforcement of rule of law, that ensure market efficiency. The latter encompasses the State's abilities to complement market activities, including the capabilities to accelerate the transfer of assets and resources to more productive industries, and to facilitate the absorption and learning of new technologies.
7. The share subject to quota has been reduced and the mandatory production plan was terminated in 1985.
8. India developed a decentralized system after its independence and thus the experience of West Bengal does not apply to the entire country (see Kochhar and others, 2006).
9. Not all land reforms have been successful, in particular when land redistribution involves resettlement of farmers. In Africa and Latin America and the Caribbean, resettlement is common and the selection of farmers often becomes an obstacle to implementation (see United Nations, 2000, chap. V).
10. Reflecting another important aspect of policy was the fact that the country had supported the development of the sugar industry, instead of taxing it, and that trading partners gave the country preferential access in sugar to their markets.
11. Export processing zones in other parts of the developing world faced similar governance-related constraints (see, for example, Willmore, 1994).
12. World Bank (2005b) emphasized the need for policy diversity and for selective and modest reforms.
13. See also Reddy and Minoiu (2005) for a similar finding.

Appendices

APPENDIX A

TECHNICAL NOTE ON THE DECOMPOSITION OF LABOUR PRODUCTIVITY GROWTH AND OF THE EMPLOYMENT-TO-POPULATION RATIO

The decomposition of labour productivity is used here to trace the contribution of the agriculture, industry and service sectors to economy-wide labour productivity growth. The approach follows Syrquin (1986). The sum of the productivity growth rates of each sector and their respective reallocation effects should add up to aggregate labour productivity growth. The relevant identity for decomposing labour productivity growth is $\sum_i X_0^i = X_0$, with the X_0^i term representing output levels by sector ($i = 1,2,....n$).

Let $\theta_0^i = X_0^i / X_0$ be the share of sector i in real output in period zero. Similarly, for employment: $\varepsilon_0^i = L_0^i / L_0$ with $\sum_i L_0^i = L_0$. The level of labour productivity in sector i is X_0^i / L_0^i and its growth rate is defined as $\xi_0^i = (\hat{X}^i - \hat{L}^i)$. After a bit of manipulation, the following exact expression for the rate of growth of economy-wide labour productivity is obtained:

$$\xi_0^i = \sum_i [\theta_0^i (\hat{X}^i - \hat{L}^i) + (\theta_0^i - \varepsilon_0^i)\hat{L}_i]$$

Labour productivity growth, ξ_L, can be decomposed into two parts. One is the sum of the weighted average of sectoral rates of productivity growth as conventionally measured, that is to say, $\sum_i \theta_0^i (\hat{X}^i - \hat{L}^i)$. The weights are the output shares, θ_0^i. The second term $\sum_i (\theta_0^i - \varepsilon_0^i)\hat{L}_i$ captures the "reallocation effects". If $\theta_0^i > \varepsilon_0^i$, then the output share of sector i is larger than its employment share, implying that the sector has a relatively high average labour productivity. Employment growth in that sector (or a negative $\hat{L}^i$ in a sector with $\theta_0^i < \varepsilon_0^i$) will increase aggregate productivity growth.

An alternative is to decompose the growth in the economy-wide employment-to-population ratio into the growth rates of the ratio for each sector and the sectoral employment shares. The employment ratio of a particular sector will rise if the sector's output per capita exceeds labour productivity growth in the sector. The original insight is from Passinetti (1981). Strong economic performance is characterized by both sustained productivity growth and a rising employment/population ratio overall. To observe the details, one can start with the identity $\phi_0 = L_0/P_0 = \sum_i (L_0^i/X_0^i)(X_0^i/P_0)$ in which P_0 is the population and ϕ_0 is the share of the population employed at the beginning of the period. Labour-output ratios (the inverse of the average productivity levels) for each sector are defined as $b_0^i = L_0^i/X_0^i$ and sectoral output levels per capita are $\chi_0^i = X_0^i/P_0$. The growth rate of the share of the employed population, $\hat{\phi}$, can be expressed as $\hat{\phi} = \sum_j \varepsilon_0^i (\hat{\chi}^i + \hat{b}^i)$ with ε_0^i being the sectoral employment shares. Each sector's growth rate of labour productivity is $\xi_0^i = (\hat{X}^i - \hat{L}^i)$ so that the growth rate of the labour/output ratio becomes $\hat{b}^i (1 + \hat{X}^i) = -\xi_L^i (1 + \hat{L}^i)$. A final expression for $\hat{\phi}$ is obtained as: $\hat{\phi} = \sum_i \varepsilon_0^i (\hat{\chi}^i - \xi_L^i)$. In other words, the growth rate of the employment/population ratio is a weighted average of differences between sectoral growth rates of output per capita and productivity. Sectors with higher shares of total employment ε_0^i contribute more strongly to the average. One might expect that $\hat{\chi}^i > \xi_L^i$ in the case of a "dynamic" sector and that the inverse will hold in the case of a "declining" or "mature" sector.

APPENDIX B

ON DATA AND METHODOLOGY FOR THE ANALYSIS OF TRADE PATTERNS AND GROWTH IN CHAPTER III

The United Nations Statistics Division of the Department of Economic and Social Affairs maintains a commodity trade statistics database (COMTRADE) on annual trade statistics (volume, value and trading partners) as reported by the relevant statistical authorities of countries or areas. Statistical offices, however, do not necessarily report trade statistics on each commodity for every year or use the same standard commodity classification. These data limitations may pose challenges for long-term analysis on trends at the commodity level and for comparative country analysis. The National Bureau of Economic Research (NBER), combining COMTRADE with other available trade databases, and using a variety of estimation methods, generated a comprehensive world bilateral trade database covering 163 countries on the basis of a common standard classification—the Standard International Trade Classification, Revision 2 (SITC) (United Nations, 1975)—for the period 1962-2000 (Feenstra and others, 2005). This database can be accessed at www.nber.org/data and was used for the analysis presented in the present chapter.

Period of analysis: The period is divided in two sub-periods (1962-1980 and 1980-2000) to account for structural changes taking place during these periods and their implications for growth.

Unit of account: Data are reported in current United States dollars. There is no comparable comprehensive database on trade volumes at the commodity level for a large number of countries. Price estimations are available for primary commodities, but not for manufactures. Volume data for the latter are particularly difficult to estimate as product quality changes over time and across countries. In order to partially offset the influence of price fluctuations, averages for relatively long periods of observation (instead of a single year) are used.

Regions: The same broad country groupings as defined in chapter II are used in this exercise, but they include a larger number of countries, when consistent data were available for the period 1962-1980. A total of 105 countries are thus considered in the analysis.[a] For country groupings, see explanatory notes.

Classification of products by technological content: Products are grouped into five categories according to natural resource and technological content on the basis of a methodological classification developed by Lall (2001). Products classified in SITC divisions 3 (fuel and energy) and 9 (non-classified products) are excluded from the analysis. While some degree of discretion is unavoidable in this regard, Lall's classification is based on indicators of technological activity in manufacturing. The five categories are:

1. **Primary products (PP)**, consisting of food and live animals, and crude materials (except fuels) as well as silver, platinum, copper, nickel, aluminium, lead, zinc and tin.

2. **Natural resource-based manufactures (NRB)**, including mainly processed foods and tobacco, simple wood products, refined petroleum products, dyes, leather (but not leather products), precious stones and organic chemicals. The products can be simple and labour-intensive (simple foods or leather processing) or intensive in terms of capital, scale and skills (modern processed foods). Competitive advantage in these products generally—but not always—arises from the local availability of natural resources.

3. **Low-technology manufactures (LT)**, including mainly textiles, garments, footwear, other leather products, toys, simple metal and plastic products, furniture and glassware. These products tend to have stable, well-diffused technologies largely embodied in capital equipment, and low R&D expenditures and skill requirements, as well as low economies of scale. Labour often dominates the cost structure of such products. Products tend to be undifferentiated, at least at the mass-produced (non-fashion) end of the scale. Barriers to entry are relatively low; competitive advantages in these products come from price rather than quality or brand names.

4. **Medium-technology manufactures (MT)**, including heavy industry products such as automobiles, industrial chemicals, machinery and relatively standard electrical and electronic products. The products tend to have complex but not fast-changing technologies, with moderate levels of R&D expenditures but advanced engineering and design skills and a large scale of production. In engineering products, emphasis is on product design and development capabilities as well as extensive supplier and subcontractor networks. Barriers to entry tend to be high owing to capital requirements and strong learning effects in operation, design and (for some products) product differentiation. Innovation and learning in the engineering segment increasingly involve cooperation in the value chain between manufacturers, suppliers and sometimes customers (for large items of equipment).

5. **High-technology manufactures (HT)**, including complex electrical and electronic (including telecommunications) products, aerospace, precision instruments, fine chemicals and pharmaceuticals. These products, with advanced and fast-changing technologies and complex skill needs,

have the highest entry barriers. The most innovative ones call for large R&D investment, advanced technology infrastructure and close interaction between firms, universities and research institutions; but many activities, particularly in electronics, may have final processes with simple technologies, where low wages can be an important competitive factor. The high value-to-weight ratio of these products (electronics products, for example, have a higher unit value relative to their weight than have automotive products) allows segments of the value chain to be broken up and located across long distances.

Trade specialization patterns: Trade specialization/diversification patterns are analysed with reference to the five product groups defined above. Diversification is broadly defined as a decline of the share of primary products and an increase in the share of manufacture products in total merchandise exports of a country or a region.

Dynamic products and sectors: Dynamic products can be defined in different ways. For the purposes of this exercise, dynamic products and sectors are defined as those that increased their market share in global exports in a given period of time.

Trade specialization (diversification) indicator: Estimates presented in statistical annex table A.5 show diversification over time, combined with the relative importance of a given country in total exports (by developing countries) in each category of product, as observed by the end of the period of analysis. The indicator thus presents the change in the share of any of the five categories of product in total exports for a given country, multiplied by the share of the country in total developing countries' exports of that particular category of product. Formally,

$$\text{Trade specialization indicator} = \left[\left(\frac{X_{ij}}{\sum_{i=1}^{n} X_j} \right)_{t+1} - \left(\frac{X_j}{\sum_{i=1}^{n} X_j} \right)_t \right] * \left[\frac{X_j}{\sum_{j=1}^{n} X_j} \right]_{t+1} * 100$$

where X = value of exports, i = goods, j = country concerned, t = period.

The indicator for a particular category of product may be relatively small if changes in the structure of exports of a particular country had been relatively large but the country failed to gain market share relative to the exports of developing countries in that category of product. As conceived, this measure combines export diversification with market penetration efforts. Countries are classified as PP, NRB manufacture or LT, MT or HT manufacture exporters according to the particular category of products in which the indicator reached its highest value, that is to say, the category where specialization was most significant relative to total merchandise exports of developing countries.

Appendix C

Annex tables

Annex Table A.1.
Decomposition of international inequality (Theil coefficient) by region, 1960, 1980 and 2000

	All countries Contribution to overall inequality 1960			All countries (without China) Contribution to overall inequality 1960		
Regions	Between Regions	Within Regions	Total	Between Regions	Within Regions	Total
Developed Countries	0.61	0.04	0.65	0.52	0.04	0.57
Eastern Europe	0.04	0.00	0.04	0.01	0.00	0.01
Latin America	0.01	0.01	0.02	-0.01	0.01	0.00
East Asia (15 larger countries)[a]	-0.17	0.00	-0.16	-0.11	0.00	-0.11
Rest of East Asia	-0.01	0.00	-0.01	-0.01	0.00	-0.01
West Asia	0.00	0.00	0.00	-0.01	0.00	0.00
Africa	-0.03	0.01	-0.03	-0.04	0.01	-0.04
Former USSR	na	na	na	na	na	na
Total inequality	0.45	0.07	0.51	0.35	0.07	0.42
	Contribution to overall inequality 1980			Contribution to overall inequality 1980		
Regions	Between Regions	Within Regions	Total	Between Regions	Within Regions	Total
Developed Countries	0.67	0.01	0.69	0.60	0.01	0.61
Eastern Europe	0.04	0.00	0.04	0.02	0.00	0.02
Latin America	0.01	0.01	0.02	0.00	0.01	0.00
East Asia (15 larger countries)[a]	-0.18	0.02	-0.16	-0.13	0.02	-0.11
Rest of East Asia	-0.01	0.00	-0.01	-0.01	0.00	-0.01
West Asia	0.01	0.01	0.01	0.00	0.01	0.01
Africa	-0.04	0.01	-0.03	-0.05	0.01	-0.04
Former USSR	na	na	na	na	na	na
Total inequality	0.51	0.05	0.56	0.42	0.05	0.48
	Contribution to overall inequality 2000			Contribution to overall inequality 2000		
Regions	Between Regions	Within Regions	Total	Between Regions	Within Regions	Total
Developed Countries	0.69	0.01	0.70	0.72	0.01	0.73
Eastern Europe	0.00	0.00	0.00	0.00	0.00	0.00
Latin America	0.00	0.01	0.00	-0.01	0.01	-0.01
East Asia (15 larger countries)[a]	-0.17	0.05	-0.13	-0.14	0.05	-0.09
Rest of East Asia	-0.01	0.00	-0.01	-0.01	0.00	-0.01
West Asia	0.00	0.00	0.00	-0.01	0.01	0.00
Africa	-0.05	0.01	-0.04	-0.06	0.01	-0.05
CIS	-0.01	0.00	-0.01	-0.02	0.00	-0.02
Total inequality	0.45	0.08	0.53	0.48	0.09	0.56

Annex Table A.1 (cont'd)

Source: UN/DESA, based on Maddison (2001).

Notes: To avoid having end-years as outliers, five-year averages were used for both GDP and population, that is to say, for 1960, the average was taken for the period 1958-1962; for 1980, for the period 1978-1982; and for 2000, for the period 1998-2001 (2001 was the latest available observation year).

Country groupings as specified in Maddison (2001).

Methodology note: Income (GDP) is expressed in 1990 Geary-Khamis constant dollars. The Theil coefficient is a measure of inequality based on information theory (general entropy). If all countries (or individuals) had the same per capita income, the Theil index would be equal to zero. The Theil index compares the income share of a country or individual with its population share. When all income is received by one country (or individual), then the Theil index assumes the value of log N, where N is the number of countries or individuals. The advantage of the Theil index over several other inequality measures (such as the Gini coefficient) is that it is easily decomposable and can show how much different subgroups of countries or individuals contribute to overall inequality and is also additive for the components attributable to between- and within-group differentials. In the above decomposition only international inequality is considered, that is to say, income inequality between countries. No account is taken of within-country inequality.

The numbers in the table confirm that most of world income is earned within the developed world (an average of 52 per cent for 1998-2001) despite the fact that it encompasses only 14 per cent of world population. As a result, inequality between developed regions and the rest of the world has contributed most to global income inequality. Over time an increasing share of world income in developed countries, despite a reduction of their share in world population, has led to a rise in their contribution to growing global inequality. Overall, the contribution of inequality within regions to international inequality is small. Because of their larger income shares, the developed countries and, from 1980, the larger countries in developing Asia have carried the weight of the contribution of intraregional inequality to world inequality. Within the developed-country region, convergence has taken place as is attested by the lower contribution of within-region income differences. The larger countries in East and South Asia, in contrast, have shown some tendency towards divergence, though the contribution to international inequality as measured by the Theil index remains small.

a   China, India, Indonesia, Philippines, Republic of Korea, Taiwan Province of China, Thailand, Bangladesh, Hong Kong Special Administrative Region of China, Malaysia, Myanmar, Nepal, Pakistan, Singapore and Sri Lanka.

Annex Table A.2.
Decomposition of developing world inequality (Theil coefficient) by region, 1960, 1980 and 2000

	All Developing Countries Contribution to overall inequality 1960			All Developing Countries (without China and India) Contribution to overall inequality 1960		
Regions	Between Regions	Within Regions	Total	Between Regions	Within Regions	Total
Eastern Europe	0.31	0.01	0.32	0.24	0.01	0.25
Latin America	0.15	0.02	0.17	0.10	0.03	0.13
East Asia (15 larger countries)[a]	-0.20	0.01	-0.19	-0.10	0.01	-0.09
Other East Asian and South Asian	-0.01	0.00	-0.01	-0.02	0.00	-0.02
West Asia	0.03	0.01	0.04	0.01	0.01	0.02
Africa	-0.03	0.01	-0.01	-0.07	0.02	-0.06
Former USSR	na	na	na	na	na	na
Total inequality	0.25	0.06	0.32	0.17	0.07	0.24
	Contribution to overall inequality 1980			Contribution to overall inequality 1980		
Regions	Between Regions	Within Regions	Total	Between Regions	Within Regions	Total
Eastern Europe	0.27	0.00	0.27	0.20	0.00	0.20
Latin America	0.17	0.01	0.19	0.11	0.02	0.13
East Asia (15 larger countries)[a]	-0.20	0.05	-0.15	-0.09	0.04	-0.05
Other East Asian and South Asian	-0.01	0.00	-0.01	-0.02	0.00	-0.02
West Asia	0.07	0.01	0.08	0.05	0.01	0.06
Africa	-0.04	0.02	-0.02	-0.08	0.02	-0.06
Former USSR	na	na	na	na	na	na
Total inequality	0.26	0.09	0.36	0.17	0.10	0.27
	Contribution to overall inequality 2000			Contribution to overall inequality 2000		
Regions	Between Regions	Within Regions	Total	Between Regions	Within Regions	Total
Eastern Europe	0.02	0.00	0.03	0.03	0.01	0.03
Latin America	0.11	0.01	0.12	0.13	0.02	0.14
East Asia (15 larger countries)[a]	-0.04	0.10	0.05	0.02	0.12	0.14
Other East Asian and South Asian	-0.01	0.00	-0.01	-0.02	0.00	-0.02
West Asia	0.04	0.01	0.05	0.05	0.01	0.07
Africa	-0.05	0.02	-0.04	-0.10	0.03	-0.07
Former USSR	0.02	0.00	0.02	0.01	0.01	0.02
Total inequality	0.08	0.15	0.23	0.12	0.19	0.31

Source: UN/DESA, based on Maddison (2001).

Notes: To avoid having end-years as outliers, five-year averages were used for both GDP and population, that is to say, for 1960, the average was taken for the period 1958-1962; for 1980, for the period 1978-1982; and for 2000, for the period 1998-2001 (2001 was the latest available observation year).

Country groupings as specified in Maddison (2001).

[a] China, India, Indonesia, Philippines, Republic of Korea, Taiwan Province of China, Thailand, Bangladesh, Hong Kong Special Administrative Region of China, Malaysia, Myanmar, Nepal, Pakistan, Singapore and Sri Lanka.

Annex Table A.3.
Exports share of selected country grouping to exports of developing countries by category of products, 1962-1965 to 1995-2000

	Product Category	1962-1965	1965-1970	1970-1975	1975-1980	1980-1985	1985-1990	1990-1995	1995-2000
Sub-Saharan Africa	Primary products	9.6	9.7	9.6	10.1	7.7	6.2	5.1	5.2
	NRB manufactures	9.0	7.8	6.6	5.3	3.7	3.1	2.9	2.2
	LT manufactures	0.5	0.8	0.8	0.8	0.5	0.6	0.5	0.4
	MT manufactures	1.5	1.3	1.1	0.8	0.6	0.4	0.2	0.1
	HT manufactures	1.8	1.2	0.6	0.8	0.4	0.2	0.1	0.1
Latin America	Primary products	37.6	37.5	35.9	38.9	39.8	36.4	35.6	36.4
	NRB manufactures	29.5	28.6	30.9	29.5	29.9	24.7	23.4	23.6
	LT manufactures	6.4	8.2	10.4	10.7	10.0	8.6	8.5	10.2
	MT manufactures	9.6	9.9	15.6	18.3	19.6	18.6	18.6	20.8
	HT manufactures	26.8	30.4	25.5	18.7	14.0	9.4	7.3	8.6
South Asia	Primary products	8.5	6.3	5.8	5.3	5.2	5.4	4.9	5.5
	NRB manufactures	7.3	6.2	4.6	4.3	4.3	5.6	5.8	6.0
	LT manufactures	29.1	20.8	12.3	8.2	6.5	6.2	6.2	6.1
	MT manufactures	4.5	6.1	4.4	3.1	1.6	1.4	1.6	1.6
	HT manufactures	5.0	3.7	1.9	1.1	0.7	1.0	0.5	0.5
China	Primary products	3.1	4.1	4.8	4.1	6.7	10.2	10.0	9.2
	NRB manufactures	1.9	2.5	2.5	2.5	4.4	6.4	8.2	10.2
	LT manufactures	9.1	9.3	8.4	7.7	12.4	19.6	32.3	37.7
	MT manufactures	5.0	5.0	4.6	3.2	5.4	8.6	13.2	16.3
	HT manufactures	2.8	3.1	2.2	1.5	2.2	4.9	10.0	15.1
NIEs and South-Eastern Asia	Primary products	16.8	15.1	16.0	20.7	21.3	22.1	23.4	20.4
	NRB manufactures	21.5	23.1	27.3	32.5	32.8	34.2	36.6	32.2
	LT manufactures	31.4	36.7	44.4	54.6	58.0	54.7	41.5	32.4
	MT manufactures	15.3	17.5	25.9	40.3	42.5	46.1	50.8	42.6
	HT manufactures	24.2	35.6	52.2	59.8	66.1	72.3	76.7	69.4
Middle East and North Africa	Primary products	7.6	8.6	9.4	7.0	6.5	6.4	6.1	5.9
	NRB manufactures	9.0	6.9	6.6	7.1	7.6	9.5	8.3	8.9
	LT manufactures	7.0	7.9	8.2	6.8	4.8	3.9	3.8	3.8
	MT manufactures	6.9	8.4	10.9	9.5	6.9	6.1	4.7	4.3
	HT manufactures	6.9	5.6	4.8	5.0	4.6	3.3	2.6	2.4
Central and Eastern Europe	Primary products	3.0	4.2	4.9	4.1	4.1	4.6	4.8	4.7
	NRB manufactures	8.4	8.2	7.6	6.8	6.6	6.3	6.8	7.9
	LT manufactures	12.1	12.5	12.7	9.5	6.7	5.1	5.5	6.9
	MT manufactures	26.1	28.9	23.2	16.1	15.4	11.4	6.5	9.6
	HT manufactures	18.1	12.9	7.0	4.4	5.4	4.6	1.6	2.8
CIS	Primary products	2.6	3.7	4.2	3.2	3.3	4.2	6.6	9.8
	NRB manufactures	6.6	8.5	7.2	7.0	6.7	6.9	5.4	7.2
	LT manufactures	3.1	2.6	1.8	0.8	0.5	0.5	0.8	1.7
	MT manufactures	27.1	20.4	11.9	6.6	5.5	5.7	4.1	4.3
	HT manufactures	12.6	5.8	4.5	6.7	3.6	2.7	0.8	0.9
LDCs not included above	Primary products	11.0	10.7	9.1	6.2	4.8	4.1	3.3	2.6
	NRB manufactures	6.7	8.0	6.4	4.5	3.7	3.2	2.4	1.8
	LT manufactures	1.0	0.8	0.6	0.7	0.6	0.4	0.3	0.5
	MT manufactures	3.3	1.5	1.5	0.9	0.8	0.7	0.2	0.2
	HT manufactures	1.0	0.5	0.5	1.3	1.2	0.5	0.1	0.1

Annex Table A.3 (cont'd)

	1962-1965	1965-1970	1970-1975	1975-1980	1980-1985	1985-1990	1990-1995	1995-2000
Memo items: All products								
Sub-Saharan Africa	8.1	7.4	6.1	5.3	3.2	2.1	1.3	1.0
Latin America	30.9	29.4	27.9	26.9	24.3	19.1	16.5	16.8
South Asia	10.2	8.2	6.4	5.2	4.3	4.3	3.9	3.5
China	3.4	4.4	4.7	4.3	7.2	11.5	17.4	20.2
NIEs and SE Asia	19.7	20.8	26.4	35.6	40.8	45.3	46.9	43.1
Middle East and North Africa	7.9	8.0	8.4	7.2	6.2	5.7	4.8	4.4
Central and Eastern Europe	6.5	7.9	8.7	7.4	7.4	6.5	5.1	6.3
CIS	4.8	5.8	5.3	4.2	3.7	3.7	3.0	3.7
LDCs not included above	8.4	8.0	5.8	3.7	2.5	1.7	1.0	0.7

Source: UN/DESA, based on Feenstra and others (2005).
Abbreviations: NRB, natural resource-based; LT, low-tech; MT, medium-tech; HT, high-tech.

Annex Table A.4.
Fast growing exports in world markets by groups of products, 1962-1980 and 1980-2000 (annual average rate of growth)

SITC	Product	Annual average rate of growth
	A. 1962-1980	
	Primary commodities	
681	Silver, platinium, etc.	29.1
36	Shellfish, fresh, frozen	18.7
271	Fertilizers, crude	18.3
684	Aluminium	17.6
274	Sulphur, unroasted iron pyrites	17.3
685	Lead	17.2
44	Maize unmilled	16.7
34	Fish, fresh, chilled, frozen	16.3
245	Fuel wood n.e.s., Charcoal	16.0
11	Meat, fresh, chilled, frozen	15.6
	Average (above items)	18.3
	Natural Resource based manufactures	
689	Non-fer base metals n.e.s.	41.2
688	Uranium, thorium, alloys	40.2
289	Precious metals ares, waste n.e.s.	30.4
511	Hydrocarbons n.e.s., Derivatives	28.2
111	Non-alcoholic beverages n.e.s.	23.1
667	Pearl, precious, semi-precious stone	22.6
515	Organo-inorganic compounds etc	22.3
514	Nitrogen-function compounds	21.9
288	Non-ferrous metal and scrap, n.e.s.	21.7
61	Sugar and honey	20.8
	Average (above items)	27.2
	Low-tech manufactures	
893	Articles of plastic, n.e.s.	48.1
843	Womens outerwear nonknit	31.1
844	Under garments not knit	24.7
821	Furniture, parts thereof	23.0
898	Musical instruments parts	21.0
691	Structures and parts n.e.s.	20.9
848	Headgear, non-textile clothing	20.8
842	Mens outerwear not knit	20.6
831	Travel goods, handbags	20.5
851	Footwear	19.6
	Average (above items)	25.0
	Medium-tech manufactures	
714	Engines and motors n.e.s.	40.2
742	Pumps for liquids etc	36.5
583	Polymerization products etc	22.8
786	Trailers, non-motor vehicle, n.e.s.	22.5
512	Alcohols, phenols, etc	21.7
513	Carboxylic acids etc	21.4
884	Optical goods n.e.s.	21.0
582	Products of condensation	20.7
872	Medical instruments n.e.s.	20.6
266	Synthetic fibres to spin	20.6
	Average (above items)	24.8

Annex Table A.4 (cont'd)

SITC	Product	Annual average rate of growth
	High-tech manufactures	
716	Rotating electric plant	924.4
524	Radioactive etc material	44.0
771	Electric power machinery n.e.s.	33.4
759	Office, adp machinery parts, accessories	30.1
752	Automatic data processing equipment	28.5
761	Television receivers	23.8
776	Transistors, valves etc	23.4
718	Other power generating machinery	23.3
774	Electro-medecal, x-ray equipments, n.e.s.	20.7
881	Photograpic apparatus, equipments, n.e.s.	20.5
	Average (above items, excluding SITC 716)	27.5

Memo items:

Annual average rate of growth of world mercahndise trade	
1962-1980	15.7
1980-2000	5.8

B. 1980-2000		
SITC	Product	Annual average rate of growth
246	Pulpwood, chips, wood waste	10.3
683	Nickel	9.0
686	Zinc	8.4
34	Fish, fresh, chilled, frozen	8.1
36	Shellfish, fresh, frozen	7.9
684	Aluminium	7.7
245	Fuel wood n.e.s., Charcoal	7.2
273	Stone, sand and gravel	6.5
681	Silver, platinium, etc.	6.2
244	Cork, natural, raw, waste	5.7
	Average (above items)	7.7
688	Uranium, thorium, alloys	66.7
286	Uranium, thorium ore, concentrates	32.1
689	Non-fer base metals n.e.s.	26.9
111	Non-alcohl beverages n.e.s.	10.5
514	Nitrogen-function compounds	10.4
98	Edible products, preparations, n.e.s.	9.5
515	Organo-inorganic compounds etc	9.1
592	Starch, inulin, gluten, etc	9.1
664	Glass	8.8
628	Rubber articles n.e.s.	8.7
	Average (above items)	11.6
893	Articles of plastic n.e.s.	38.6
845	Outerwear knit nonelastic	36.0
843	Womens outerwear nonknit	23.1
846	Under garments knitted	22.0
844	Under garments not knit	21.4
898	Musical instruments pts	11.0
894	Toys, sporting goods, etc	10.5

Annex Table A.4 (cont'd)

SITC	Product	Annual average rate of growth
831	Travel goods, handbags	10.4
655	Knitted, etc fabrics	9.8
821	Furniture, parts thereof	9.7
	Average (above items)	19.3
742	Pumps for liquids etc	32.7
714	Engines and motors n.e.s.	17.1
728	Other machinery for spcial industries	12.7
553	Perfumery, cosmetics, etc	12.2
872	Medical instruments n.e.s.	11.2
772	Switchgear etc, parts n.e.s.	10.5
773	Electricity distributing equipment	10.3
812	Plumbing, heating, lighting equipments	9.4
783	Road motor vehicles n.e.s.	9.4
533	Pigments, paints, etc	9.0
	Average (above items)	13.4
771	Electric power machinery n.e.s.	37.3
716	Rotating electric plant	35.7
759	Office, adp machinery parts, accessories	35.7
776	Transistors, valves etc	17.0
871	Optical instruments	16.2
752	Automatic data processing equipment	15.4
764	Telecommunications equipments, parts, accessories, n.e.s.	14.0
874	Measuring, controling instruments	13.5
541	Medicinal, pharmaceutical prodcuts	10.8
778	Electrical machinery n.e.s.	9.6
	Average (above items)	20.5

Memo items:

Annual average rate of growth of world mercahndise trade	
1962-1980	15.7
1980-2000	5.8

Source: UN/DESA, based on Feenstra and others (2005).

Note: Current values.

Abbreviations: n.e.s., not elsewhere specified or included; ADP: automatic data processing; SITC: Standard International Trade Classification.

Annex Table A.5.
Trade specialization, selected economies, 1962-1980 and 1980-2000

A. 1962-1980

Country	Primary products	NRB manufactures	LT manufactures	MT manufactures	HT manufactures	Per capita GDP average annual growth 1962-1980
HT manufacture exporters						**2.8**
Singapore	-0.5161	-0.0790	0.0521	0.9227	2.7744	7.4
Israel	-0.0897	-0.0802	0.0648	0.0461	0.0951	4.2
Mexico	-0.9119	-0.0670	0.1255	0.3871	1.4068	3.8
Russian Federation	-0.0816	0.0095	-0.0149	-0.1345	0.3472	2.5
Philippines	-0.0338	-0.6468	0.0912	0.0157	0.1153	2.4
Gabon	0.0005	-0.0599	0.0000	0.0001	0.0120	2.0
El Salvador	-0.0584	0.0025	-0.0038	0.0013	0.0335	1.1
Niger	-0.0272	0.0507	0.0000	0.0000	0.4989	-0.9
MT manufacture exporters						**3.1**
Oman	-0.0106	0.0000	0.0003	0.0536	0.0345	7.6
Saudi Arabia	-0.0306	0.0036	0.0078	0.4342	-0.0374	6.3
Libyan Arab Jamahiriya	-0.0045	-0.0007	-0.0001	0.0531	0.0001	6.2
Hong Kong SAR[a]	0.0012	-0.0250	-1.4322	0.6432	0.1929	6.0
Algeria	-0.0016	-0.0393	0.0012	0.0147	0.0005	4.5
Iraq	-0.0209	-0.0004	0.0005	0.0201	0.0002	4.2
Brazil	-2.1565	0.5868	0.2397	0.8342	0.0648	4.1
Romania	-0.1334	-0.2075	0.4226	0.4255	0.0026	4.1
Trinidad and Tobago	-0.0024	-0.0278	0.0066	0.0111	0.0005	3.6
Panama	-0.0650	0.0284	0.0116	0.1068	-0.0764	3.6
Bulgaria	-0.0795	-0.0058	0.0293	0.1274	0.0055	3.4
Costa Rica	-0.0473	-0.0011	0.0054	0.0062	0.0022	3.2
Poland	-0.0097	-0.3303	0.1318	0.4869	0.0290	3.1
Syrian Arab Republic	-0.1394	0.0025	0.0186	0.1664	0.0016	3.0
Jordan	-0.0483	0.0047	0.0048	0.0138	0.0038	3.0
Dominican Republic	-0.0164	-0.1481	0.0095	0.0751	0.0004	3.0
Republic of the Congo	-0.0025	-0.0118	0.0000	0.0069	0.0001	2.4

Appendix C • 191

Annex Table A.5 (cont'd)

Country	Primary products	NRB manufactures	LT manufactures	MT manufactures	HT manufactures	Per capita GDP average annual growth 1962-1980
Argentina	-0.9621	0.0350	0.1083	0.1632	0.0151	2.1
Lebanon	-0.0700	0.0151	0.0457	0.1140	-0.0041	1.9
South Africa	-0.2897	-0.0625	0.0465	0.0750	0.0196	1.8
Zimbabwe	-0.0108	-0.0017	-0.0003	0.0380	0.0000	1.8
Bolivarian Republic of Venezuela	0.0250	-0.1509	0.0011	0.0159	0.0018	0.6
Liberia	-0.0034	-0.0679	0.0000	0.0451	0.0000	-0.3
Kuwait	-0.0223	-0.0036	0.0521	0.2684	-0.0037	-3.8
LT manufacture exporters						**3.2**
Republic of Korea	-0.1883	-0.2637	1.0627	0.8899	0.5204	7.5
Taiwan Province of China	-0.1824	-0.7865	2.7668	0.8594	1.0397	7.4
Thailand	-0.5591	0.0135	0.0796	0.0226	0.0347	4.5
Tunisia	-0.0535	-0.0489	0.1661	0.0146	0.0001	4.3
China	-0.5081	-0.0081	0.9342	0.0000	0.0170	3.7
Egypt	-0.1598	0.0062	0.0814	0.0043	0.0005	3.7
Islamic Republic of Iran	-0.0756	-0.0024	0.1344	0.0073	0.0008	3.2
Turkey	-0.4577	0.0089	0.1580	0.0084	0.0001	3.2
Morocco	-0.0706	-0.0500	0.0372	0.0054	0.0003	2.9
Pakistan	0.1078	-0.0569	0.3190	0.0050	0.0000	2.9
Colombia	-0.2820	0.0125	0.0319	0.0051	0.0003	2.8
Hungary	-0.0582	0.0040	0.0629	0.0144	0.0205	2.6
Czech Republic	-0.0072	-0.0215	0.1352	-0.0381	-0.0031	2.3
Uruguay	-0.1063	0.0016	0.0934	0.0068	0.0000	1.7
Mauritius	0.0001	-0.1101	0.0190	0.0003	0.0027	1.7
Haiti	-0.0181	-0.0203	0.0776	0.0019	0.0216	1.1
Afghanistan	-0.0266	-0.0004	0.0167	0.0002	0.0001	-0.2
NRB manufacture exporters						**1.7**
Malaysia	-1.1617	0.8100	0.0198	0.0195	0.6442	4.6
Indonesia	-0.6577	0.9411	-0.0028	0.0010	0.0053	3.3
Ecuador	-0.0974	0.0163	0.0005	0.0006	0.0000	3.2

Annex Table A.5 (cont'd)

Country	Primary products	NRB manufactures	LT manufactures	MT manufactures	HT manufactures	Per capita GDP average annual growth 1962-1980
Guatemala	-0.0736	0.0105	0.0015	0.0037	0.0084	2.6
Albania	-0.0096	0.0090	0.0043	0.0008	0.0001	2.5
Cameroon	-0.0756	0.0249	0.0004	0.0000	0.0000	2.0
Sri Lanka	-0.0925	0.0086	0.0069	0.0002	0.0000	2.0
Honduras	-0.0457	0.0140	0.0006	0.0007	0.0000	1.7
Myanmar	-0.0603	0.0641	0.0001	0.0001	0.0000	1.7
Cuba	-0.0052	0.1295	0.0000	-0.0002	0.0000	1.4
Guinea	-0.0027	0.0860	0.0000	0.0000	0.0000	1.3
Chile	-0.2673	0.1695	0.0005	0.0024	0.0000	1.3
Peru	-0.1385	0.0352	0.0084	0.0029	0.0001	1.3
India	-0.2309	0.2093	-0.2026	0.1113	0.0077	1.2
Jamaica	-0.0052	0.0747	-0.0007	0.0009	0.0002	0.8
United Arab Emirates	-0.0374	0.0119	0.0086	0.0008	0.0044	0.7
Senegal	-0.0184	0.0125	-0.0003	0.0016	0.0002	-0.7
Viet Nam	-0.0165	0.0056	0.0013	-0.0001	0.0000	-0.9
PP exporters						**1.5**
Paraguay	0.1304	-0.0755	0.0004	0.0000	0.0000	3.9
Côte d'Ivoire	0.0774	-0.0814	0.0009	0.0013	0.0001	2.6
Nigeria	0.0542	-0.0166	0.0020	0.0008	0.0008	2.6
Burundi	0.0102	-0.0009	0.0000	0.0000	0.0000	2.6
Bolivia	0.0439	-0.1431	0.0002	0.0001	0.0000	2.5
Bahrain	0.0162	-0.0038	0.0033	0.0021	-0.0022	2.3
Rwanda	0.0588	-0.0147	0.0000	0.0000	0.0000	1.8
Tanzania	0.1175	-0.0475	0.0028	0.0000	0.0000	1.3
Sierra Leone	0.0086	-0.0280	0.0000	0.0000	0.0000	1.3
Madagascar	0.0267	-0.0113	0.0011	0.0000	0.0000	-0.4
Ghana	0.0969	-0.0284	0.0000	0.0000	0.0000	-1.1
Angola	0.0313	-0.0251	0.0000	0.0001	0.0001	-1.8

Annex Table A.5 (cont'd)

Country	Primary products	NRB manufactures	LT manufactures	MT manufactures	HT manufactures	Per capita GDP average annual growth 1962-1980
No apparent diversification trend						1.0
Republic of Yemen	-0.0049	-0.0003	0.0002	0.0010	0.0016	4.9
Seychelles	0.0013	-0.0028	0.0000	0.0000	0.0000	3.5
Mongolia	-0.0030	0.0002	0.0002	0.0001	0.0000	3.0
Equatorial Guinea	0.0044	-0.0007	0.0000	0.0000	0.0000	2.9
Malawi	-0.0310	0.0045	0.0003	0.0001	0.0000	2.8
Kenya	-0.0291	-0.0050	0.0045	0.0008	0.0004	2.1
Mauritania	0.0010	-0.0176	0.0000	0.0000	0.0000	2.1
Togo	-0.0020	0.0000	0.0000	0.0000	0.0000	2.0
Mali	0.0037	-0.0006	0.0000	0.0000	0.0000	1.9
Ethiopia	-0.0130	0.0007	0.0001	0.0000	0.0000	1.9
Guinea-Bissau	-0.0010	0.0000	0.0000	0.0000	0.0000	1.6
Gambia	-0.0008	0.0007	0.0000	0.0000	0.0000	1.6
Lao People's Democratic Republic	-0.0008	0.0019	0.0004	0.0000	0.0000	1.3
Benin	0.0019	-0.0022	0.0001	0.0001	0.0000	1.1
Cambodia	-0.0026	0.0006	0.0001	0.0002	0.0000	1.0
Nepal	0.0020	-0.0014	0.0004	-0.0001	0.0000	0.2
Burkina Faso	-0.0008	0.0000	0.0001	0.0000	0.0000	0.1
Zambia	-0.0283	0.0021	0.0000	0.0000	0.0000	0.0
Nicaragua	-0.0255	-0.0020	0.0012	0.0045	0.0003	-0.2
Djibouti	-0.0041	0.0006	0.0004	0.0010	0.0000	-0.3
Sudan	-0.0298	0.0020	0.0000	0.0000	0.0001	-0.6
Mozambique	-0.0104	-0.0084	0.0024	0.0015	0.0000	-0.8
Central African Republic	-0.0013	0.0026	0.0000	0.0000	0.0000	-0.9
Uganda	-0.0052	0.0000	0.0000	0.0000	0.0013	-1.0
Somalia	-0.0058	0.0003	0.0000	0.0001	0.0000	-1.4
Chad	-0.0040	0.0000	0.0002	0.0000	0.0000	-3.0

Annex Table A.5 (cont'd)

B. 1980-2000

Country	Primary products	NRB manufactures	LT manufactures	MT manufactures	HT manufactures	Per capita GDP average annual growth 1980-2000
HT manufacture exporters						3.8
Republic of Korea	-0.0352	-0.0007	-1.5603	1.0785	1.9362	6.4
China	-1.4143	-0.3516	-0.2903	1.2522	1.6077	6.0
Taiwan Province of China	-0.0458	-0.0876	-1.5764	0.5384	2.5494	5.3
Thailand	-1.3038	-0.2161	-0.0212	0.2251	1.1304	4.6
Singapore	-0.0563	-0.1249	-0.0679	-0.3213	3.0904	4.6
Malaysia	-0.3625	-1.3909	0.0596	0.3097	3.2395	3.9
Hong Kong SAR[a]	-0.0010	0.0213	-0.6424	-0.1129	0.5967	3.6
Israel	-0.0502	-0.1001	-0.0236	-0.0009	0.2050	1.9
Costa Rica	-0.2958	0.0017	0.0147	0.0015	0.0330	1.2
Philippines	-0.1276	-0.3013	-0.0638	0.0116	1.8225	0.0
MT manufacture exporters						0.0
Mexico	-0.4989	-0.1397	0.1371	1.0430	0.3755	0.7
Panama	-0.0106	-0.0052	0.0015	0.0128	0.0006	0.6
Hungary	-0.1341	-0.0725	-0.0253	0.1874	0.1185	0.6
Trinidad and Tobago	-0.0001	-0.0309	0.0011	0.0103	0.0000	0.5
Argentina	-0.6848	0.0657	0.0015	0.0977	0.0005	0.2
South Africa	-0.3654	-0.1239	0.0228	0.1415	-0.0012	-0.3
Jordan	-0.0277	-0.0005	0.0003	0.0106	0.0010	-0.5
Bolivarian Republic of Venezuela	-0.1041	0.0102	-0.0029	0.0532	0.0004	-0.9
Kuwait	-0.0007	-0.0039	-0.0013	0.0159	0.0003	-1.3
Republic of Liberia	-0.0015	-0.0068	0.0000	0.0133	0.0000	-1.5
United Arab Emirates	-0.0686	-0.0021	0.0103	0.0174	0.0054	-2.5
Libyan Arab Jamahiriya	0.0004	-0.0062	0.0004	0.0103	-0.0002	-5.5
LT manufacture exporters						
Mauritius	0.0001	-0.0353	0.0373	-0.0002	0.0000	4.6
Viet Nam	-0.4771	-0.0195	0.2942	0.0113	0.0006	4.4

194 • Uneven Economic Development

Annex Table A.5 (cont'd)

Country	Primary products	NRB manufactures	LT manufactures	MT manufactures	HT manufactures	Per capita GDP average annual growth 1980-2000
India	-0.2572	-0.0288	0.1113	0.0397	0.0039	3.6
Sri Lanka	-0.1107	-0.0076	0.1716	0.0003	0.0008	3.5
Indonesia	-1.0284	-0.5122	0.5319	0.1515	0.0910	2.7
Pakistan	-0.1221	-0.0008	0.2596	0.0053	0.0000	2.5
Myanmar	-0.0063	-0.0431	0.0125	0.0000	0.0000	2.5
Turkey	-0.4061	0.0178	0.2589	0.0644	0.0075	2.5
Nepal	-0.0009	-0.0002	0.0051	0.0001	0.0000	2.3
Dominican Republic	-0.0317	-0.0260	0.1621	0.0034	0.0005	2.2
Tunisia	-0.0123	-0.0228	0.1104	-0.0115	0.0011	2.2
Egypt	-0.1319	0.0036	0.0590	0.0063	0.0008	1.7
Lao People's Democratic Republic	-0.0005	-0.0168	0.0097	0.0000	0.0000	1.5
Poland	-0.2157	0.0199	0.2472	0.0269	-0.0142	1.2
Cambodia	-0.0194	-0.0048	0.0666	0.0000	0.0000	1.1
Colombia	-0.5507	0.0271	0.0295	0.0284	0.0010	0.9
Morocco	-0.2085	-0.0298	0.1037	0.0022	0.0080	0.8
El Salvador	-0.1214	0.0001	0.1183	0.0000	-0.0009	0.7
Syrian Arab Republic	-0.0232	-0.0005	0.0052	-0.0001	0.0000	0.7
Jamaica	0.0001	-0.0957	0.0175	0.0014	0.0000	0.6
Albania	-0.0023	-0.0040	0.0157	-0.0003	0.0000	0.6
Czech Republic	0.0037	0.0878	0.2209	-0.4605	-0.0083	0.4
Honduras	-0.2374	-0.0066	0.1850	0.0000	0.0000	0.1
Guatemala	-0.2191	0.0003	0.0770	-0.0001	0.0000	-0.4
Bulgaria	0.0130	0.0069	0.0415	-0.0318	-0.0051	-0.6
Romania	-0.0026	-0.0075	0.1240	-0.0612	0.0004	-1.6
Nicaragua	-0.0587	0.0007	0.0119	0.0000	0.0000	-1.6
Russian Federation	-0.2930	-0.1573	0.1433	0.1237	-0.0257	-1.9
Madagascar	-0.0483	0.0001	0.0119	0.0000	0.0000	-2.0
Haiti	-0.0007	0.0000	0.0094	-0.0002	-0.0001	-2.3
Saudi Arabia	-0.0121	-0.0141	0.0085	0.0009	0.0014	-2.5

Annex Table A.5 (cont'd)

Country	Primary products	NRB manufactures	LT manufactures	MT manufactures	HT manufactures	Per capita GDP average annual growth 1980-2000
NRB manufacture exporters						**0.5**
Equatorial Guinea	-0.0033	0.0097	0.0000	0.0000	0.0000	8.8
Chile	-0.5230	0.1379	0.0023	0.0072	0.0001	2.7
Oman	-0.0092	0.0086	0.0049	-0.0061	-0.0020	2.7
Seychelles	-0.0093	0.0105	0.0000	0.0000	0.0000	2.0
Islamic Republic of Iran	-0.0333	0.0219	-0.0286	0.0083	0.0001	0.9
Uruguay	-0.0346	0.0144	-0.0155	0.0068	0.0003	0.9
Bahrain	0.0157	0.0065	-0.0017	-0.0008	-0.0006	0.7
Ghana	-0.1081	0.0482	0.0000	0.0000	0.0006	0.5
Brazil	-0.5208	0.1645	-0.0046	0.1424	0.0146	0.3
Mongolia	-0.0194	0.0287	-0.0001	0.0000	0.0000	0.1
Lebanon	-0.0116	0.0103	0.0026	0.0001	0.0000	-0.2
Cameroon	-0.0812	0.0571	0.0000	0.0000	0.0000	-0.3
Republic of the Congo	-0.0007	0.0189	0.0000	0.0000	0.0000	-0.4
Cuba	-0.0108	0.0394	0.0000	0.0000	0.0002	-0.5
Paraguay	-0.0508	0.0075	0.0007	0.0000	0.0000	-0.5
Gambia	-0.0088	0.0192	0.0000	0.0000	0.0000	-0.7
Central African Republic	-0.0050	0.0183	0.0000	0.0000	0.0000	-0.9
Angola	-0.0050	0.0429	0.0000	0.0000	0.0000	-1.0
Ecuador	-0.1123	0.0071	0.0006	0.0006	0.0000	-1.4
Zambia	-0.0712	0.0113	0.0002	0.0000	0.0000	-1.5
Gabon	-0.0004	0.0526	0.0000	0.0000	-0.0010	-2.7
PP exporters						**-0.1**
Mozambique	0.0228	-0.0011	-0.0006	-0.0005	0.0000	0.8
Benin	0.0126	-0.0004	0.0000	0.0000	0.0000	0.8
Senegal	0.0081	-0.0030	0.0000	0.0000	0.0000	0.5
Mauritania	0.0106	-0.0099	0.0000	0.0000	0.0000	0.1
Zimbabwe	0.0183	-0.0001	0.0026	-0.0057	0.0000	-0.1
Peru	0.0569	-0.0422	0.0047	-0.0002	0.0000	-0.7
Côte d'Ivoire	0.0473	-0.0098	-0.0001	0.0000	0.0000	-2.3

Annex Table A.5 (cont'd)

Country	Primary products	NRB manufactures	LT manufactures	MT manufactures	HT manufactures	Per capita GDP average annual growth 1980-2000
No apparent diversification trend						**0.0**
Uganda	-0.0037	0.0000	0.0000	0.0000	0.0000	1.6
Burkina Faso	-0.0043	0.0001	0.0001	0.0000	0.0000	1.3
Chad	0.0009	0.0000	0.0000	0.0000	0.0000	1.1
Mali	-0.0029	-0.0001	0.0000	0.0001	0.0002	0.7
Republic of Yemen	-0.0023	0.0003	0.0000	0.0001	0.0000	0.6
Sudan	-0.0126	0.0009	0.0001	0.0000	0.0000	0.3
Malawi	-0.0008	-0.0008	0.0005	0.0000	0.0000	0.3
Guinea	0.0013	-0.0113	0.0000	0.0000	0.0000	0.2
Bolivia	-0.0084	-0.0120	0.0033	0.0000	0.0000	0.0
Kenya	-0.0156	0.0006	0.0003	0.0001	0.0000	0.0
Ethiopia	-0.0123	0.0000	0.0002	0.0001	0.0001	-0.1
Burundi	0.0016	0.0000	0.0000	0.0000	0.0000	-0.4
Guine Bissau	-0.0032	0.0000	0.0001	0.0000	0.0000	-0.5
Algeria	0.0023	0.0034	0.0000	-0.0032	0.0000	-0.6
Tanzania	-0.0076	0.0006	0.0001	0.0000	0.0000	-0.6
Rwanda	-0.0028	0.0002	0.0000	0.0000	0.0000	-0.7
Somalia	-0.0019	0.0000	0.0000	0.0001	0.0000	-0.9
Nigeria	-0.0481	0.0044	0.0041	0.0001	0.0000	-1.0
Afghanistan	0.0015	0.0002	-0.0006	0.0000	0.0000	-1.4
Djibouti	-0.0003	0.0001	0.0000	0.0001	0.0000	-2.0
Niger	-0.0001	0.0001	0.0000	0.0000	-0.0003	-2.7
Togo	-0.0064	0.0001	0.0000	0.0001	0.0000	-3.0
Sierra Leone	-0.0024	-0.0008	0.0001	0.0003	0.0000	-5.3
Iraq	-0.0003	0.0002	0.0000	0.0000	0.0000	-7.9

Source: UN/DESA, based on World Development Indicators 2005 database and Feenstra and others (2005).
Note: See appendix to chapter III for definitions and methodology.
Abbreviations: NRB, natural resource-based; LT, low-tech; MT, medium-tech; HT, high-tech; PP, primary products.
[a] Special Administrative Region of China.

Annex Table A.6.
Service exports by sectors and sub-sectors, developing countries and world, 1980-2003

		Millions of dollars						Average annual growth rate		
		1980	1985	1990	1995	2000	2003	1980-2003	1980-1990	1990-2003
Total services	World total	366,118	393,832	803,747	1,195,501	1,527,264	1,836,861	7.3	8.2	6.6
	Developing countries[a]	64,194 (17.5%)	73,519	13,5145	254,455	359,259	423,686 (23.1%)	8.6	7.7	9.2
Transport	World total	121,844	104,946	191,065	288,196	340,790	397,346	5.3	4.6	5.8
	Developing countries[a]	19,350 (15.9%)	22,159	33,991	64,375	90,845	108,416 (27.3%)	7.8	5.8	9.3
Travel	World total	95,302	109,771	250,410	385,792	463,790	520,437	7.7	10.1	5.8
	Developing countries[a]	22,730 (23.9%)	24,556	52,724	94,239	127,441	147,394 (28.3%)	8.5	8.8	8.2
Other services	World total	148,972	157,468	320,883	521,509	719,982	919,078	8.2	8.0	8.4
	Developing countries[a]	22,114 (14.8%)	26,804	48,426	95,837	138,271	167,876 (18.3%)	9.2	8.2	10.0
Communications	World total	..	..	7,923	23,419	32,351	39,976	..	..	..
	Developing countries[a]	..	..	1,173	6,852	8,714	9,499 (23.8%)	..	..	..
Construction	World total	..	..	1,2294	35,037	28,942	36,954	..	..	..
	Developing countries[a]	..	..	818	2,775	4,553	6,264 (17.0%)	..	..	..
Computer and information services	World total	..	..	2,188	11,297	45,596	71,524	..	..	..
	Developing countries[a]	..	..	9	465	6,285	14,634 (20.5%)	..	..	..
Insurance	World total	..	..	17,450	24,380	28,421	52,382	..	..	..
	Developing countries[a]	..	..	2,508	5,374	6,147	5,972 (11.4%)	..	..	..
Financial services	World total	..	..	27,500	45,990	95,899	95,391	..	..	..
	Developing countries[a]	..	..	87	3,517	7,937	8,861 (9.3%)	..	..	..
Royalties and license fees	World total	..	..	27,444	54,243	79,725	94,231	..	..	..
	Developing countries[a]	..	..	398	1,068	2,267	3,300 (3.5%)	..	..	..

Annex Table A.6 (cont'd)

		Millions of dollars						Average annual growth rate		
		1980	1985	1990	1995	2000	2003	1980-2003	1980-1990	1990-2003
Other business services	World total	..	..	178,448	270,779	348,104	451,484	..	..	..
	Developing countries[a]	..	..	36,082	66,040	90,978	103,998 (23.0%)	..	..	..
Personal, cultural and recreational services	World total	..	..	3,266	10,557	20,708	24,637	..	..	..
	Developing countries[a]	..	..	18	2,466	3,609	3,995 (16.2%)	..	..	..
Government services n.i.e.	World total	..	..	45,346	46,136	40,309	52,500	..	..	..
	Developing countries[a]	..	..	7,334	7,324	7,785	11,353 (21.6%)	..	..	..
Memo item:										
Commercial services	World total	..	..	758,401	1,149,365	1,486,956	1,784,362	..	..	..
	Developing countries[a]	..	..	127,812	247,131	351,474	412,333 (23.1%)	..	..	..

Sources: UNCTAD Handbook of Statistics on CD-ROM (United Nations publication, Sales No. E/F.05.II.D.30); and UN/DESA.

Note: Average annual growth rates for the components of the other services sector were not reflected owing to lack of uniformity in reporting information during the period.

[a] Including the group of non-developed countries in transition.

Annex Table A.7.
Computer and information services exports, selected economies, 2000-2004

	Millions of dollars				
	2000	2001	2002	2003	2004
India	4,727.4	7,407.4	8,889.3	11,365.7	..
Israel	4,246.1	3,470.8	3,143.3	3,656.5	4,321.8
China	355.9	461.0	638.2	1,102.2	..
Singapore	247.2	311.6	315.7	318.6	..
Hong Kong, SAR[a]	59.7	154.0	207.6	245.4	..
Malaysia	81.6	176.3	181.6	216.0	..
Russian Federation	59.0	128.0	137.3	175.0	255.8
Costa Rica	59.7	124.7	153.4	166.8	200.3
Argentina	138.4	188.8	115.6	153.2	176.9
Taiwan, Province of China	117.0	154.0	115.0	110.0	110.0
Romania	44.0	50.0	78.0	108.0	143.0
Cyprus	57.8	86.8	104.0	92.1	249.8
Slovenia	53.9	64.1	79.8	88.4	97.5
Chile	33.4	42.8	62.9	81.4	70.5
Sri Lanka	..	66.0	50.0	80.0	..
Croatia	33.5	43.8	45.7	62.2	65.0
Syrian Arab Republic	..	..	..	50.0	1.0
Jamaica	40.4	36.6	34.1	36.0	..
Pakistan	22.0	19.0	21.0	34.0	37.7
Latvia	20.2	21.9	24.8	32.7	43.6
Estonia	21.2	23.3	24.3	31.1	38.8
Korea, Republic of	10.6	16.1	19.5	29.7	23.3
Brazil	34.0	27.0	36.4	29.1	53.4
Lithuania	15.5	24.2	18.8	28.6	31.0
Philippines	76.0	22.0	21.0	28.0	33.0
Memorandum item:					
Ireland	7,489.7	8,925.7	10,447.1	14,372.4	18,316.5
United Kingdom	4,321.5	4,682.8	5,770.1	7,892.5	10,549.9
Germany	3,798.2	4,805.0	5,491.3	6,679.9	7,877.5
United States	5,622.0	5,457.0	5,431.0	5,431.0	5,436.0

Sources: UNCTAD Handbook of Statistics on CD-ROM (United Nations publication, Sales No. E/F.05.II.D.30); and UN/DESA.

[a] Special Administrative Region of China.

References

Acemoglu, Daron, Simon Johnson and James A. Robinson (2001). The colonial origins of comparative development: an empirical investigation. *American Economic Review*, vol. 91, No. 5 (December), pp. 1369-1401.

Acemoglu, Daron (2003). An African success story: Botswana. In *In Search of Prosperity. Analytic Narratives on Economic Growth*, Dani Rodrik ed. Princeton, New Jersey: Princeton University Press.

Acemoglu, Daron (2005). The rise of Europe: Atlantic trade, institutional trade and economic growth. *American Economic Review*, vol. 95, No. 3 (June), pp. 546-579.

Addison, Tony, Basuser Guha-Khasnobis and George Mavrotas (2006). Introduction and overview. *The World Economy*, vol. 29, No. 1 (January), pp. 1-8.

Agénor, Pierre-Richard (1991). Output, devaluation and the real exchange rate in developing countries. *Weltwirtschaftliches Archiv*, vol. 127, pp. 18-41.

Aghion, Philippe, and Peter Howitt (2005). Appropriate growth policy: a unifying framework.The 2005 Joseph Schumpeter Lecture at the Twentieth Annual Congress of the European Economic Association, Amsterdam, 25 August, 2005.

Aghion, Philippe, Robert Barro and Ioana Marinescu (2006). Cyclical budgetary policies: their determinants and effects on growth. Work in progress.

Agosin, Manuel R., and Ricardo J. Mayer (2000). Foreign investment in Developing Countries: Does it Crowd in Domestic Investment? UNCTAD Discussion Papers, No. 146. Geneva: UNCTAD. UNCTAD/OSG/DP/146. February.

Aitken, B., and A. Harrison (1999). Do domestic firms benefit from foreign investment? Evidence from Venezuela. *American Economic Review*, vol. 89, No. 3 (June).

Aizenman, Joshua, and Yothin Jinjarak (2006). Globalization and developing countries: a shrinking tax base? NBER Working Paper, No. 11933. Cambridge, Massachusetts: National Bureau of Economic Research. January.

Akyüz, Yilmaz (2004). Trade growth and industrialization: issues, experience and policy challenges. Geneva: Third World Network. Mimeo. December.

Akyüz, Yilmaz (2005). The WTO negotiations on industrial tariffs: what is at stake for developing countries? Geneva: Third World Network. May. Available from www.twnside.org.sg/title2/akyuz_papers/NamaIndFin.pdf (accessed 16 March 2006).

Akyüz, Yilmaz, ed. (2003). *Developing Countries and World Trade: Performance and Prospects*. Geneva: UNCTAD; Penang: Third World Network; and London: Zed Books.

Ascherson, Neal (1963). *The King Incorporated: Leopold the Second and the Congo*. London: George Allen and Unwin.

Azam, Jean-Paul (1998). Politiques macro-économiques et réduction de la pauvreté. Paper presented in the African Economic Research Consortium (AERC) seminar on "Poverty, income distribution, and issues related to labour market", held in Abidjan, 8–13 October.

Banerjee, Abhijit, Paul J. Gertler and Maitreesh Ghatak (2002). Empowerment and efficiency: tenancy reform in West Bengal. *Journal of Political Economy*, vol. 110, No. 2 (April), pp. 239–280.

Barro, Robert J. (1999). Human capital and growth in cross-country regressions. *Swedish Economic Policy Review*, vol. 6, No. 2, pp. 237–277.

Barro, Robert J., and Xavier Sala-i-Martin (1992). Convergence. *Journal of Political Economy (Chicago, Illinois)*, vol. 100, No. 2 (April), pp. 223–251.

Ben-David, Dan (1995). Convergence clubs and diverging economies. Foerder Institute for Economic Research Working Paper, No. 40–95 (November). Tel-Aviv University, Israel.

Blomström M., R. Lipsey and M. Zejan (1992). What explains developing country growth? NBER Working Paper, No. 4132. Cambridge, Massachusetts: National Bureau of Economic Research. August.

Blomström M., and A. Kokko (2003). Human Capital and Inward FDI, CEPR Working Paper, No.167, London: Centre for Economic Policy Research.

Bloom, David, David Canning and Jaypee Sevilla (2004). The effect of health on economic growth: a production function approach. *World Development*, vol. 32, No. 1, pp.1–13.

Bonaglia, Federico, and Kichiro Fukasaku (2003). Export diversification in low-income countries: an international challenge after Doha. OECD Development Centre. Working Paper, No. 209. Paris: OECD. June.

Borensztein E., J. De Gregorio and W. Lee (1995). How does foreign direct investment affect economic growth? NBER Working Paper, No. 5057. Cambridge, Massachusetts: National Bureau of Economic Research. March.

Borjas, George J., and Lawrence F. Katz (2005). The evolution of the Mexican born workforce in the United States. NBER Working Paper, No. 11281. Cambridge, Massachusetts: National Bureau of Economic Research. April.

Bourguignon, François, and Christian Morrisson (2002). Inequality among world citizens, 1820–1992. *American Economic Review*, vol. 92, No. 4 (September), pp. 727–744.

Braunstein, E., and G. Epstein (2004). Bargaining power and foreign direct investment in China: can 1.3 billion consumers tame the multinationals? In *Labor and the Globalization of Production: Causes and Consequences of Industrial Upgrading*, W. Milberg, ed. London: Palgrave.

Briault, C. (1995). The costs of inflation. *Quarterly Bulletin* (Bank of England), vol. 8 (February), pp. 33–45.

Brock, William A., and Steven N. Durlauf (2001). Growth empirics and reality. *World Bank Economic Research*, vol. 15, No. 2, pp. 229–272.

Calderón, César, and Luis Servén (2003). Latin America's infrastructure in the era of macroeconomic crises. In *The Limits of Stabilization: Infrastructure, Public Deficits, and Growth in Latin America*, William Easterly and Luis Servén, eds., Palo Alto, California, and Washington, D.C.: Stanford University Press and World Bank, pp. 21–94.

Calderón, César, William Easterly and Luis Servén (2003). Infrastructure compression and public sector solvency in Latin America. In *The Limits of Stabilization: Infrastructure, Public Deficits, and Growth in Latin America*, William Easterly and Luis Servén, eds., Palo Alto, California, and Washington, D.C.: Stanford University Press and World Bank, pp. 119-138.

Calderón, César, Norman Loayza and Klaus Schmidt-Hebbel (2005). Does openness imply greater exposure? World Bank Policy Research Working Paper, No. 3733. Washington, DC.: World Bank. October.

Canning, David (1999). Infrastructure's contribution to aggregate output, World Bank Policy Research Working Paper, No. 2246. Washington, D.C.: World Bank.

Carkovic, Maria, and Ross Levine (2002). Does foreign direct investment accelerate economic growth? Minneapolis, Minnesota: University of Minnesota. Mimeo. May.

Carmel, Erran (2003). Taxonomy of new software exporting nations. *The Electronic Journal on Information Systems in Developing countries*, vol. 13, No. 2 (May), pp. 1-6. Available from http://www.ejisdc.org/ojs/viewissue.php?id=66 (accessed 22 March 2006).

Chang, Ha-Joon (1999). Industrial policy and East Asia: the miracle, the crisis, and the future. Revised version of paper presented at the World Bank workshop on "Rethinking the East Asian miracle", San Francisco, California, 16 and 17 February 1999. May.

Chang, Ha-Joon (2003). Kicking away the ladder: the "real" history of free trade. Foreign Policy In Focus special report. December. Available from http://www.fpif.org/pdf/papers/SRtrade2003.pdf (accessed 14 March 2006).

Chang, Roberto, L. Kaltani and N. Loayza (2005). Openness can be good for growth: the role of policy complementarities. NBER Working Paper, No. 11787. Cambridge, Massachusetts: National Bureau of Economic Research. November.

Chenery, Hollis B. (1979). *Structural Change and Development Policy*. New York: Oxford University Press.

Chenery, Hollis B., and Lance Taylor (1968). Development patterns among countries and over time: *The Review of Economics and Statistics*, vol. 50, No. 4, pp. 391-416.

Cimoli, Mario, and Jorge Katz (2002). *Structural Reforms, Technological Gaps and Economic Development: a Latin American Perspective*. Desarrollo Productivo Series, No. 129. Sales No. E.02.II.G.89. Santiago: ECLAC. August.

Claessens, Stijn, Michael P. Dooley and Andrew M. Warner (1995). Portfolio capital flows: hot or cold? *World Bank Economic Review*, vol. 9, No. 1, pp. 153-174.

Collier, Paul (2006). War and military expenditure in developing countries and their consequences for development. *The Economics of Peace and Security Journal*, vol. 1 No. 1, pp. 1-4.

Collier, Paul, and Jan Willem Gunning (1999). Explaining African economic performance. *Journal of Economic Literature*, Vol. XXXVII, No. 1 (March), pp. 64-111.

Commission for Africa (2005). *Our Common Interest: Report of the Commission for Africa*. Available from http://www.commissionforafrica.org/english/home/newsstories.html.

Cooper, Richard (1971). Currency devaluation in developing countries. In *Government and Economic Development*, Gustav Ranis, ed. New Haven, Connecticut: Yale University Press.

Cosbey, Aaron, Simon Tay, Hank Lim and Matthew Walls (2004). The rush to regionalism: sustainable development and regional/bilateral approaches to trade and investment liberalization. Scoping paper prepared for the International Development Research Centre (IDRC), Canada. Winnipeg, Manitoba: International Institute for Sustainable Development. November.

Dasgupta, Sukti, and Ajit Singh (2005). Manufacturing, services, jobless growth and the informal economy: will services be the new engine of Indian economic growth? Paper presented at the United Nations University World Institute for Development Economics Research (WIDER) Jubilee Conference, Helsinki, 17 and 18 June 2005.

Davis, Graham A., and John E. Tilton (2005). The resource curse. *Natural Resources Forum: A United Nations Sustainable Development Journal*, vol. 29, Issue 3 (August), pp. 233–242. Oxford, United Kingdom: Blackwell Publishing.

De Ferranti, David, Guillermo E. Perry, Indermit Gill, J. Luis Guasch, William F. Maloney, Carolina Sánchez-Páramo, Norbert Schady (2003). *Closing the Gap in Education and Technology*. World Bank Latin American and Caribbean Studies. Washington, D.C: World Bank.

de Mello, L. (1997). Foreign direct investment in developing countries and growth: a selective survey. *Journal of Development Studies*, vol. 34, No. 1, pp. 1–34.

Demetriades, Panicos O., and Theofanis P. Mamuneas (2000). Intertemporal output and employment effects of public infrastructure capital: evidence from 12 OECD economies. *Economic Journal* (Royal Economic Society), vol. 110, No. 465 (July), pp. 687–712.

Dixit, Avinash (2005). Evaluating recipes for development success. Princeton, New Jersey: Princeton University. 1 June.

Dollar, David (1992). Outward-oriented developing economies really do grow more rapidly: evidence from 95 LDCs, 1976–1985. *Economic Development and Cultural Change*, vol. 40, No. 3, pp. 523–544.

Dornbusch, Rudiger, and Stanley Fischer (1993). Moderate inflation. *World Bank Economic Review*, vol. 7, No. 1 (January), pp 1–44.

Dowrick Steve, and Jane Golley (2004). Trade openness and growth: who benefits? *Oxford Review of Economic Policy*, vol. 20, No. 1, pp. 38–56.

Driffield, Nigel, and James H. Love (2005). Intra-industry foreign direct investment, uneven development and globalisation: the legacy of Stephan Hymer. *Contributions to Political Economy*, vol. No. 24, pp. 55–78.

Driffield, Nigel, and Karl Taylor (2002). Spillovers from FDI and skill structures of host-country firms. Discussion Papers in Economics, No. 02/4. Leicester, United Kingdom: Department of Economics, University of Leicester.

Easterly, William (2001). The lost decades: developing countries' stagnation in spite of policy reform 1980–1998. *Journal of Economic Growth*, vol. 6, No. 2, pp. 135–157.

Easterly, William (2005). How to assess the needs for aid? The answer: don't ask. Paper prepared for the Third Agénce Française de Développement/European Development Research Network (AFD/EUDN) Conference on "Financing Development: What Are the Challenges in Expanding Aid Flows?", Paris, 14 December 2005.

Easterly, William, and Sergio Rebelo (1993). Fiscal policy and economic growth: an empirical investigation. *Journal of Monetary Economics*, vol. 32, pp. 417-458.

Easterly, William, Roumeen Islam, and Joseph E. Stiglitz (2001). Shaken and stirred: volatility and macroeconomic paradigms for rich and poor countries. In *Annual World Bank Conference on Development Economics 2000*, Boris Pleskovic and Nicholas Stern eds., Washington, D.C.: World Bank, pp. 191-212.

Edwards, Sebastian (1986). Are devaluations contractionary? *Review of Economics and Statistics*, vol. 68, No. 3 (August), pp. 501-508.

Eichengreen, Barry (2004). Financial instability. Paper written for the Copenhagen Consensus, and presented in Copenhagen on 25-28 May 2004.

Evans, P. (1979). *Dependent Development: The Alliance of Multinationals, State and Local Capital in Brazil*. Princeton, New Jersey: Princeton University Press.

Feenstra, Robert C., Robert E. Lipsey, Haiyan Deng, Alyson C. Ma and Hengyong Mo (2005). World trade flows: 1962-2000. NBER Working Paper, No. 11040. Cambridge, Massachussetts: National Bureau of Economic Research. January. Available from http://www.nber.org/papers/w11040 (accessed 15 February 2006).

Feld, Serge (2005). Labour force trends and immigration in Europe. *International Migration Review*, vol. 39, issue 3 (Fall), pp. 637-662. New York: Center for Migration Studies.

Ffrench-Davis, Ricardo (2006). *Reforming Latin America's Economies: After Market Fundamentalism*. London: Palgrave-Macmillan.

Fiess, Norbert (2002). Chile's new fiscal rule. Washington, D.C.: World Bank. Mimeo. May.

Fischer, Stanley, and Franco Modigliani (1978). Towards an understanding of the real effects and costs of inflation. *Weltwirtschaftliches Archiv*, vol. 114, No. 4, pp. 810-833.

FitzGerald, Valpy (2008). Financial development and economic growth: a critical survey. In *Growth Divergences. Explaining Differences in Economic Performance*, José Antonio Ocampo, Jomo K.S. and Rob Vos eds., New York, London, Hyderabad and Penang: Orient Longman, Zed Books and Third World Network, pp. 204-235.

Gabriele, Alberto (2004). Exports of services and economic growth in developing countries. Geneva: UNCTAD. UNCTAD/DITC/TNCD/MISC/2003/6. 3 June. Available from http://www.unctad.org/en/docs//ditctncdmisc20036_en.pdf (accessed 22 March 2006).

Gala, Paulo, and Claudio R. Lucinda (2006). Exchange rate misalignment and growth: old and new econometric evidence. Sao Paulo, Brazil: Sao Paulo School of Business Administration and Sao Paulo School of Economics. Mimeo.

Gallup, John Luke, Jeffrey D. Sachs and Andrew D. Mellinger (1998). Geography and economic development. NBER Working Paper, No. 6849. Cambridge, Massachusetts: National Bureau of Economic Research. December.

Gates, Scott, and Anke Hoeffler (2004). Global Aid Allocation: Are Nordic Donors Different? Centre for the Study of African Economies Working paper Series, No.234. Oxford University, Oxford.

Ghose, Ajit K. (2004). Capital inflows and investment in developing countries. ILO Employment Strategy Paper, No. 2004/11. Geneva: International Labour Office. November.

Gillson, Ian, Adrian Hewitt and Sheila Page (2004). Forthcoming changes in the EU banana/sugar markets: a menu of options for an effective EU transitional package: report. London: Overseas Development Institute. Available from http://www.odi.org.uk/iedg/Projects/EU_banana_sugar_markets/SUGARreport.pdf (accessed 13 March 2006).

Glaeser, Edward L., Rafael la Porta, Florencio Lopez-de-Silane and Andrei Shleifer (2004). Do institutions cause growth? NBER Working Paper, No. 10568. Cambridge, Massachusetts: National Bureau of Economic Research. June.

Gorg, Holger, and David Greenaway (2001). Foreign direct investment and intra-industry spillovers. Paper prepared for the Economic Commission for Europe/European Bank for Reconstruction and Development regional expert meeting on "Finance for Development: enhancing the benefits of FDI and improving the flow of corporate finance in the transition economies", Geneva, 3 December 2001.

Gottschalk, Ricardo (2005). The macro content of PRSP: assessing the need for a more flexible macroeconomic policy framework. *Development Policy Review*, vol. 23, No. 4, pp. 419–442.

Griffith-Jones, Stephany, Miguel Angel Segoviano and Stephen Spratt (2003). Submission to the Basel Committee on Banking Supervision: CP3 and the developing world. Institute of Development Studies, University of Sussex, Brighton, United Kingdom. Available from http://www.stephanygj.com.

Grilli, Enzo R., and Maw Cheng Yang (1988). Primary commodity prices, manufactured goods prices, and the terms of trade of developing countries: what the long run shows. *World Bank Economic Review*, vol. 2, No. 1, pp. 1–47.

Guillaumont, Patrick (2005). Macro vulnerability in low income countries and aid responses. Paper presented at the Annual World Bank Conference on Development Economics. Amsterdam, 24 and 25 May.

Gupta, Poonam, Deepak Mishra and Ratna Sahay (2003). Output response to currency crises. IMF Working Paper, No. 03/230, Washington, D.C.: International Monetary Fund.

Gupta, Sanjeev, Robert Powell and Yongzheng Yang (2006). Macroeconomic Challenges of Scaling Up Aid to Africa: A checklist for Practitioners. Washington, D.C.: International Monetary Fund. March.

Hadjimichael, Michael T., and Michel Galy (1997). The CFA franc zone and the EMU. IMF Working Paper, No: 97/156, Washington D.C.: International Monetary Fund. November.

Haggard, Stephan (2004). Institutions and growth in East Asia. *Studies in Comparative International Development*, vol. 38, No. 4 (winter), pp. 53–81.

Hanson, Gordon H., Raymond J. Mataloni, Jr., and Matthew J. Slaughter (2001). Expansion Strategies of U.S. multinational firms. In *Brookings Trade Forum*

2001, Susan M. Collins and Dani Rodrik, eds., Washington, D.C.: Brookings Institution Press, pp. 245–282.

Harrison, Ann E., and Margaret S. McMillan (2002). Does direct foreign investment affect domestic firms credit constraints? Berkeley, California: University of California, Berkeley. Mimeo. January.

Hausmann, Ricardo, Jason Hwang and Dani Rodrik (2006). What you export matters. NBER Working Paper, No. 11905. March. Cambridge, Massachusetts: National Bureau of Economic Research.

Hausmann, Ricardo, Lant Pritchett and Dani Rodrik (2004). Growth accelerations. NBER, Working Paper, No. 10566, June. Cambridge, Massachusetts: National Bureau of Economic Research.

Hausmann, Ricardo, Dani Rodrik and Andrés Velasco (2005). Growth diagnostics (revised). Cambridge, Massachusetts: Harvard University, Kennedy School of Government. March. Available from http://ksghome.harvard.edu/~drodrik/barcelonafinal march2005.pdf.

Helleiner, Gerald K. (1973). Manufacturing exports from less developed countries and multinational firms. *Economic Journal*, vol. 83, No. 329, pp. 21–47.

Herman, Barry (2005). How well do measurements of an enabling domestic environment for development stand up? In *The IMF and the World Bank at Sixty,* Ariel Buira, ed. London: Anthem Press, pp. 281–310.

Hochschild, Adam (1999). *King Leopold's Ghost.* New York: Mariner Books.

Houde M., and K. Yannaca-Small (2004). Relationship between international investment agreements, Organization for Economic Cooperation and Development Working Papers on International Investment 2004/1, Paris: Organization for Economic Cooperation and Development Publishing.

Hummels, David, Jun Ishii and Kei-Mu Yi (1998). Vertical specialization and the changing nature of world trade. *Economic Policy Review* (Federal Reserve Bank of New York), pp. 79–99, June.

Hymer, Stephen H. (1976). *The International Operations of National Firms: A Study of Direct Foreign Investment.* Cambridge, Massachusetts: The MIT Press.

Imbs, Jean, and Romain Wacziarg (2003). Stages of diversification. *American Economic Review,* vol. 93, No. 1 (March), pp. 63–86.

International Monetary Fund (1998). World Economic Outlook: May 1998. Washington D.C. International Monetary Fund.

International Monetary Fund (2005). The macroeconomics of managing increased aid inflows: experiences of low-income countries and policy implications. Washington, D.C.: Policy Development and Review Department, International Monetary Fund. 8 August.

International Monetary Fund (2006). *Finance and Development*, vol. 43, No. 1 (March).

Jenkins, Rhys, and Chris Edwards (2004). How does China's growth affect poverty reduction in Asia, Africa and Latin America? Overseas Development Group, University of East Anglia, Norwich, United Kingdom. Expanded report for the Department for International Development, United Kingdom. 10 December.

Johnson, Simon, Jonathan D. Ostry and Arvind Subramanian (2006). Levers for growth. *Finance and Development*, vol. 43, No. 1 (March).

Kaldor, Nicholas (1957). A model of economic growth. *Economic Journal*, vol. 67, pp. 591-624.

Kaldor, Nicholas (1978). Causes of the slow rate of growth of the United Kingdom. In *Further Essays on Economic Theory*. London: Duckworth.

Kamaly, Ahmed (2003). Mergers and acquisitions: the forgotten facet of FDI. Cairo: Department of Economics, University of Cairo. Mimeo. September.

Kaminsky, Graciela, Carmen M. Reinhart and Carlos A. Végh (2004). When it rains, it pours: procyclical capital flows and macroeconomic policies. NBER Working Paper, No. 10780. Cambridge, Massachusetts: National Bureau of Economic Research. September.

Kapur, Devesh, and John McHale (2005). *Give Us Your Best and Brightest: The Global Hunt for Talent and its Impact on the Developing World*. Washington, D.C.: Center for Global Development.

Kaufmann, Daniel, Aart Kraay and Massimo Mastruzzi (2004). Governance matters III: governance indicators for 1996-2002. World Bank. 5 April (revised).

Kaufmann, Daniel (2005). Measuring governance using cross-country perceptions data. World Bank. August.

Keck, Alexander, and Patrick Low (2004). Special and differential treatment in the WTO: why, when and how? World Trade Organization Staff Working Paper, No. ERSD-2004-03. Geneva: Economic Research and Statistics Division, World Trade Organization. May.

Khan, Mushtaq H. (2007). Governance, economic growth and development since the 1960s. In *Growth Divergences. Explaining Differences in Economic Performance*, José Antonio Ocampo, Jomo K.S. and Rob Vos eds., New York, London, Hyderabad and Penang: Orient Longman, Zed Books and Third World Network, pp. 285-324.

King, Robert. G., and Ross Levine (1993). Finance, entrepreneurship, and growth: theory and evidence. *Journal of Monetary Economics*, vol. 32, No. 3, pp. 513-542.

Klinger, Bailey, and Daniel Lederman (2004). Discovery and development: an empirical exploration of "new" products, World Bank Policy Research Working Paper, No. 3450. Washington, D.C.: World Bank. November.

Kochhar, Kalpana, Utsav Kumar, Raghuram Rajan, Arvind Subramanian and Ioannis Tokatlidis (2006). India's pattern of development: what happened, what follows? IMF Working Paper, No. WP/06/22. January. Available from http://www.imf.org/external/pubs/ft/wp/2006/wp0622.pdf (accessed 22 March 2006).

Kornai Janos (1993). Transformational recession: a general phenomenon examined through the example of Hungary's development. *Economie Appliquée*, vol. 46, No. 2, pp. 181-227.

Kornai Janos (1994). Transformational recession: the main causes. *Journal of Comparative Economics*, vol. 19, No. 1, pp. 39-63.

Kose, M. Ayhan, Eswar S. Prasad and Marco E. Terrones (2005). Growth and volality in an era of globalization. *IMF Staff Papers*, vol. 52, special issue, pp. 31-63. Washington, D.C.: International Monetary Fund.

Kozul-Wright, Richard, and Paul Rayment (2006). *The Resistable Rise of Market Fundamentalism*. London: Zed Press.

Kregel, Jan (1996). Some risks and implications of financial globalization for national policy autonomy. *United Nations Conference on Trade and Development Review* (Geneva), pp. 55–62.

Krugman, Paul (1995). Growing world trade: causes and consequences. In *Brookings Papers on Economic Activity*, No. 1. Washington, D.C.: the Brookings Institution.

Krugman, Paul, and Lance Taylor (1978). The contractionary effects of devaluation. *Journal of International Economics*, vol. 8, pp. 445–458.

Kumar, Nagesh, and Jaya Prakash Pradhan (2002). Foreign direct investment, externalities and economic growth in developing countries: some empirical explorations and implications for WTO negotiations on investment. RIS Discussion Paper, No. RIS–DP27/2002. New Delhi: Research and Information System for the Non-Aligned and Other Developing Countries.

Kuznets, Simon (1966). *Modern Economic Growth: Rate, Structure, and Spread*. New Haven: Yale University Press.

Lall, Sanjaya (2000). Selective industrial and trade policies in developing countries: theoretical and empirical issues. QEH Working Paper, No. 48. Oxford, United Kingdom: Queen Elizabeth House, University of Oxford. August.

Lall, Sanjaya (2001). *Competitiveness, Technology and Skills*. Cheltenham: Edward Elgar.

Lall, Sanjaya (2003). Reinventing industrial strategy: the role of government policy in building industrial competitiveness. Working paper prepared for the Intergovernmental Group on Monetary Affairs and Development (G–24). Second draft. September.

Lee, Jong-Wha (1997). Economic growth and human development in the Republic of Korea, 1945–1992. Occasional Paper, No. 24. New York: United Nations Development Programme.

Lim, Ewe-Ghee (2001). Determinants of, and the relation between, foreign direct investment and growth: a summary of the recent literature. IMF Working Paper, No.01/175. Washington, D.C.: International Monetary Fund.

Lucas, Robert E., Jr. (1988). On the mechanics of economic development. *Journal of Monetary Economics*, vol. 22, No. 1 (February), pp. 3–42.

Lucas, Robert E., Jr. (2000). Some macroeconomics for the 21st century. *Journal of Economic Perspectives*, vol. 14, no. 1 (winter), pp. 159–168.

Lucas, Robert E.B. (2001). Diaspora and development: highly skilled migrants from East Asia. Report prepared for the World Bank. November.

Maddison, Angus (1995). *Monitoring the World Economy 1820–1992*. Development Centre Studies. Paris: Organization for Economic Cooperation and Development Development Centre.

Maddison, Angus (2001). *The World Economy: A Millennial Perspective*. Development Centre Studies. Paris: Organization for Economic Cooperation and Development Development Centre.

McGillivray, Mark, and Oliver Morrisey (2001). A review of the evidence on the fiscal effects of aid. CREDIT Research Paper, No. 01/13. Nottingham, United Kingdom: University of Nottingham.

Milanovic, Branko (2005). *Worlds Apart: Measuring International and Global Inequality*. Princeton, New Jersey: Princeton University Press.

Milanovic, Branko, and Shlomo Yitzhaki (2001). Decomposing world income distribution: does the world have a middle class? World Bank Policy Research Working Paper, No. 2562. Washington, D.C.: World Bank Poverty and Human Resources, Development Research Group. 31 March.

Minoiu, Camelia, and Sanjay G. Reddy (2008). Aid does matter after all: revisiting the relationship between aid and growth. In *Growth Divergences. Explaining Differences in Economic Performance*, José Antonio Ocampo, Jomo K.S. and Rob Vos eds., New York, London, Hyderabad and Penang: Orient Longman, Zed Books and Third World Network, pp. 236–258.

Milberg, William (2004). Globalized production: structural challenges for developing country workers. In *Labour and the Globalization of Production; Causes and Consequences of Industrial Upgrading*, William Milberg, ed. New York: Palgrave-Macmillan.

Mody, Ashoka (2004). Is FDI integrating the world economy? Paper presented at the Thirteenth World Congress of the International Economics Association, Lisbon, September 2002.

Mosley, Paul, (1999). "Micro-macro linkages in financial markets: the impact of financial liberalisation on access to rural credit in four African countries. Finance and Development Research Programme Working Paper No. 4. Manchester, United Kingdom: Institute for Development Policy and Management, University of Manchester. March.

Murshed, S. Mansoob (2001). Short-run models of natural resource endowment. In *Resource Abundance and Economic Development*, Richard Auty ed. Oxford, United Kingdom: Oxford University Press.

Murshed, S. Mansoob (2002). Civil war, conflict and underdevelopment. *Journal of Peace Research*, vol. 34, no. 4, pp. 387–393.

Murshed, S. Mansoob (2008). Turning swords to ploughshares and little acorns to tall trees: the conflict-growth nexus and the poverty of nations. In *Growth Divergences. Explaining Differences in Economic Performance*, José Antonio Ocampo, Jomo K.S. and Rob Vos eds., New York, London, Hyderabad and Penang: Orient Longman, Zed Books and Third World Network, pp. 325–351.

Myrdal, Gunnar (1957). *Economic Theory and Underdeveloped Regions*. London: Duckworth.

Nielson, Julia, and Daria Taglioni (2004). Services trade liberalisation: identifying opportunities and gains. OECD Trade Policy Working Paper, No. 1. Paris: Working Party of the Trade Committee, Organization for Economic Cooperation and Development. TD/TC/WP(2003)23/FINAL. February. Available from http://www.olis.oecd.org/olis/2003doc.nsf/LinkTo/td-tc-wp(2003)23-final (accessed 20 March 2006).

Norwegian Refugee Council (2006). Internal displacement: global overview of trends and developments in 2005, Geneva: International Displacement Monitoring Centre and Norwegian Refugee Council. March.

Nunnenkamp, Peter, and Julius Spatz (2004). FDI and economic growth in developing countries: how relevant are host-economy and industry characteristics? *Transnational Corporations* (New York and Geneva), vol.13, No. 3 (December), pp. 53–83.

Ocampo, José Antonio (2003). Capital-account and counter-cyclical prudential regulations in developing countries. In *From Capital Surges to Drought: Seeking Stability for Emerging Markets*, Ricardo Ffrench-Davis and Stephany Grifith-Jones, eds., London: Palgrave-Macmillan, pp. 217–244.

Ocampo, José Antonio, and Juan Martin (coordinators) (2003), *Globalization and Development: A Latin American and Caribbean Perspective*, Palo Alto, Stanford University Press, ECLAC and World Bank.

Ocampo, José Antonio, and María Ángela Parra (2003). The terms of trade for commodities in the twentieth century. *CEPAL Review* (Santiago), No. 79. (April), pp. 7–35. LC/G.2200-P.

Ocampo, José Antonio (2004). Latin America's growth and equity frustration during structural reforms. *Journal of Economic Perspectives* (American Economic Association), vol. 18, No. 2 (Spring), pp. 67–88.

Ocampo, José Antonio (2005a). A broad view of macroeconomic stability. DESA Working Paper, No. 1, New York. October. Available from http://www.un.org/esa/desa/papers.

Ocampo, José Antonio (2005b). The quest for dynamic efficiency: structural dynamics and economic growth in developing countries. In *Beyond Reforms: Structural Dynamics and Macroeconomic Vulnerability*, José Antonio Ocampo, ed. Palo Alto, California, and Washington, D.C.: Stanford Economics and Finance, Stanford University Press, and World Bank.

Ocampo, José Antonio (2005c). The dual divergence: growth successes and collapses in the developing world since 1980. Paper presented at the ECLAC, Santiago, Chile, Seminar on Economic Growth with Equity: Challenges for Latin America, 1 and 2 September, 2005, Santiago. In Ricardo Ffrench-Davis and José Luis Machinea (eds.), *Economic Growth with Equity; Challenges for Latin America*, Palgrave, London. DESA Working Paper No. 24. May 2006. Available from http://www.un.org/esa/desa/papers.

Ocampo, José Antonio (2006). Market, social cohesion and democracy. DESA Working Paper, No. 9. February. Available from http://www.un.org/esa/desa/papers.

Ocampo, José Antonio, Jan Kregel and Stephany Griffith-Jones (2006) *International Finance and Development*, New York, London, Hyderabad and Penang: Orient Longman, Zed Books and Third World Network.

Ocampo, José Antonio, and Stephany Griffith-Jones (2006). Counter-cyclical framework for a development-friendly international financial architecture. Paper presented at the International Development Research Centre workshop on "International Financial Architecture, Macroeconomic Volatility and Institutions", United Nations Headquarters, New York, 17 and 18 April 2006.

Ocampo, José Antonio and Rob Vos (2006) Policy space and the changing paradigm in conducting macroeconomic policies in developing countries, Paper presented at FONDAD–UN/DESA seminar on 'Policy Space for Developing Countries in a Globalized World, New York, 7–9 December.

Ocampo, José Antonio, Jomo K.S., and Rob Vos eds., (2008). *Growth Divergences. Explaining Differences in Economic Performance*, New York, London, Hyderabad and Penang: Orient Longman, Zed Books and Third World Network.

Okita, Saburo (1985). Special presentation: prospects of Pacific economies. *Pacific Cooperation: Issues and Opportunities*: Report of the Fourth Pacific Economic Cooperation Conference, Seoul, April 29–May 1, 1985. Seoul: Korea Development Institute.

Palma, Gabriel (2003). The three routes to financial crises: Chile, Mexico and Argentina [1]; Brazil [2]; and Korea, Malaysia and Thailand [3]. In *Rethinking Development Economics*, Ha-Joon Chang, ed., London: Anthem Press.

Palma, Gabriel (2004). Flying-geese and lame ducks: regional powers and the different capabilities of Latin America and East Asia to "demand-adapt" and "supply-upgrade" their export productive capacity. Unpublished. August.

Palma, Gabriel (2006). Growth after globalization: a structuralist-Kaldorian game of musical chairs. Background paper prepared for the *World Economic and Social Survey 2006: Diverging Growth and Development*. February. Available from http://www.un.org/esa/policy/wess/index.html.

Pang, Tikki, Mary Ann Lansang and Andy Haines (2002). Brain drain and health professionals: a global problem needs global solutions. *British Medical Journal* vol. 324, pp. 499–500. 2 March.

Passinetti, Luigi (1981). *Structural Change and Economic Growth: A Theoretical Essay on the Dynamics of the Wealth of Nations*. Cambridge, United Kingdom: Cambridge University Press.

Perry, Guillermo E., Omar S. Arias, J. Humberto López, William F. Maloney and Luis Servén (2006). *Poverty Reduction and Growth: Virtuous and Vicious Circles*. Washington, D.C.: World Bank.

Plender, J. (2003). *Going off the Rails: Global Capital and the Crisis of Legitimacy*. Chichester, United Kingdom: John Wiley and Sons, Ltd.

Podkaminer, Leon (2006). External liberalization, growth and distribution: the Polish experience. In *External Liberalization in Asia, Post-Socialist Europe, and Brazil*, Lance Taylor, ed. New York: Oxford University Press.

Polak, Jacques J. (1957). Monetary analysis of income formation and payments problems. *IMF Staff Papers*, vol. 6 (November), pp. 1–50.

Polanyi, Karl (1944). *The Great Transformation*. Boston, Massachusetts: Beacon Press.

Prasad, Eswar S., Kenneth Rogoff, Shang-Jin Wei and M. Ayhan Kose (2003). Effects of financial globalization on developing countries: some empirical evidence. IMF Occasional Paper, No. 220. Washington, D.C.: International Monetary Fund.

Przeworski, Adam (2003). Institutions matter? New York: New York University, Department of Politics. Paper prepared for the meeting on Institutions, Behavior and Outcomes, Centro Brasileiro de Analise e Planejamento (CEBRAP), São Paulo, Brazil, 12 March 2003.

Qian, Yingyi (2003). How Reform Worked in China. *In Search of Prosperity: Analytic Narratives on Economic Growth*, Dani Rodrik, ed. Princeton, New Jersey: Princeton University Press, pp. 297–333.

Qian, Yingyi, and Wu, Jinglian (2000). China's transition to a market economy: how far across the river? Paper prepared for the conference on Policy Reform in China at the Center for Research on Economic Development and Policy Reform (CEDPR), Stanford University, Palo Alto, California, 18–20 November 1999.

Quah, Danny T. (1996). Twin peaks: growth and convergence in models of distribution dynamics. *The Economic Journal*, vol. 106, No. 437 (July), pp. 1045-1055.

Rada, Codrina, and Lance Taylor (2008). Developing and transition economies in the late 20th century: diverging growth rates, economic structures, and sources of demand. In *Growth Divergences. Explaining Differences in Economic Performance*, José Antonio Ocampo, Jomo K.S. and Rob Vos eds., New York, London, Hyderabad and Penang: Orient Longman, Zed Books and Third World Network.

Rajan, Raghuram G., and Arvind Subramanian (2005). What undermines aid's impact on growth. IMF Working Paper, No. 05/126, Washington, D.C.: International Monetary Fund.

Ramey, Garey, and Valerie Ramey (1995). Cross-country evidence on the link between volatility and growth. *American Economic Review*, vol. 85, No. 5 (December), pp. 1138-1151.

Ranis, Gustav, and Frances Stewart (2005). Dynamic links between the economy and human development. DESA Working Paper, No. 8. November. Available from http://www.un.org/esa/desa/papers.

Rawls, John (1999). *A theory of Justice*, revised ed. Cambridge, Massachusetts: Harvard University Press.

Raychaudhuri, Ajitava (2004). Lessons from the land reform movement in West Bengal, India. Paper presented at Scaling Up Poverty Reduction: A Global Learning Process and Conference, Shanghai, China, 25-27 May 2004.

Reddy, Sanjay G., and Camelia Minoiu (2005). Real income stagnation of countries, 1960-2001. Department of Economics, Barnard College, Columbia University, and Department of Economics, Columbia University, New York. Background paper prepared for the *World Economic and Social Survey 2006: Diverging Growth and Development*. February. Available from http://www.un.org/esa/policy/wess/index.html.

Rodriguez, Francisco (2006a). Cleaning up the kitchen sink: on the consequences of the linearity assumption for cross-country growth empirics. Wesleyan University Working Papers, No. 2006-004. Middletown, Connecticut: Department of Economics, Wesleyan University. 19 January. Also in: *Growth Divergences. Explaining Differences in Economic Performance*, José Antonio Ocampo, Jomo K.S. and Rob Vos eds., New York, London, Hyderabad and Penang: Orient Longman, Zed Books and Third World Network (2008), pp. 128-147.

Rodriguez, Francisco (2006b). Have collapses in infrastructure spending led to cross-country divergence in per capita GDP? Background paper prepared for the *World Economic and Social Survey 2006: Diverging Growth and Development*. Available from http://www.un.org/esa/policy/wess/index.html. Also in: *Growth Divergences. Explaining Differences in Economic Performance*, José Antonio Ocampo, Jomo K.S. and Rob Vos eds., New York, London, Hyderabad and Penang: Orient Longman, Zed Books and Third World Network (2008), pp. 259-284.

Rodriguez, Francisco (2006c). Openness and growth: what have we learned? Wesleyan Economic Working Papers, No. 2006-11. Middletown, Connecticut:

Department of Economics, Wesleyan University. Also in: *Growth Divergences. Explaining Differences in Economic Performance*, José Antonio Ocampo, Jomo K.S. and Rob Vos eds., New York, London, Hyderabad and Penang: Orient Longman, Zed Books and Third World Network (2008), pp. 172–203.

Rodrik, Dani (1999). *The New Global Economy and Developing Countries: Making Openness Work.* Washington, D.C.: Overseas Development Council.

Rodrik, Dani (2000a). Exchange rate regimes and institutional arrangements in the shadow of capital flows. Paper presented at the Conference on Central Banking and Sustainable Development, held in Kuala Lumpur, 28–30 August, in honour of Tun Ismail Mohamed Ali.

Rodrik, Dani (2000b). Trade policy reform as institutional reform. Cambridge, Massachusetts: Harvard University. August.

Rodrik, Dani (2004a). Getting institutions right. Cambridge, Massachusetts: Harvard University. April.

Rodrik, Dani (2004b). Industrial policy for the twenty-first century. Paper prepared for the United Nations Industrial Development Organization. September.

Rodrik, Dani (2004c). Growth Strategies. A paper for the *Handbook of Economic Growth*, Philippe Aghion and Steven Durlauf, eds., Amsterdam: North-Holland. Revised October 2004.

Rodrik, Dani (2005). Why we learn nothing from regressing economic growth on policies. Cambridge, Massachusetts: Harvard University. 25 March.

Rodrik, Dani (2006a). Goodbye Washington Consensus, hello Washington Confusion? Cambridge, Massachusetts: Harvard University. January.

Rodrik, Dani (2006b). What's so special about China's exports? NBER Working Paper, No. 11947. Cambridge, Massachusetts: National Bureau of Economic Research. January.

Rodrik, Dani, ed. (2003). *In Search of Prosperity: Analytic Narratives on Economic Growth*, Princeton, New Jersey: Princeton University Press.

Roller, Lars-Hendrik, and Leonard Waverman (2001). Telecommunications infrastructure and economic development: a simultaneous approach. *American Economic Review*, vol. 91, No. 4, pp. 909–923.

Roodman, D. (2004). The anarchy of numbers: aid, development and cross-country empirics. Washington, D.C.: Center for Global Development. Mimeo.

Ros, Jaime (2000). *Development Theory and the Economics of Growth.* Ann Arbor, Michigan: University of Michigan Press.

Rowthorn, R. E. (1992). Intra-industry trade under oligopoly: the role of market size. *Economic Journal*, vol. 102, issue 411, pp. 402–414.

Sachs, Jeffrey, and Andrew Warner (1995). Economic reform and the process of global integration. *Brookings Papers on Economic Activity*, No. 1, pp. 1–118. Washington, D.C.: Brookings Institution Press.

Sánchez, Marco V. (2005). Reformas económicas, régimen cambiario y choques externos: efectos en el desarrollo económico, la desigualidad y la pobreza en Costa Rica, El Salvador y Honduras. *Serie de Estudios y Perspectivas*, No. 36, Mexico. United Nations, Economic Commission for Latin America and the Caribbean.

Sánchez-Robles, B. (1998). Infrastructure investment and growth: some empirical evidence. *Contemporary Economic Policy*, vol. 16, No. 1 (January), pp. 98–108.

Schady, Norbert (2005). Changes in the global distribution of life expectancy and health. Washington, D.C.: World Bank. Mimeo.

Schmidt-Hebbel, Klaus, Luis Servén and Andrés Solimano (1996). Saving and investment: paradigms, puzzles, policies. *World Bank Research Observer*, vol. 11, No. 1, pp. 87–117.

Schultz, Theodore W. (1961). Investment in human capital. *The American Economic Review*, vol. LI (March), pp. 1–17.

Shapiro, Helen (2008). Industrial policy and growth. In *Growth Divergences. Explaining Differences in Economic Performance*, José Antonio Ocampo, Jomo K.S. and Rob Vos eds., New York, London, Hyderabad and Penang: Orient Longman, Zed Books and Third World Network, pp. 148–171.

Singh, Nirvikar (2003). India's information technology sector: what contribution to broader economic development? OECD Development Centre Working Paper, No. 207. Paris: Organization for Economic Cooperation and Development Development Centre. DEV/DOC(2003)05. March. Available from http://www.oecd.org/dataoecd/59/12/2503442.pdf (accessed 22 March 2006).

Slaughter, Matthew J. (1998). International trade and per capita income convergence: a difference-in-differences analysis. NBER Working Paper, No. 6557. Cambridge, Massachusetts: National Bureau of Economic Research. May.

Sokoloff, Kenneth, and Stanley Engerman (2000). Institutions, factor endowments, and paths of development in the New World. *Journal of Economic Perspectives*, Vol. 14, No. 3. (Summer), pp. 217–232.

Spiezia, V. (2004). Trade, foreign direct investment and employment: some empirical evidence. In *Understanding Globalization, Employment and Poverty Reduction*, E. Lee and M. Vivarelli, eds, London: Macmillan.

Stallings, Barbara, and Jürgen Weller (2001). *Job Creation in Latin America in the 1990s: The Foundation for Social Policy*. Serie macroeconomía del desarrollo, No. 5. Sales No. E.01.II.G.15. Santiago: Economic Commission for Latin America and the Caribbean, Economic Development Division.

Stiglitz, Joseph E., and Andrew Charlton (2004). The development round of trade negotiations in the aftermath of Cancún. Report prepared for the Commonwealth Secretariat with the Initiative for Policy Dialogue.

Stiglitz, Joseph E. (2006). Aid for trade: a report for the Commonwealth Secretariat, London. March.

Stiglitz, Joseph, José Antonio Ocampo, Shari Spiegel, Ricardo Ffrench-Davis and Deepak Nayyar (2006). *Stability with Growth*. Oxford, United Kingdom: Oxford University Press.

Subramanian, Arvind, and Devesh Roy (2001). Who can explain the Mauritian miracle: Meade, Romer, Sachs or Rodrik? Available from http://ksghome.harvard.edu/~drodrik/Growth%20volume/Subramanian-Mauritius.doc (accessed 16 March 2006).

Syrquin, Moshe (1986). Productivity growth and factor reallocation. In *Industrialization and Growth*, Hollis B. Chenery, Sherman Robinson and Moshe Syrquin, eds., New York: Oxford University Press.

UN Millennium Project (2005). *Investing in Development: Practical Plan to Achieve the Millennium Development Goals*. London: Earthscan.

United Nations (1975). *Standard International Trade classification, Revision 2*. Statistical Papers, No. 34/Rev.2. Sales No. E.75.XVII.6.
United Nations (2000). *World Economic and Social Survey 2000*. Sales No. E.00.II.C.1.
United Nations (2002a). *Report of the International Conference on Financing for Development, Monterrey, Mexico, 18–22 March 2002*. Sales No. E.02.II.A.7. Chap. I, resolution 1, annex.
United Nations (2002b). *World Economic and Social Survey 2002*. Sales No. E.02.II.C.1.
United Nations (2004a). *International Trade Statistics Yearbook, 2003*, vol. II, *Trade by Commodity*. Sales No. E/F.05.XVII.2, vol. II.
United Nations (2004b). *World Economic and Social Survey 2004: International Migration*. Sales No. E.04.II.C.3.
United Nations (2005a). *The Inequality Predicament: Report on the World Social Situation 2005*. Sales No. E.05.IV.5.
United Nations (2005b). *World Economic and Social Survey 2005: Financing for Development*. Sales No. E.05.II.C.1.
United Nations (2006). *World Economic Situation and Prospects 2006*. Sales No. E.06.II.C.2.
United Nations, Economic Commission for Africa (2001). *Transforming Africa's Economies: Overview*. Addis Ababa. Available from http://www.uneca.org/eca_resources/Publications/books/transforming_africas_economies/index.htm.
United Nations, Economic Commission for Latin America and the Caribbean (2000). Equity, Development and Citizenship. Santiago: ECLAC. LC/G.2071(SES.28/3). March.
United Nations (2003). *A decade of Light and Shadow: Latin America and the Caribbean in the 1990s*. Sales No. E.03.II.G.79. Santiago: ECLAC. July.
United Nations (2004). Productive development in open economies. Santiago: ECLAC. LC/G.2234(SES.30/3). June.
United Nations Conference on Trade and Development (1992). *Trade and Development Report, 1992*. Sales No. E.92.II.D.7.
United Nations Conference on Trade and Development (1996). *Trade and Development Report, 1996*. Sales No. E.96.II.D.6.
United Nations Conference on Trade and Development (1999). *Trade and Development Report, 1999: Fragile Recovery and Risks: Trade, Finance and Growth*. Sales No. E.99.II.D.1.
United Nations Conference on Trade and Development (2000). *World Investment Report, 2000: Cross-border Mergers and Acquisitions and Development*. Sales No. E.00.II.D.20.
United Nations Conference on Trade and Development (2002). *Trade and Development Report, 2002: Developing Countries in World Trade*. Sales No. E.02.II.D.2.
United Nations Conference on Trade and Development (2003). *Trade and Development Report 2003: Capital Accumulation, Growth and Structural Change*. Sales No. 03.II.07.
United Nations Conference on Trade and Development (2005a). *Trade and Development Report 2005: New Features of Global Interdependence*. Sales No. E.05.II.D.13.

United Nations Conference on Trade and Development (2005b). *UNCTAD Handbook of Statistics, 2005*. Sales No. E/F.05.II.D.29.

United Nations Conference on Trade and Development (2006). Trade in services and development implications: note by the UNCTAD secretariat. TD/B/COM.1/77. Geneva, 16 January. Also available from http://www.unctad.org/en/docs/c1d77_en.pdf (accessed 22 March 2006).

United Nations Development Programme (2005). *Human Development Report 2005. International Cooperation at a Crossroads: Aid, Trade and Security in an Unequal World*. New York: United Nations Development Programme.

United Nations Industrial Development Organization (2005). *Industrial Development Report, 2005: Capacity Building for Catching-up: Historical, Empirical and Policy Dimensions*. Vienna: UNIDO.

van Pottelsberghe de la Potterie, Bruno, and Frank Lichtenberg (2001). Does foreign direct investment transfer technology across borders? *Review of Economics and Statistics*, vol. 83, No. 3 (1 August), pp. 490–497.

Verdoorn, P. J. (1949). Fattori che regolano lo sviluppo della produttività del lavoro. *L'Industria*, vol. 1, pp. 3–10.

Villanueva, D., and A. Mirakhor (1990). Strategies for financial reforms. *IMF Staff Papers*, vol. 37, No. 3, pp. 509–536.

Vos, Rob (1994). *Debt and Adjustment in the World Economy*. London: Macmillan.

Vos, Rob, and Samuel Morley (2006). Bad luck or wrong policies? external shocks, domestic adjustment, and the growth slowdown in Latin America and the Caribbean. In: *Who Gains from Free Trade? Export-led Growth, Inequality and Poverty in Latin America*, Rob Vos, Enrique Ganuza, Samuel Morky and Sherman Robinson, eds., London: Routledge.

Wade, Robert Hunter (2004). *Governing the Market: Economic Theory and the Role of Government in East Asian Industrialization*, 2nd paperback ed. Princeton, New Jersey: Princeton University Press.

Wade, Robert Hunter (2005). Escaping the squeeze: lessons from East Asia on how middle-income countries can grow faster. Available from http://www.lse.ac.uk/collections/DESTIN/pdf/Galbraithvolume.nov04.pdf (accessed 8 March 2006).

White, Howard, ed. (1998). *Aid and Macroeconomic Performance: Theory, Empirical Evidence and Four Country Cases*. London: Macmillan.

Willmore, Larry (1994). Export processing in the Caribbean: the Jamaican experience. *CEPAL Review*, vol. 52 (April), pp. 91–104.

Winters, Alan L. (2002). The economic implications of liberalising Mode 4 trade. Paper prepared for the Joint WTO-World Bank Symposium on the Movement of Natural Persons (Mode 4) under the GATS, World Trade Organization, Geneva, 11–12 April. London: Centre for Economic Policy Research and Centre for Economic Performance, London School of Economics.

World Bank (1993). *The East Asia Miracle: Economic Growth and Public Policy*. World Bank Policy Research Report. New York: Oxford University Press.

World Bank (1999). *Global Economic Prospects 1998/99: Beyond Financial Crisis*. Washington, D.C.: World Bank.

World Bank (2003). China: promoting growth with equity: country economic memorandum. Poverty Reduction and Economic Management Unit, East Asia and Pacific Region. Report No. 24169–CHA. 15 October.

World Bank (2004). The Marrakech Action Plan for Statistics: Better Data for Better Results. An Action Plan for Improving Development Statistics. Paper prepared by the Staff of the Development Data Group of the World Bank and presented at the Second International Roundtable on Managing for Development Results, Marrakech, Morocco, 4 and 5 February 2004. Available from http://unstats.un.org/unsd/statcom/doc04.marrakech.pdf.

World Bank (2005a). *World Development Report 2006: Equity and Development*. Washington, D.C.: World Bank; and New York: Oxford University Press.

World Bank (2005b). *Economic Growth in the 1990s: Learning from a Decade of Reforms*, Washington, D.C.: World Bank. April. Also available from http://www1.worldbank.org/prem/lessons1990s/ (accessed 9 March 2006).

World Bank (2005c). *Global Development Finance, 2005: Mobilizing Finance and Managing Vulnerability*. Washington, D.C.: World Bank.

World Bank (2006). *Global Economic Prospects. Economic Implications of Remittances and Migration*. Washington, D.C.: World Bank.

World Bank, and International Monetary Fund (2006). *Global Monitoring Report 2006: Millennium Development Goals: Strengthening Mutual Accountability—Aid, Trade and Governance*. Washington, D.C.: World Bank.

World Trade Organization (2005). Doha work programme: draft ministerial declaration: revision. Agreed at the Sixth Ministerial Conference of the World Trade Organization, Hong Kong, 13–18 December 2005. WT/MIN(05)/W/3/Rev.2, 18 December 2005.

World Trade Organization (2006). Measuring trade in services. Training module produced by the Economic Research and Statistics Division. March.

World Trade Organization, Committee on Subsidies and Countervailing Measures (2001). Procedures for extensions under article 27.4 for certain developing country members. G/SCM/39. 20 November.

Young, Alwyn A. (1928). Increasing returns and economic progress. *The Economic Journal*, vol. 38, pp. 527–542.

Young, H. Peyton (1998). *Individual Strategy and Social Structure: An Evolutionary Theory of Institutions*. Princeton, New Jersey: Princeton University Press.

Index

Afghanistan, 69, 155, 167 table V.1, 193 table A.5, 199 table A.5
Africa, 5, 6 table I.1, 7, 11, 12 fig. I.3B, 15, 17, 20, 21, 26–28 fig. I.10, 30, 37, 38–39 fig. II.1–2, 42–44 table II.1, 45 fig. II.3, 47 fig. II.4–fig. II.5, 50–53 fig. II.7–10, 54–56, 67 fig. III.2, 72, 79, 82, 83, 84, 87, 90, 106 table IV.1, 107, 108 fig. IV.1–IV.2, 109, 111 fig. IV.3, 112, 113, 114 fig. IV.4, 115, 121, 122 table IV.2, 130, 131 table IV.3, 134, 138, 141, 143, 150–51, 154, 166–69, 171–73, 184 table A.1, 186–87 table A.2–3, 195 tableA.5. *See also* Northern Africa; Sub-Saharan Africa
agriculture
    in Andean countries, 54
    annual growth rates, 39 fig. II.2
    contribution to job creation, 50 fig. II.7
    contribution to labour productivity growth, 177
    decrease in developing economies, 37, 56
    essential to economic development, 174
    export subsidies, 98
    insufficient attention to, 169
    Malaysia and Thailand, 66
    modernization, 35, 168
    preferential treatment, 41
    residual employer, 52
    share of employment, 49
    share of output, 38 fig. II.1C, 39, 47 fig. II.5
    structural change, 42, 55
    in Sub-Saharan Africa, 42
aid. *See* official development assistance (ODA)
Albania, 194 table A.5
Algeria, 192 table A.5, 199 table A.5
Angola, 171, 194 table A.5, 198 table A.5
Argentina, 19, 20, 49, 73, 75, 84, 111, fig. IV.3, 122 table IV.2, 125 fig. IV.7, 133 fig. IV.10, 154, 155, 193 table A.5, 196 table A.5, 202 table A.7
Asia, 5, 6 table I.1, 7, 11, 12 fig. I.3, 15, 17, 19, 23, 28 fig. I.10, 33, 37, 44, 51, 53, 55, 56, 66, 72, 75, 80, 81, 83, 107, 111 fig. IV.3, 113, 115, 119, 120, 122 table IV.2, 158, 171 *See also* East Asia; South Asia; South-East Asia; Western Asia
Austria, 137
Australia, 5, 126 fig. IV.8, 154, 168

Bahrain, 194 table A.5, 198 table A.5
Bangladesh, 19, 24, 125 fig. IV.7, 154
Benin, 195 table A.5, 198 table A.5
bonds
    commodity-linked, 142
    domestic market for, 114–15
    GDP-linked, 142
    importance of, 115, 119–120
boom-bust cycles, 13, 101n14, 119, 151
Bolivia, 19, 125 fig. IV.7, 133 fig. IV.10, 167 table V.1, 194 table A.5, 199 table A.5
Botswana, 20, 21, 30, 66 box III.1, 109, 126 fig. IV.8, 150, 157, 168-70

Brazil, 20, 73, 101n11, 109, 122 table IV.2, 125 fig. IV.7, 126 fig.IV.8, 133 fig. V.10, 166, 192 table A.5, 202 table A.7
Bretton Woods system
    collapse of, 106
Bulgaria, 192 table A.5
Burkina Faso, 128, 195 table A.5, 199 table A.5
Burundi, 194 table A.5, 199 table A.5

Cambodia, 15, 83, 195 table A.5, 197 table A.5
Cameroon, 122 table IV.2, 125 fig. IV.7, 167 table V.1, 194 table A.5
Canada, 49, 126 fig. IV.8, 137, 155
capital flows, 101n14, 120
    volatility, 117, 123, 127, 142
    private, 27, 117, 118, 119
        cyclical pattern of, 117, 119
        pro-cyclical (nature of), 28, 104, 119–120, 142
        volatility, 119–120
Caribbean, 20, 38–39 fig.II.1–2, 44 table II.1, 47 fig. II.4–5, 50–52 fig.II.7–9, 53–54, 56, 67 fig. III.2, 71, 79, 90, 106 table IV.1, 108 fig. IV.1, 155
Central African Republic, 195 table A.5, 198 table A.5
Central America, 17, 37, 38 fig. II.1, 41, 44 table II.1, 47 fig. II.4–5, 50–52 fig. II.7–9, 53, 54, 72, 79, 81–83
Central and Eastern Europe, 12 fig. I.3, 37, 38 fig. II.1, 41, 43, 44 table II.1, 45, 46 box II.1, 47 fig. II.4, 50 fig. II.7, 51 fig. II.8, 52 fig. II.9, 53, 56, 67 fig. III.2, 72, 187-88 table A.3. *See also* Eastern Europe
Chad, 195 table A.5, 199 table A.5
Chile, 20, 23, 54, 125, 126 fig. IV.8, 128, 133 fig. IV.10, 140, 166, 169, 194 table A.5, 198 table A.5, 202 table A.7
China, 1, 4, 6 table I.18, 16, 19, 24–26, 37–39 fig. II.1–2, 43, 44 table II.1, 45 fig. II.3, 47 fig. II.4–5, 50 fig. II.7, 51–53 fig.II.8–10, 55, 67 fig. III.2, 68, 71, 78, 81, 83, 87, 95, 112, 122 table IV.2, 126 fig. IV.8, 133 fig. IV.10, 158–59, 161, 163, 165, 173, 187–88 table A.3, 193 table A.5, 196 table A.5, 202 table A.7
classical development thinking, 35–36
Colombia, 20, 122 table IV.2, 125, 126 fig. IV.8, 128, 133 fig. IV.10, 193, 197
Commonwealth of Independent States (CIS), 19, 20, 28 fig. I.10, 37, 38–39 fig. II.1–2, 41, 43, 44 table II.1, 45 fig. II.3, 46, 47 fig. II.4, 50–53 fig. II.7–10, 54, 184 table A.1, 187–88 table A.3
conflict
    conflict management, 150, 161, 170–73, 175
    and economic growth, 23, 31, 43, 69
    governance and, 31, 152, 170–73
convergence, 97–100, 142
    capital flows, 101n14
    convergence clubs, 15, 17, 18, 151, 157
    developing versus developed countries, 5–8, 59
    development aid, 30, 28
    endogenous, 36 and FDI, 77–79, 80, 83, 85
    and good governance, 31
    and human development, 21, 23, 24 fig. I.8
    income, 1, 14, 27, 77, 98
    inequality, 32n2
    and investment increase, 43
    MT exporters, 69
    non-NRB exporters, 69
    patterns, 3–5, 91
    regional, 20–21
    virtuous cycle group, 23
    See also growth
Costa Rica, 54, 71, 89, 125, 126 fig. IV.8, 192 table A.5, 196 table A.5, 202 table A.7

Côte d'Ivoire, 84, 122 table IV.2, 125 fig. IV.7, 167 table V.1, 194 table A.5, 198 table A.5
Croatia, 202 table A.7
Cuba, 167 table V.1, 194 table A.5, 198 table A.5
currency crisis, 119, 120, 125
cyclicality
    of fiscal and monetary policies, 121, 122 table IV.2, 123 fig. IV.6
Cyprus, 202 table A.7

debt relief, 28, 59, 138
de-industrialization, 37, 41, 56, 92
Democratic Republic of Congo, 167 table V.1, 192 table A.5, 198 table A.5
Denmark, 126 fig. IV.8
development aid, 28, 30, 137, 143. *See also* official development assistance (ODA)
development patterns, 35, 77
divergence, 3–5, 6 table I.1, 15, 105–17
    downward (growth) divergence, 7, 17
    dual divergence, 8, 147
    upward (growth) divergence, 7
    See also growth
Djibouti, 167 table V.1, 195 table A.5, 199 table A.5
Doha round, 29, 96, 99, 100
domestic bond market, 114–15 fig. IV.5, 116, 145n3
domestic market integration, 97, 99
Dominican Republic, 17, 79, 125, 133 fig. IV.10, 192 table A.5, 197 table A.5
Dutch disease, 166
dynamic comparative advantage, 89–90

East Asia, 4, 15, 30, 40, 43, 67 fig. III.2, 72, 79, 81–82, 90–91, 106 table IV.1, 107, 108 fig. IV.2, 118, 121, 129, 130, 131 table IV.3, 132, 133 fig. IV.10, 134, 141, 143, 150, 153, 157, 161, 162, 184 table A.1, 186 table A.2.
    See also Asia
Eastern Europe, 5, 6 table I.1, 7, 114 fig. IV.4, 131, 149 box IV.1, 184 table A.1, 186 table A.2.
    See also Central and Eastern Europe
economies of scale, 34, 61, 62, 63, 138, 180
Ecuador, 125 fig. IV.7, 193 table A.5, 198 table A.5
Egypt, 125 fig. IV.7, 154, 193 table A.5
El Salvador, 19, 125 fig. IV.7, 133 fig. IV.10, 192 table A.5, 197 table A.5
employment, 74, 82, 103–105, 134, 139, 141, 161, 172
    "employer of last resort", 52
    informal sector, 35, 51, 58n8
    and labour productivity growth, 33–34, 49–56, 53 fig. II.10, 54–56, 177–78
    structure, 34, 49
employment-to-population ratio, 53 fig. II.10, 177–78
Equatorial Guinea, 69, 195 table A.5, 198 table A.5
Ethiopia, 125 fig. IV.7, 155, 195 table A.5, 199 table A.5
European Union, 17, 46, 80
exchange rate, 115, 164
    appreciation, 124, 125 fig. IV.7, 126, 138
    and economic growth, 140, 141
    devaluation
        and short-term effects on growth, 15, 125–26
    overvaluation, 105, 124, 139, 141
    peg, 40, 123–24
    policies, 123, 124
export-led growth strategies, 39, 89, 124, 162
export processing zone, 76, 89, 95–96, 161–62
export diversification, 27, 40, 73, 141, 181
    and specialization patterns, 60
    strategy, 89

exports, 60–61
   of manufactures, 64, 181
      high-tech, 63, 64 fig. III.1, 65,
         68, 72, 97, 180–81
      low-tech, 64 fig. III.1, 65, 68,
         98, 180–81
      medium-tech, 64 fig. III.1,
         65, 72, 180–81
      natural resource-based,
         64 fig. III.1, 65–66,
         180–81
   of primary commodities, 27, 41,
      65–66, 68, 166
   of services (service exports), 62,
      73–77 fig. II.4, 98–99, 200
      table A.6, 202 table A.7
   technology- and skill-
      intensive, 61, 82
   and FDI, 36, 83

financial crises, 20, 23, 29, 41, 105, 107,
   113, 118, 141
   Asian, 15, 66, 117
   and governance, 154
   recovery, 120
   Russian, 46
financial deepening, 113–14
   and savings rate, 113, 114 fig. IV.4
financial development, 117, 124
   and growth, 104, 112–17
financial reforms, 1, 40, 113, 158
financial sector, 116
   liberalization, 153
   and growth, 112, 117
   regulation, 105, 116, 139, 141
   "repressed", 113
Finland, 66 box III.1, 122 table IV.2
fiscal behaviour, 123, 140
   pro-cyclical, and rate of long-term
      growth, 19, 104, 122 table
      IV.2, 123, 129
fiscal policies, 141, 152
   cyclicality of, 121, 144
fiscal space, 31, 105, 121, 134, 143
flying geese formation, 19, 24, 40, 76–77

foreign direct investment (FDI)
   concentration of, 79–81
   and domestic capital formation, 84
   flows, 77, 78 fig. III.5, 79, 81, 82, 84,
      101n10, 119, 171
   and growth convergence, 60, 77–79,
      80, 83–85
   and integrated production networks
      (IPN), 81–85
   liberalization of, 78–80
   in manufacturing, 79, 81–83
   in modern service sectors, 80
   and privatization, 79, 80, 81
   sectoral composition of, 79
   sectoral trends of, 78–79
   stock of, 79, 80
   and technological spillovers, 84
Former Soviet Union, 7, 41, 45, 56
France, 114 fig. IV.4, 122 table IV.2

Gabon, 20, 192 table A.5, 198 table A.5
Gambia, 195 table A.5, 198 table A.5
Germany, 114 table IV.4, 122 table IV.2,
   202 table A.7
Ghana, 21, 125 fig. IV.7, 138, 194 table A.5,
   198 table A.5
golden age, 3, 7–8, 11, 20
governance
   and civil strife and conflict, 19, 43,
      170–73
   conditionalities, 31, 139, 144
   growth-enhancing governance
      capabilities, 100n3, 139,
      176n6
   measures, 155–56, 175
      critiques of, 153–56
   quality of, 151, 153, 154, 147
      correlation with income
         per capita, 152
      two-way relationship
         with economic
         performance, 153
   transformations
      successful , 147–48, 157–65

varieties of governance structures, 156–57
growth
    binding constraints on, 39, 43, 148, 158
    collapses, 5, 8–15, 15–21, 31, 166
    and conflict, 31, 173
    convergence, 3–5
    determinants of economic growth, 4, 26, 34
    divergence, 3–4, 7–8, 23–24, 60–64, 68–69, 75, 90, 93, 97, 112–17, 121, 129, 132, 134, 139, 143, 147
    failure, 4, 11, 31, 172, 173
        sources of, 166–73
    and human development, 21–24, 143
    low-growth development trap, 42
    output of the global economy, 25 fig. I.9
    per capita GDP growth, 10 fig. I.2, 13 fig. I.4
    and regional convergence clubs, 15, 19, 157
    and structural change, 33, 37–43, 38 fig. II.1, 134, 143
    successes, 5, 8–15, 11, 15–21, 35
growth theories
    endogenous, 4, 36, 176n2
    neo-classical, 34
    non-neoclassical, 35–36
Guatemala, 194 table A.5, 197 table A.5
Guinea, 154, 194 table A.5, 199 table A.5
Guinea Bissau, 195 table A.5
Guyana, 126 fig. IV.8

Haiti, 167 table V.1, 193 table A.5, 197 table A.5
heavily indebted poor countries (HIPC), 59
Herfindahl-Hirschmann index, 28
Honduras, 20, 194 table A.5, 197 table A.5
Hong Kong, 8, 19, 71, 76, 83, 102n25, 133 fig. IV.10, 192 table A.5, 196 table A.5, 202 table A.7

human development
    growth and, 22–23, 143
    growth divergence and, 21–24
    and vicious cycle, 22–23, 134
    and virtuous cycle, 22–23, 134
Hungary, 71, 126 fig. IV.8, 193 table A.5, 196 table A.5

Iceland, 137
imports
    global market, 75, 98–99
    of services, 34, 59–60, 61–62, 73–74 fig. III.4, 97
import substitution, 38, 87, 89, 91, 162
increasing returns to scale, 35
India, 1, 6 table I.1, 7–9, 19, 40, 56, 70, 75, 76–77, 125 fig. IV.7, 159, 194 table A.5, 197 table A.5, 202 table A.7
Indonesia, 19, 53, 72, 112, 122 table IV.2, 125 fig. IV.7, 126 fig. IV.8, 166, 193 table A.5, 197 table A.5
industrial development, 33, 35, 40, 51, 90, 96. See also industrialization
industrial policy (policies) 19, 93, 96, 141, 162
    space for, 93-97
industrialization, 33, 35, 37, 40, 71, 72, 79, 86–87, 89, 93, 168–69. See also industrial development
industry, 37, 40, 41, 43, 45, 46, 47 fig. II.5, 48, 49, 50
    contribution to job creation, 50 fig. I.7
    export revenues from, 180
infant protection, 89, 96
    and labour productivity growth, 177
    local, 92
    mineral, 168–69
    productivity growth, 54, 56
inequality
    developing world income equality
        Theil decomposition of, 16 table I.3, 186 table A.2
    Gini coefficient of, 164, 185
    global income inequality, 9 fig. I.1, 22, 24, 29–30, 82

international income inequality
    Theil decomposition of, 16 table I.2
    Theil coefficient of, 32n6, 184 table A.1, 185
infant mortality rates, 22, 23, 24 fig. I.8
inflation
    and growth performance, 108 fig. IV.2, 104, 107–109
    hyperinflation, 19, 107
    volatility, 106 table IV.1
inflation targeting, 128, 141
infrastructure
    and growth, 129–130
    indivisibilities, 46–47, 129, 143
    public investment in, 105, 129–130 fig. IV.9, 132, 141
    return to investment in, 130–32
information (and communication) technology 76, 95
information services, 73, 75, 76, 200 table A.6, 202 table A.7
integrated production networks (IPN), 61, 82
    FDI and, 82, 83, 84, 85
international emerging market bonds, 120
international inequality. *See* divergence
institutional change, 46, 118, 147, 149
    in China, 163, 168
institutional development, 35, 116
institutions
    and governance structure, 147, 151–57, 172–73
    and growth divergence, 148–51
    quality of, 148, 104
Intellectual Property Rights, 89, 94–95, 97, 102n26, 165
interest rate shock, 11, 13
international capital markets, 117
investment
    composition of, 46
    (gross fixed capital formation), 44 table II.1, 45 fig. II.3, 48 fig. II.6
    in infrastructure, 105, 130, 132, 136, 141
    patterns, 43–49
    private, 27, 82, 88, 103, 107, 132, 136, 138
    public, 114, 130 fig. IV.9
    in human development, 24, 27, 41, 89, 121, 129, 133–35, 136, 143–44
    in (physical) infrastructure, 86, 121, 129–33
    uncertainty, 45, 102, 120, 140
    volatility, 33, 45, 47 fig. II.4, 106
Iran, Islamic Republic of, 42, 125 fig. IV.7, 193 table A.5, 198 table A.5
Iraq, 167 table V.1, 192 table A.5, 199 table A.5
Israel, 19, 75, 76, 192 table A.5, 196 table A.5, 202 table A.7

Jamaica, 167 table V.1, 125 fig. IV.7, 194 table A.5, 197 table A.5, 202 table A.7
Japan, 5, 6 table I.1, 7, 19, 21, 30, 40, 48, 59, 80, 114 fig. IV.4, 122 table IV.2, 147, 155, 162
Jordan, 125 fig. IV.7, 126 fig. IV.8, 192 table A.5, 196 table A.5

Kenya, 21, 113, 122 table IV.2, 125 fig. IV.7, 167 table V.1, 195 table A.5, 199 table A.5
Keynesian approach, 103
Korea, Democratic People's Republic of, 167 table V.1
Korea, Republic of, 8, 15, 17, 19, 23, 30, 48 fig. II.6, 71, 82, 86, 89, 122 table IV.2, 126 fig. IV.8, 133 fig. IV.10, 134, 158, 160, 167 table V.1, 193 table A.5, 195 table A.5, 202 table A.7
Kuwait, 19, 193 table A.5, 196 table A.5

labour productivity, 56
　decomposition of, 50, 177–78
　and employment-to-population ratio, 177–78
labour underutilization, 35, 49, 56
land reform, 176n9
　in China, 158
　in India, 159–60
　and infrastructure, 39
　in Korea and Taiwan, 158, 160
　in Viet Nam, 159
Lao People's Democratic Republic, 15, 195 table A.5, 197 table A.5
Latin America, 5, 6 table I.1, 7, 15, 17, 19, 23, 26–27, 29–30, 40, 43, 56, 65, 67 fig. III.2, 71–72, 75, 79, 81, 82, 84, 89, 106 table IV.1
Latvia, 202 table A.7
learning by doing, 34, 35, 36, 87
least developed countries (LDCs), 11, 12 fig. 12.3, 27, 28 fig. I.10, 59, 67 fig. III.2, 69, 74, 99, 187–88 table A.3
Lebanon, 195 table A.5, 198 table A.5
Lesotho, 79, 113, 126 fig. IV.8
Liberia, 69, 167 table V.1, 193 table A.5, 196 table A.5
Libyan Arab Jamahiriya, 71, 167 table V.1, 192 table A.5, 196 table A.5
life expectancy, 21, 22 fig. I.7, 134, 137
Lithuania, 202 table A.7
Luxembourg, 137

macroeconomic imbalances
　and growth, 109–12, 121–22
　twin deficits, 110
macroeconomic instability, 106–107, 109, 112–13, 116–17, 119, 123, 126, 128
macroeconomic policies, 103–104, 120, 139–41
　broader approach to, 104
　counter-cyclical, 15, 28, 29, 31, 119, 120–29, 140
　　Keynesian approach to, 103
　and national development strategies, 140–41
　new orthodoxy in, 103–104
　pro-cyclical (pattern of), 103, 104, 121, 127, 129
　costs of, 126
　space for, 29, 31
macroeconomic stability, 104, 106, 125, 128
　and growth, 105–107, 109, 112–17, 139–140, 161
Madagascar, 126 fig. IV.8, 167 table V.1, 194 table A.5, 197 table A.5
Malawi, 21, 113, 195 table A.5, 199 table A.5
Malaysia, 19, 23, 66, 71, 122 table IV.2, 125 fig. IV.7, 126 fig. IV.8, 166, 193 table A.5, 196 table A.5, 202 table A.7
Mali, 195 table A.5, 199 table A.5
Mauritania, 21, 195 table A.5, 198 table A.5
Mauritius, 20, 90, 151, 161, 193 table A.5, 196 table A.5
Mexico, 20, 71–73, 79, 81–83, 89, 119, 122 table IV.2, 125, 126 fig. IV.8, 133 fig. IV.10, 192 table A.5
microcredit schemes, 113
Middle East, 37, 56, 114 fig. IV.4, 115 fig. IV.5, 171
　and Northern Africa, 12 fig. I.3, 38 fig. II.1, 39 fig. II.2, 42–45, 47 fig. II.5, 50 fig. II.7, 51, fig. II.8, 52 fig. II.9, 53 fig. II.10, 54, 67 fig. III.2, 106 table IV.1, 131 table IV.3, 187–88 table A.3.
　See also Northern Africa and Middle East
millennium development goals (MDGs), 2, 4, 31, 135, 138, 175
Mozambique, 21, 195 table A.5, 198 table A.5
monetary policies
　contractionary, 104, 125
　cyclicality of, 121, 122 table IV.2, 123

226 • Uneven Economic Development

and inflation targeting, 128, 141
Mongolia, 195 table A.5, 198 table A.5
Morocco, 125 fig. IV.7, 193 table A.5, 197 table A.5
multilateral surveillance, 142
multilateral trading environment, 62, 98
    GATT, 94, 162
multilateral trade negotiations
    Doha Round of, 29, 96, 99, 100
    and Intellectual Property Rights, 89, 94–95, 97, 102n26, 165
    and international labour migration, 62, 99
    and non-agricultural market access (NAMA), 96
    and trade in services, 62, 73, 74, 98
    Uruguay Round of, 94, 96
Myanmar, 194 table A.5, 197 table A.5

Namibia, 20, 167 table V.1
natural resource abundance
    institutional aspects of, 168–170
    natural resource curse, 138, 153, 166, 168
    and rent-seeking behaviour, 168
    and stabilization funds, 170
Nepal, 195 table A.5, 197 table A.5
Netherlands, 137, 148, 149
new comparative economics, 151, 152–53
New Zealand, 5, 49, 126 fig. IV.8, 154
newly industrialized economies
    first-tier, 19, 37–38 fig. II.1, 39–40, 43–44 table II.1, 45 fig. II.3, 47 fig. II.4–5, 50 fig. II.7, 53 fig. II.10, 55–56, 58n1, 65, 68, 82, 89, 110–11 fig. IV.3, 112
    second-tier, 19, 30, 40, 89
Nicaragua, 19, 126 fig. IV.8, 133 fig. IV.10, 167 table V.1, 195 table A.5, 197 table A.5
Niger, 69, 192 table A.5, 199 table A.5
Nigeria, 43, 125 fig. IV.7, 126 fig. IV.8, 194 table A.5, 199 table A.5
Northern Africa, 82, 83, 108 fig. IV.2
    and Middle East, 12 fig. I.3, 38 fig. II.1, 39 fig. II.2, 42-45, 47 fig. II.5, 50 fig. II.7, 51, fig. II.8, 52 fig II.9, 53 fig. II.10, 54, 67 fig. III.2, 106 table IV.1, 131 table IV.3, 187-88 table A.3.
    See also Middle East and Northern Africa

Official development assistance (ODA), 59, 105, 118
    "big pushes" in, 135, 144
    effectiveness of (aid effectiveness), 30, 136, 144
    and growth, 135–39
    growth impact of, 136, 138
    fungibility in aid spending, 136 See also development aid
oil (price) shock, 7, 11, 42
Oman, 17, 72, 192 table A.5, 198 table A.5
Organization for Economic Cooperation and Development (OECD), 10 fig. I.2, 29, 122 table IV.2

Pakistan, 19, 24, 76–77, 125 fig. IV.7, 193 table A.5, 197 table A.5, 202 table A.7
Panama, 192 table A.5, 196 table A.5
Papua New Guinea, 126 fig IV.8
Paraguay, 126 fig. IV.8, 167 table V.1, 194 table A.5, 198 table A.5
Peru, 20, 122 table IV.2, 125 fig. IV.7, 133 fig. IV.10, 194 table A.5, 198 table A.5
Philippines, 19–20, 83, 125 fig. IV.7, 126 fig. IV.8, 192 table A.5, 196 table A.5, 202 table A.7
Poland, 41, 192 table A.5, 197 table A.5
policy space, 15, 26–27, 29, 31, 94, 96–97, 99, 127, 140, 161
Portugal, 17, 19, 149
production linkages, 61, 63, 72
production sector development policies
    industrial and other, 86–88
    space for, 93–97

See also industrial policy
productivity
    and output growth, 35–36, 49
    and technological innovation, 34, 104
public investment
    in human development, 141, 143–44
    in infrastructure, 105, 129–33, 129–130 fig. IV.9, 132, 141, 143–44, 164
public development banks, 113

Qatar, 19, 167 table V.1

regional convergence clubs, 15, 17, 19, 157
remittances, 84, 99, 89
research & development (R&D), 34, 66
    R&D Institutions, 89
Romania, 192 table A.5, 197 table A.5, 192 table A.5, 197 table A.5, 202 table A.7
rule of law, 152, 154–56, 176n6
Russian Federation, 42, 54, 192 table A.5, 197 table A.5, 202 table A.7
Rwanda, 122 table IV.2, 194 table A.5, 199 table A.5

Sao Tome and Principe, 167 table V.1
Saudi Arabia, 42, 167 table V.1, 192 table A.5, 197 table A.5
semi-industrialized countries, 12 fig. I.3, 34, 37, 38 fig. II.1, 39 fig. II.2, 44, 45 fig. II.3, 47 fig. II.4-5, 50 fig. II.7, 51 fig. II.8, 52 fig. II.9, 53 fig. II.10, 54, 75, 111 fig. IV.3, 112
Senegal, 194 table A.5, 198 table A.5
services
    capital investment in, 43, 45
    contribution to job creation, 50 fig. II.7
    contributors to labour productivity, 46, 52 fig. II.9, 158
    development of modern, 93
    economic growth in, 38 fig. II.1B, 39 fig. II.2, 41
    "employer of last resort", 52
    employment in, 33, 49, 51, 68
    export processing zones, 89
    exports of, 62–64, 74 fig. III.4, 97, 200 table A.6
        of computer and information services, 76–77, 202 table A.7
        and growth, 73–77
        sectoral world exports, 74 fig. III.4
        by sectors/sub-sectors, 200–1 table A.6
    and FDI flows, 79–81, 84
    global trends in markets for, 99–100
    government provision of, 150, 162, 171
    growth, 36, 37, 38 fig. II.1B, 39 fig. II.2, 41, 74
    high income elasticity of demand, 61–62
    imports, 34, 59-60, 61
    increased flow of, 59, 60
    innovations in, 87, 93
    international trade in, 98–99
    investment towards, 33, 48–49
    medical, 171
    in multilateral trade negotiations, 98–99
    productive activities in, 60
    public services, 129, 139, 144, 150, 162
    share in total world trade, 73
    social, 105
    strong expansions in, 37, 55–56
    source of productivity, 35, 46, 51–52 fig. II.9, 54–56
        decomposition, 50
    specialization patterns in, 73–77
    technology-and skill-intensive, 75
    tradable, 40, 61
    world exports by sectors, 74 fig. III.4

Seychelles, 195 table A.5, 198 table A.5
Sierra Leone, 194 table A.5, 199 table A.5
Singapore, 8, 19, 23, 71, 89, 133 fig. IV.10, 192 table A.5, 196 table A.5, 202 table A.7
social cohesion, 148–150, 157–58, 161, 168, 170, 172, 175
Solomon Islands, 126 fig. IV.8
Somalia, 195 table A.5, 199 table A.5
South Africa, 20, 79, 84, 111 fig. IV.2, 125 fig. IV.7, 168, 193, 196 table A.5
South America, 41
South Asia, 4, 19, 37–40, 43– 45, 47, 50–53, 56, 67, 76–77, 106, 108, 131, 151, 168, 171, 186–88. *See also* Asia
South-East Asia, 37–38 fig. II.1, 40, 43–44, 47 fig. II.4–5, 50 fig. II.7, 53, 67 fig. III.2, 79, 110, 111 fig. IV.3, 124, 138 fig. II.1B. *See also* Asia
Spain, 17, 19, 149
Sri Lanka, 19, 70, 125 fig. IV.7, 194 table A.5, 197 table A.5, 202 table A.7
stabilization funds
    commodity, 128
    fiscal, 140, 170
stabilization policies, 40, 103, 109, 117, 140
structural adjustment policies, 42
structural budget rules
    in Chile, 128, 140
structural change
    dynamic, 36
    and economic growth, 33–37
    and sectoral linkages, 36
Sub-Saharan Africa, 7, 17, 21, 30, 37, 38 fig. II.1, 42, 43, 45, 52, 54, 55, 56, 68, 72, 87, 90, 107, 109, 111, 112, 124, 130, 134, 143. *See also* Africa
Sudan, 195 table A.5, 199 table A.5
surplus labour, 36, 54
Sweden, 66
Switzerland, 21, 137
Syrian Arab Republic, 125 fig. IV.7, 192 table A.5, 197 table A.5, 202 table A.7

Taiwan, 8, 19, 30, 71, 86, 89, 133 fig. IV.10, 158–160, 193 table A.5, 196 table A.5, 202 table A.7
Tanzania, United Republic of, 125 fig. IV.7, 167 table V.1, 194 table A.5, 199 table A.5
technological change, 4, 36, 43, 65, 93
technological innovation, 34, 104
technology frontier, 66, 87
terms of trade, 11, 25, 63, 66, 124, 137
    of commodities, 166
    fallacy of composition and, 63
    manufactures terms of trade, 14 fig. I.5
    non-fuel commodities terms of trade, 14 fig. I.5
    terms of trade shocks, 13, 43
Thailand, 15, 19, 66, 71, 109, 125 fig. IV.7, 126 fig. IV.8, 155, 193 table A.5, 196 table A.5
Togo, 126 fig. IV.8, 195 table A.5, 199 table A.5
trade
    in agricultural goods, 61, 65
    international, 73, 98
    merchandise, 68–73
    in services, 62, 74, 73–77
    and specialization patterns, 30–31, 64, 68–73, 73–77, 97, 181
trade integration, 59
trade liberalization, 40, 86
    and growth, 74, 91–93
trade reforms, 29, 158, 161
    in Mauritius, 161

Trinidad and Tobago, 192 table A.5, 196 table A.5, 197 table A.5
Tunisia, 17, 20, 42, 125 fig. IV.7, 193 table A.5
Turkey, 72, 109, 125 fig. IV.7, 154, 155, 193 table A.5, 197 table A.5

Uganda, 21, 113, 124, 125 fig. IV.7, 126 fig. IV.8, 167 table V.1, 195 table A.5, 199 table A.5

Ukraine, 42, 54
United Arab Emirates, 71, 167 table V.1, 194 table A.5, 196 table A.5
United Kingdom, 49, 122 table IV.2, 126 fig. IV.8, 202 table A.7
United States, 1, 48, 122 table IV.2, 126 fig. IV.8, 155
Uruguay, 20, 126 fig. IV.8, 193 table A.5, 198 table A.5
Uruguay Round of, multilateral trade agreement, 94, 96

Viet Nam, 19, 23, 70, 159, 194 table A.5, 196 table A.5
Venezuela, 19, 122 table IV.2, 125 fig. IV.7, 126 fig. IV.8, 167 table V.1, 193 table A.5, 196 table A.5

volatility
    of capital flows, 117, 119, 123, 127, 142
    exchange-rate, 124
    inflation, 106 table IV.1
    investment, 33, 45, 47 fig. II.4, 106
    macroeconomic, 106–107, 117, 141
    output, 118, 120, 106 table IV.1

Washington Consensus, 26, 158
Western Asia, 108 fig. IV.2, 167 table V.1, 186. *See also* Asia

Yemen, 19, 195 table A.5, 199 table A.5

Zambia, 21, 195 table A.5, 198 table A.5
Zimbabwe, 21, 125 fig. IV.7, 126 fig. IV.8, 193 table A.5, 198 table A.5